Hardin County

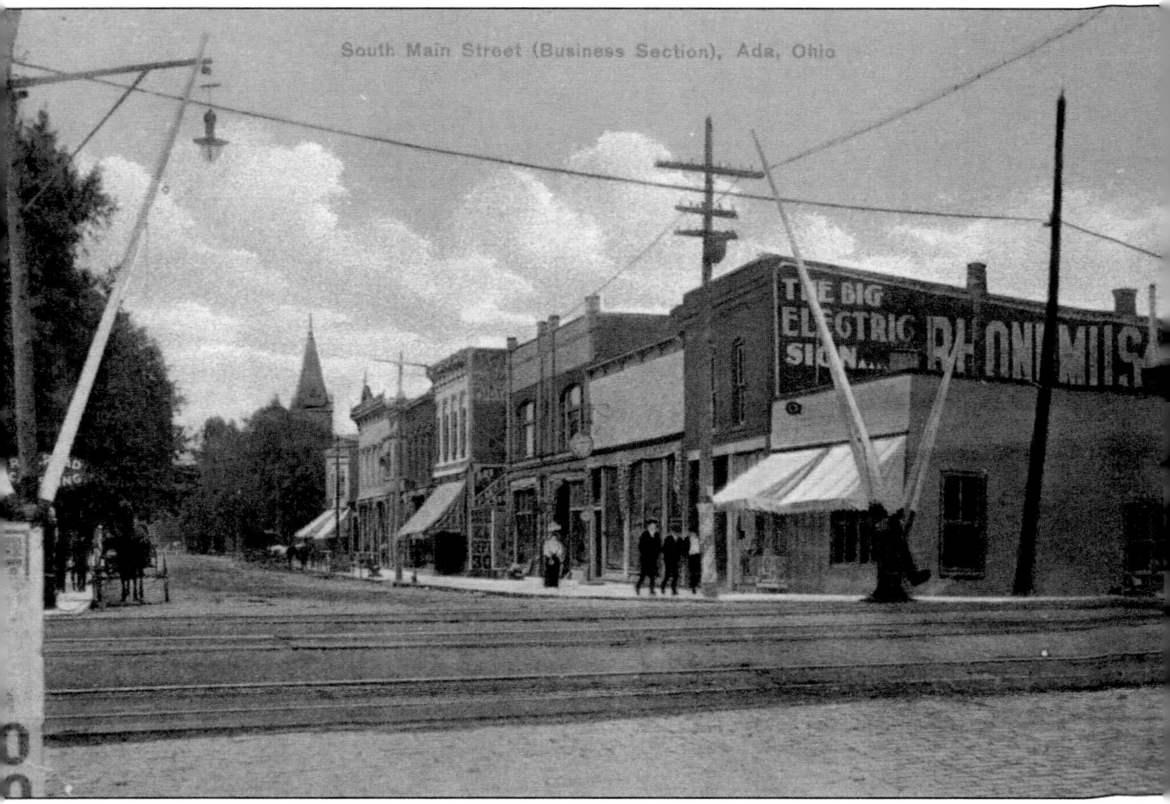

This 1910 postcard view of Ada's Main Street faces south from the Pennsylvania Railroad tracks. Businesses on the west side included the Clutter Art Gallery, Doling Bakery, Povenmire Grocery, and Paeszler Photography Studio. (Author's collection.)

FRONT COVER: Kenton was referred to as "Little Chicago" during the 1920s and 1930s. The south side of the square was said to house its unsavory element, as evidenced by the large number of saloons in this image. (Author's collection.)

BACK COVER: Locals examine the flooded ditches and fields outside McGuffey in March 1913. Up to six inches of rain was recorded in Hardin County during the flood of 1913. (Author's collection.)

POSTCARD HISTORY SERIES

Hardin County

Ronald I. Marvin Jr.

ARCADIA PUBLISHING

ISBN 978-0-7385-8251-1

Published by Arcadia Publishing
Charleston, South Carolina

Printed in the United States of America

Library of Congress Control Number: 2011923296

For all general information contact Arcadia Publishing at:
Telephone 843-853-2070
Fax 843-853-0044
E-mail sales@arcadiapublishing.com
For customer service and orders:
Toll-Free 1-888-313-2665

Visit us on the Internet at www.arcadiapublishing.com

This book is dedicated to my parents, Ronald and Ann Marvin, whose support of my museum career has been steadfast.

Contents

Acknowledgments

This book would not have been possible without the aid and support of my parents, Ronald and Ann Marvin, who helped amass the collection that this book is drawn from, provided editorial comments, and served as a sounding board for my constant research. I need to thank the Hardin County Genealogical Society for providing access to its incredible collections. I also want to thank Kathy Hines, Bill Evans, Gene Cornell, and the rest of the volunteers at the genealogical society for their helpful hints and assistance in researching the postcards. I also need to recognize the historical collections at the Mary Lou Johnson-Hardin County District Library, Hardin County Historical Museums, Ada Public Library, Forest-Jackson Historical Society, and Ohio Northern University's Heterick Library. The Ohio Library Networks collection of Sanborn maps was invaluable in pinpointing locations of buildings, residences, and businesses in the late 1800s. Special recognition needs to be made to the staff of the Hardin County Recorder's office. It is amazing how many historical questions and inaccuracies can be cleared up by original deeds and records.

I need to also extend my gratitude to the staff at Arcadia Publishing, including my original editor Melissa Basilone, who worked diligently to get this project off the ground, my final draft editors Ted Gerstle and Rob Kangas, and Midwest regional publisher John Pearson for their assistance in getting the book completed.

All images in the book are from the author's collection.

INTRODUCTION

This book explores the history of Hardin County in northwestern Ohio. It was the sixth county to be created out of the former Indian Lands in the Northwest Territory. In 1790, the Scioto River, which flows through the center of the county, was the northern tip of the Virginia Military Reserve. On February 12, 1820, the Ohio Legislature passed an ordinance resulting in the formation of the county. It would be carved out of the northern portion of Champaign County and attached to Logan County until its formal organization in 1833. Hardin County was divided into 15 townships and named for American Revolutionary War hero Col. John Hardin, who was killed in nearby Shelby County while on a peace mission to Indian leaders. In keeping with the pioneer spirit of the region, the county seat was named Kenton in honor of renowned frontiersman Simon Kenton.

The earliest known inhabitants were the Glacial Kame Culture, represented by several mounds in the area. The best example is the Zimmerman Kane near Roundhead in southwestern Hardin County. Native American tribes such as the Delaware, Miami, Ottawa, Shawnee, and Wyandotte lived in and traveled through the area, hunting game along the county rivers and marshes. Chief Stiahta (Roundhead) headed a village along the Scioto River near where the town of Roundhead was begun in 1832.

French fur trappers and traders were known to have traveled throughout the region. French explorer Celeron De Bienville was credited with naming the Scioto River in 1751. Perhaps the first true Americans to travel through the area were the soldiers under Gen. William Hull's command. They blazed a trail north through Ohio on their way to Detroit during the War of 1812. Fort McArthur was named for Gen. Duncan McArthur, the future Ohio governor. The fort was established on this trail, three miles west of Kenton, along the banks of the Scioto River. Sixteen soldiers died here during the winter of 1813 and were buried in a small cemetery nearby.

The Shawnee Trail, which led north toward Wapakoneta, crossed the Scioto River near Pfeiffer Station at the Shawnee Ford. Stagecoaches would eventually follow this trail, and the Wheeler Tavern, established in 1836 by Portius Wheeler, became one of the early stops.

The Scioto, Hog Creek, and Cranberry Marshes constituted one of the largest inland wetlands in the United States. The area, teeming with abundant vegetation and wildlife, provided game for native tribes and temporary shelter for escaped slaves. The towns of Alger, Foraker, and McGuffey were established along these marshes. During the 1920s and 1930s, this region was considered the largest producer of onions and sugar beets in the world. Additional crops such as potatoes, radishes, carrots, and peppermint were grown in the fertile soil. Large storage warehouses are still standing in the towns.

Ada boasts Hardin County's only university. The Northwestern Ohio Normal School was founded in 1870 by Dr. Henry Lehr. It was renamed Ohio Normal University in 1885, and in 1903 the name was changed to Ohio Northern University. The College of Arts and Sciences, the College of Business Administration, the College of Engineering, the College of Law, and the College of Pharmacy currently offer degrees at the school.

Hardin County has been home to several military and political figures. A few of these include Lt. Jacob Parrott (first Congressional Medal of Honor recipient); Ohio secretary of state Gen. James Robinson (Civil War); Rear Adm. Kent Melhorn (World War II); Rear Adm. Lucian Moebus (World War II); Brig. Gen. John Murray (Iraq War); Kansas governors Thomas Carney (second), Nehemiah Green (fourth), and William Stanley (fifteenth); and Ohio governor Frank Willis.

In addition to the local amusement parks of Lake Idlewild and Spring Lake Resort, the region has provided entertainment to the rest of the nation and world. The International Brotherhood of Magicians held its first two conventions in Kenton, the hometown of its original headquarters. The Kenton Hardware Company produced cast-iron KentonToys, including the Gene Autry cap pistol. Wilson Sporting Goods of Ada has been the exclusive manufacturers of National Football League footballs for over 50 years. Forest's Buckeye Machine Fabricators produced components for the IndyCar Racing Series. Some famous residents include *Etta Kett* comic strip creator Paul Robinson (Kenton), illusionist William W. Durbin (Kenton), Alaskan artist Fred Machetanz (Kenton), Major League Baseball player Billy Southworth (Kenton), National Football League coach Dean Pees (Dunkirk), and Negro League ballplayer and Hall-of-Famer Raymond Brown (Alger).

Hardin County has also hosted US presidents William Howard Taft, Theodore Roosevelt, James Garfield, William McKinley, and George Bush. A few of the other political figures who have visited include Henry Clay, Stephen Douglas, Carrie Nation, William Jennings Bryan, Dr. Martin Luther King Jr., and Ohio governor James Rhodes. Ohio Northern University's Freed Center for the Performing Arts attracts modern entertainers in the tradition of former county visitors Harry Blackstone, P.T. Barnum, Charles Dickens, Jim Thorpe, Jack Britton, and Gene Autry. Southern Hardin County also welcomed numerous champion dogs as it hosted the world-famous Kenton National Flea Market and Leafy Oak Coon Dog Trials from 1927 until 2008. Several antique and craft shops, scattered through the refurbished downtown of Mount Victory, continue to attract visitors, famous or otherwise.

Souvenir postcards are fun, simple little pieces of ephemera to collect. However, they mean much more to local historians, because they can tell the story of a town or county. By examining the cards, one can infer which people, places, and events were considered important to the local photographers and publishers at that time.

The golden era of Hardin County postcards was between 1905 and 1920. Almost every local drugstore or bookstore sold their own series of cards. This book contains an array of images available from the various publishers. I have attempted to piece together a selection of some of the most intriguing images from my personal collection.

Selecting only 225 postcards from the nearly 1,000 available was a daunting task. Inevitably, many smaller towns are going to be underrepresented, if not completely absent, while some chapters seem to favor Kenton and Ada. This has as much to do with early postcard production as with the basic survival of postcards. Unfortunately, villages such as Yelverton, Holden, and Pfeiffer Station never prospered as much as their counterparts, resulting in few postcards (if any) produced and still fewer that survive today.

I have collected, researched, and written articles about Hardin County for over 20 years. Every attempt has been made to verify the information provided and to be as thorough as possible in the descriptions. It is my intent that readers will come away with a greater understanding of the county's residents, businesses, and facilities. In selecting the cards, I have tried to stay within the heyday of the local publishers. However, some later images were necessary to show the growth of the county over time. I hope this book evokes memories and that readers find it entertaining and informative.

One

Greetings from Hardin County

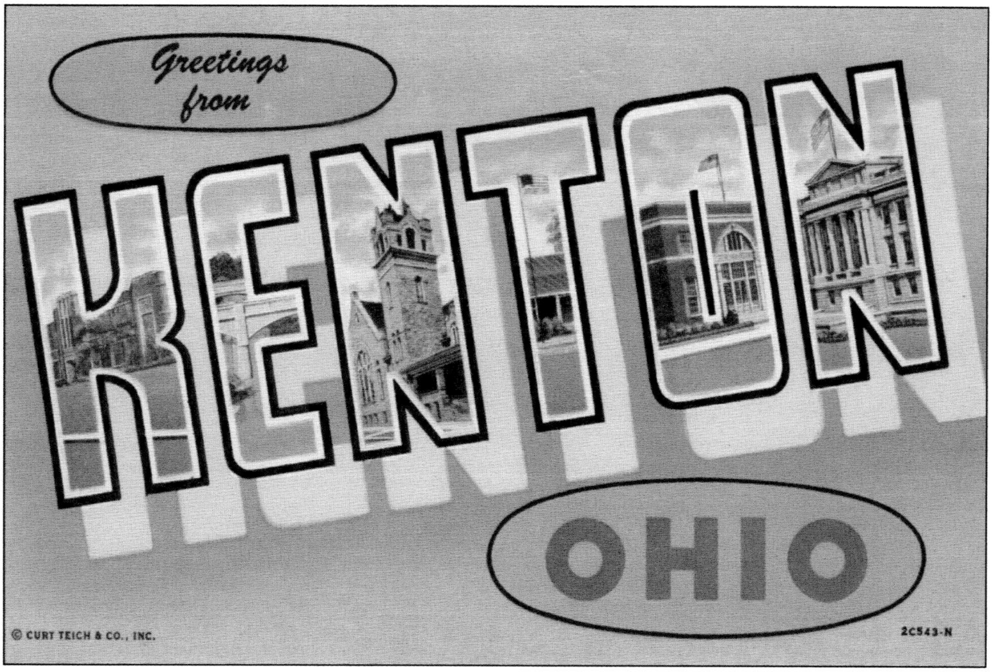

This preprinted stock postcard promoting Kenton contains pictures of landmarks from the town. Kenton was founded in 1833 and was incorporated as a village in 1845 and a city in 1886. The images include the high school, Scioto River bridges, golf course, post office, and the courthouse. More information about these structures can be found in the following chapters.

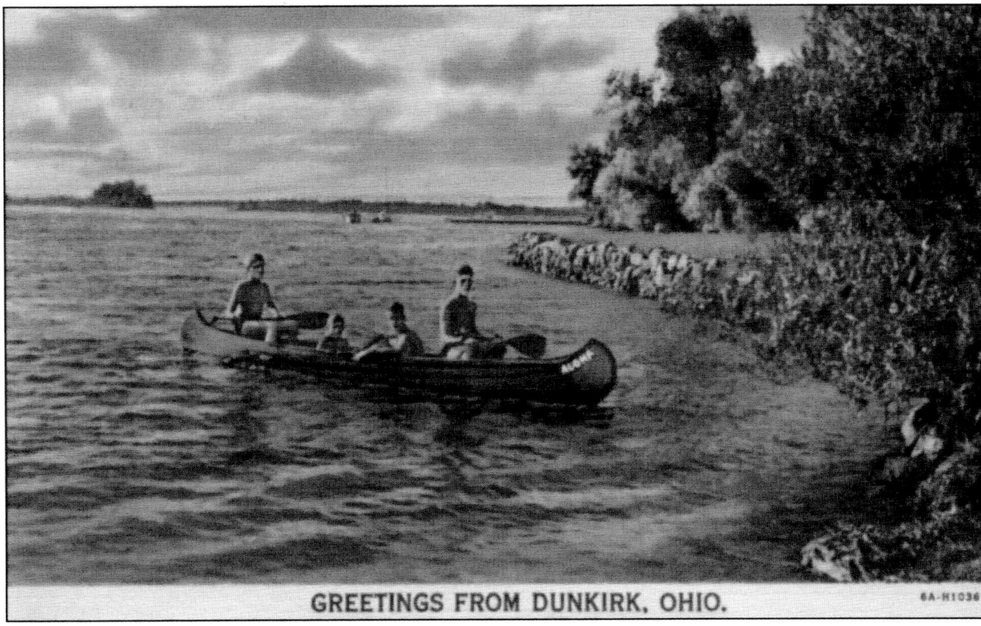

Similar to the Dunkirk Quarry, Hepburn's quarry was converted into a recreational lake. Hepburn was established near a large gravel bank along the Chicago & Atlantic Railroad in 1882. The stone was excavated, and the area was converted into Spring Lake Resort, once called "Kenton's playground." Residents could take a day excursion on the railroad to the park, where they enjoyed boating, swimming, dancing, and picnicking.

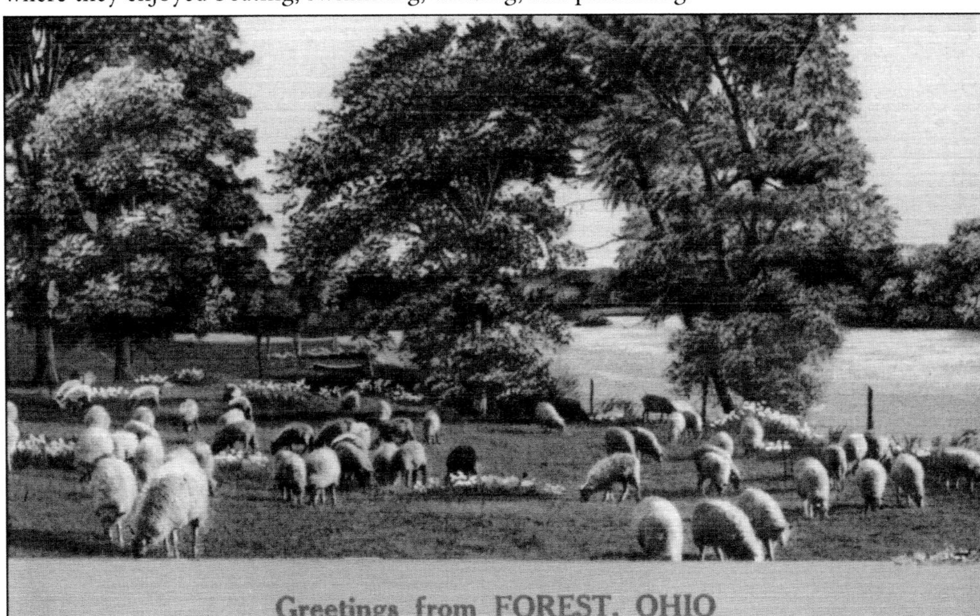

Hardin County's best-known sheep ranchers in the 1910s were the Orth Brothers (Adolph, Alexander, Frederick, and Louis) near Mount Victory, who bred Rambouillet Merino sheep. This type of sheep was raised as much for its meat as for its wool. The brothers exhibited at local fairs, the Ohio State Fair, and the International Livestock Exposition in Chicago, where they repeatedly won grand championships.

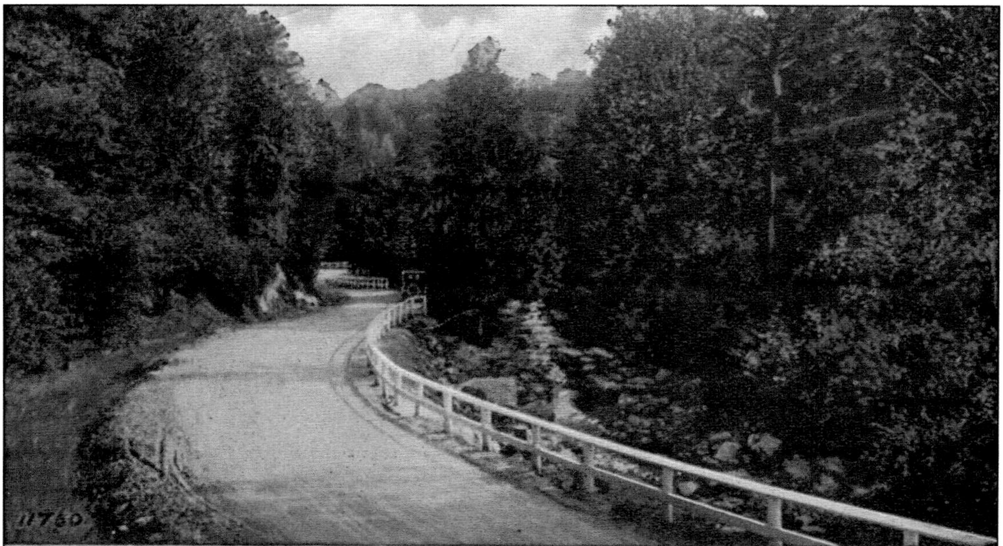

Greetings from RIDGEWAY, OHIO

The Ridgeway area is perhaps best known as the home of the Leafy Oak Coon Dog Field Trials, which began in 1927. The name was changed to the Kenton National Flea Market and Leafy Oak Coon Dog Trials about 1957 when the Ross family acquired ownership. The annual Labor Day event, which once advertised the "World's Largest Flea Market," hosted its last dog races in 2008.

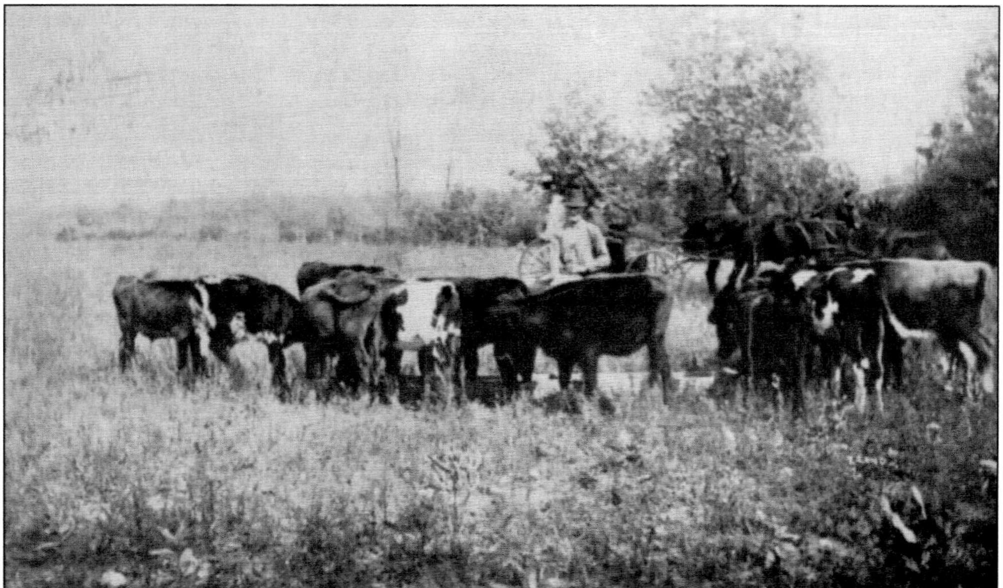

Scenes from near MT. VICTORY, Ohio

This 1930 postcard promotes the cattle farms in Hardin County. One of the most prominent farmers and cattlemen of southwestern Hardin County was Roundhead's James V. Hill (1875–1937). He owned a 280-acre farm in Roundhead Township and specialized in breeding Herford cattle. In 1921, he was recognized in the American Hereford Cattle Breeders' Association Yearbook.

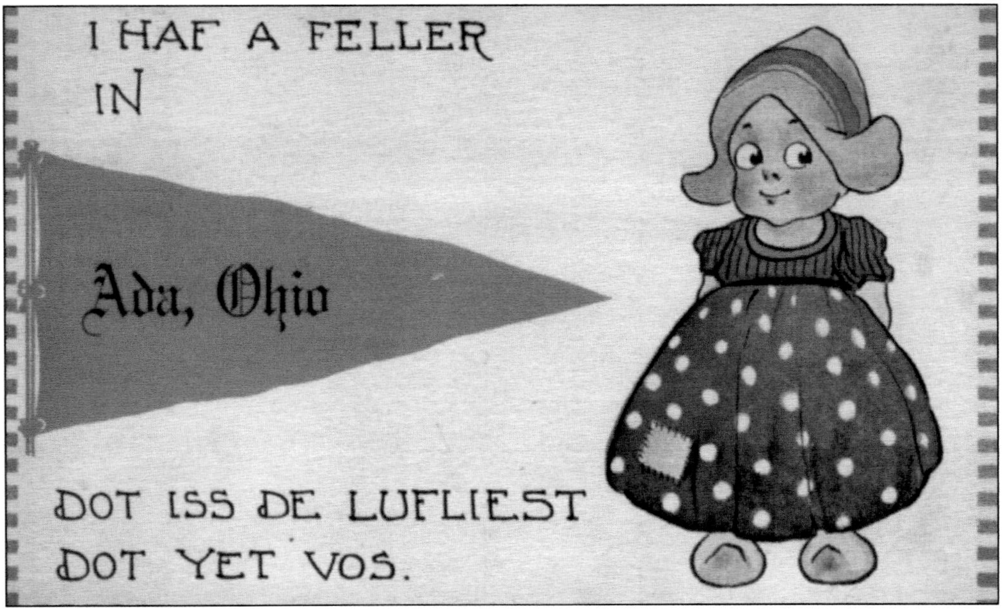

The Ada Public Library has a collection of historical photographs and vintage postcards. The library began as a collection of books in the women's restroom at Ada City Hall during the 1910s. It formally organized in June 1917, then, in October, it moved into the Brewer Block; the books moved to Highland Avenue in March 1919. A new $74,000 facility on North Main Street was dedicated in 1953.

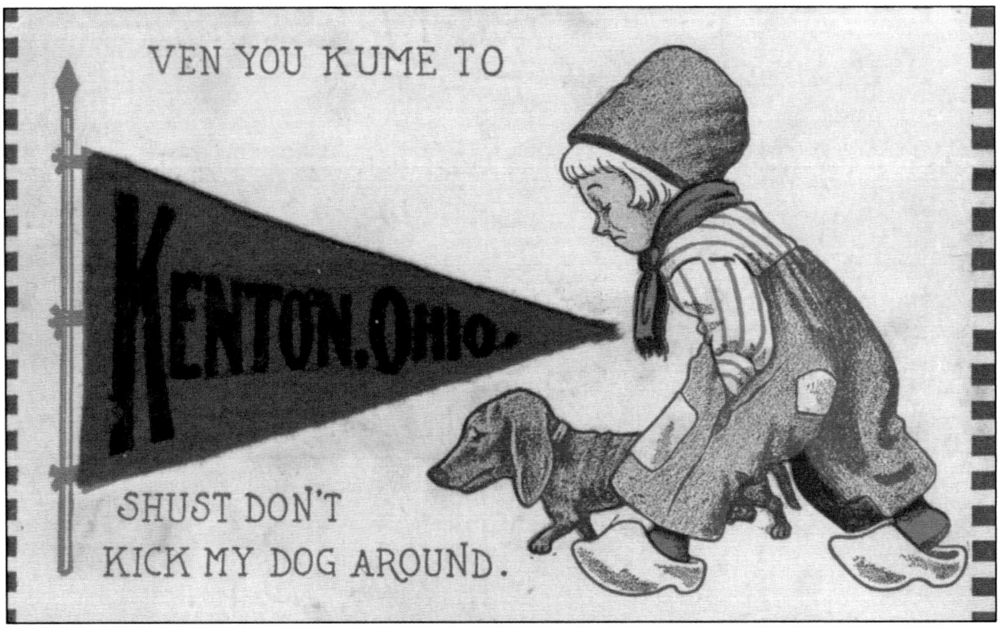

One of Kenton's longest, continuously operated businesses is the Kenton Marble & Granite Company. James D. White started the operation in 1850 as the Kenton Marble Works on East Franklin Street. The business changed hands several times before it moved to South Main Street. Carl Price purchased the company in 1903 and moved it to its current location on South Leighton Street in 1904.

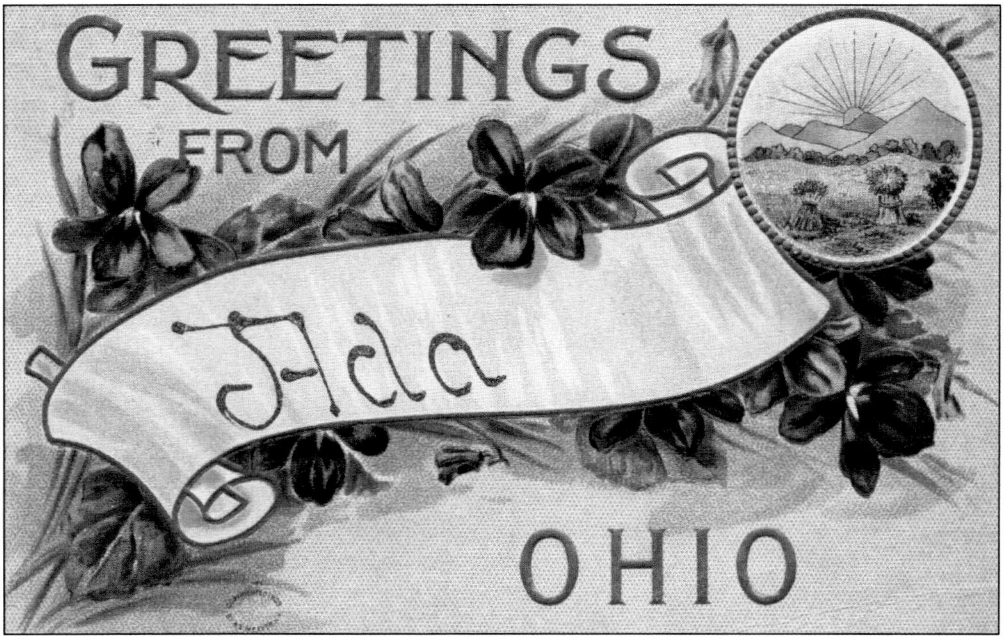

This official-looking postcard of Ada was mailed in 1909. Ada's original city hall was erected on West Buckeye Avenue and contained the police department, fire station, and post office. The opera house occupied the second floor. The current Ada town hall and police station was erected at the same location in 1937. The Ada Fire Department has since moved to North Main Street.

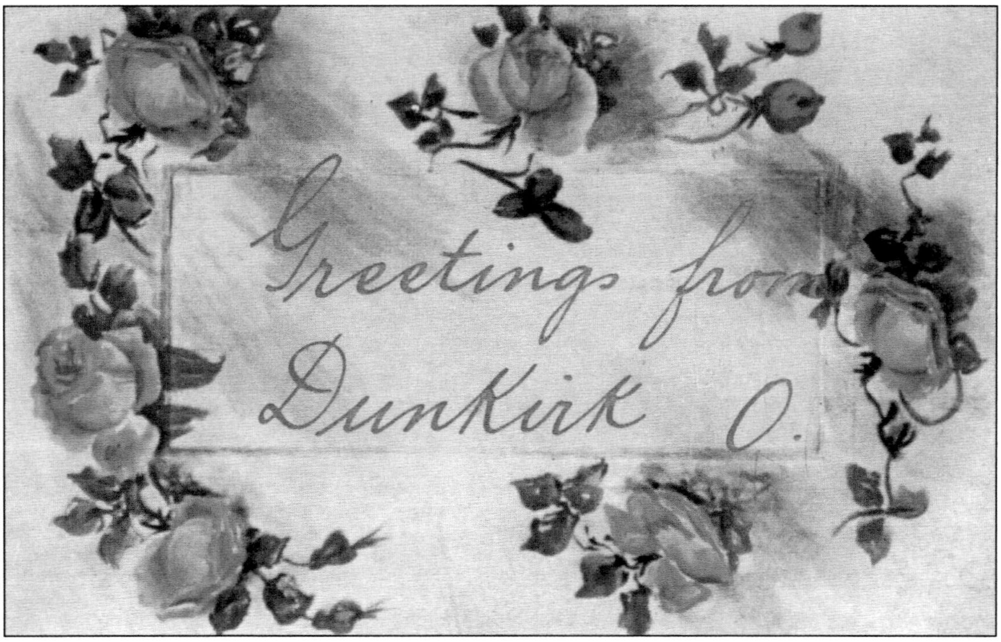

Dunkirk's city hall, containing the engine house and new city jail, was built in 1886 at the corner of Patterson and West (Buckeye) Streets. It was used until a new fire station was erected in 1966. The original jail was erected in 1861 and used as a public voting booth from 1887 until 1965. The jail is now located in Kenton at the Historic Village and Farm.

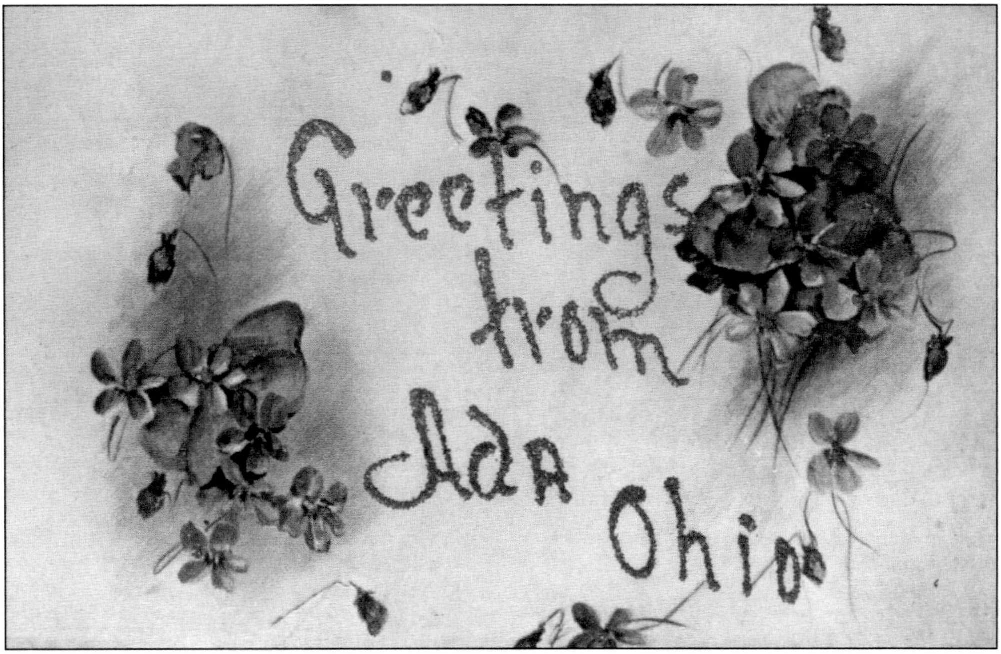

In the early 1900s, many of Hardin County's small shopkeepers sold preprinted stock postcards or crafted their own homemade postcards. Many of these, such as this early postcard from Ada, were created by tinseling, a process of dusting metallic powder over lines of glue. County residents could also purchase tinseling kits from these stores to embellish their own postal cards.

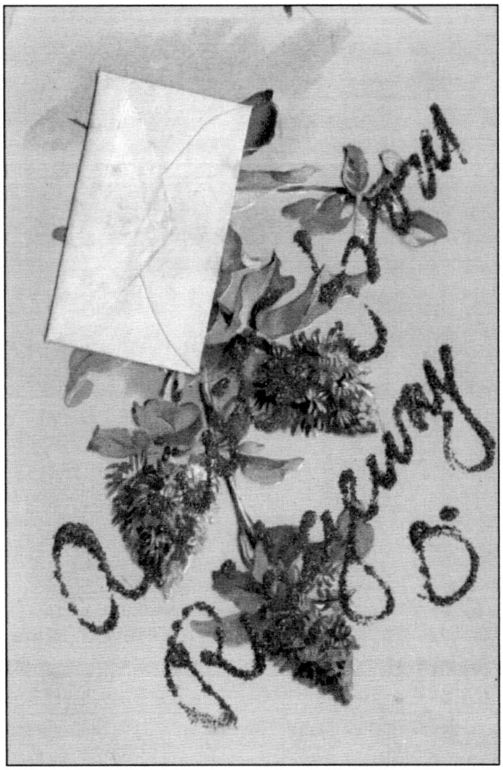

One of the most picturesque parts of Hardin County is the Old Order Amish community near Pfeiffer Station, northeast of Ridgeway. The Amish moved here in 1953 and strive to maintain their simple, plain lifestyle. Visitors to the area get a glimpse of what life was like in the county during the horse-and-buggy days.

George H. Patterson laid out a town in 1845, which was established as Petersburg by Peter Boslow in 1846. The post office was named Sylvia the next year. In 1850, the town was renamed for Robert Patterson, the secretary/treasurer of the Mad River & Lake Erie Railroad. Once one of the county's largest towns, Patterson was bypassed by the Pittsburgh, Fort Wayne & Chicago Railroad and slowly reduced in size.

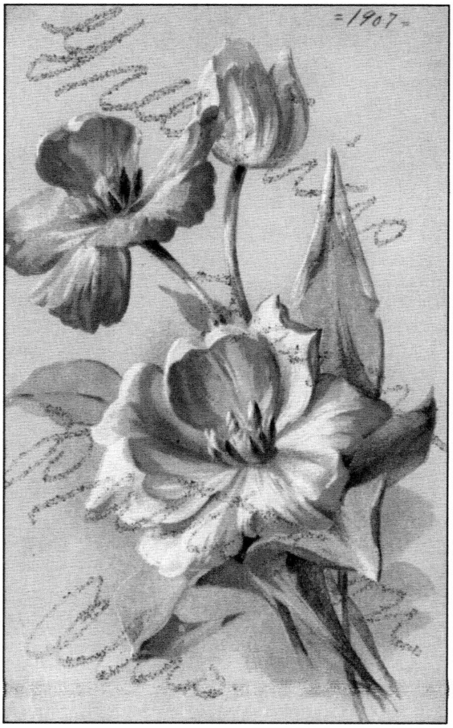

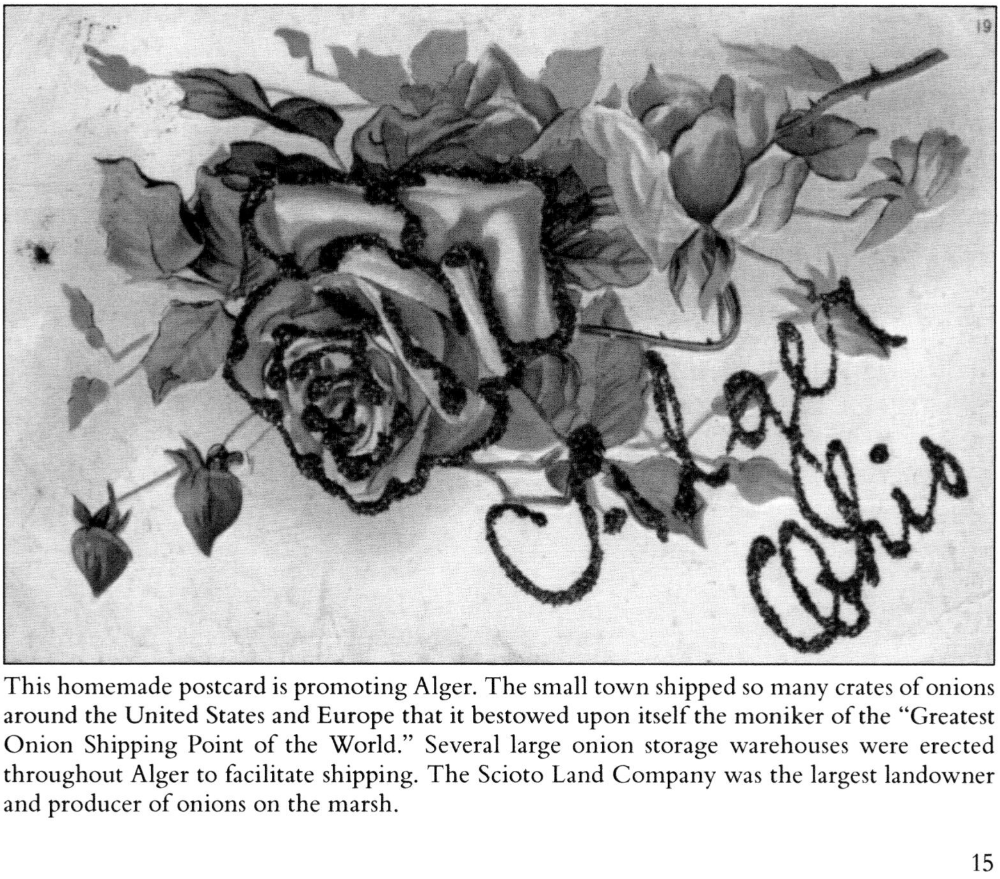

This homemade postcard is promoting Alger. The small town shipped so many crates of onions around the United States and Europe that it bestowed upon itself the moniker of the "Greatest Onion Shipping Point of the World." Several large onion storage warehouses were erected throughout Alger to facilitate shipping. The Scioto Land Company was the largest landowner and producer of onions on the marsh.

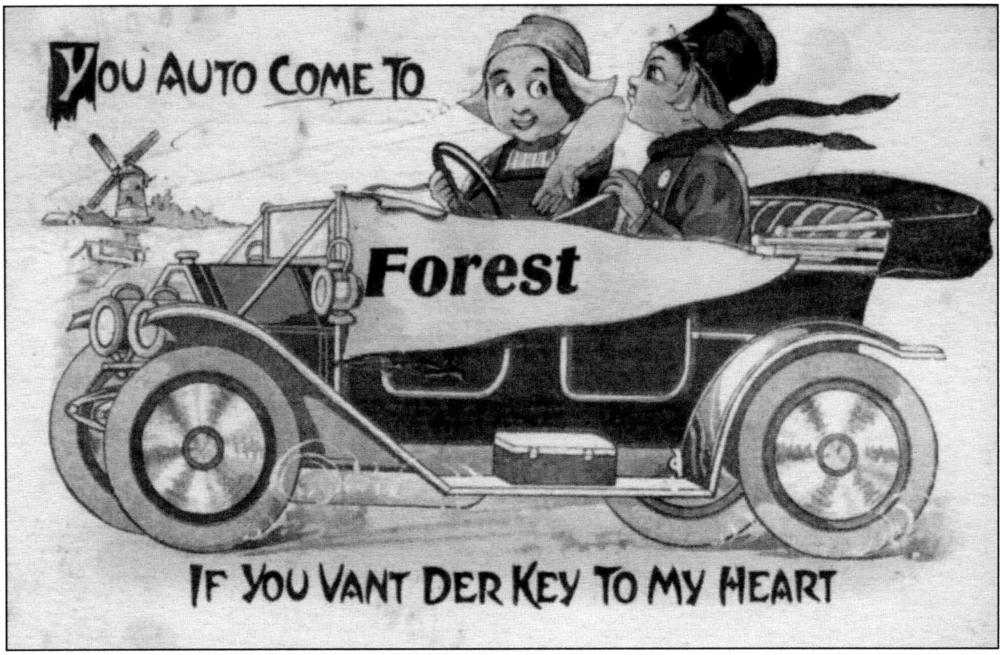

Postcard publishers took advantage of the fact that automobiles were replacing horses as the preferred mode of travel in the 1910s. This 1913 stock postcard is promoting Forest. John N. Pfeiffer was a Ford dealer in Forest and Kenton who also sold automobile accessories and supplies. He promoted his repair shop as a Lincoln Highway garage in 1916.

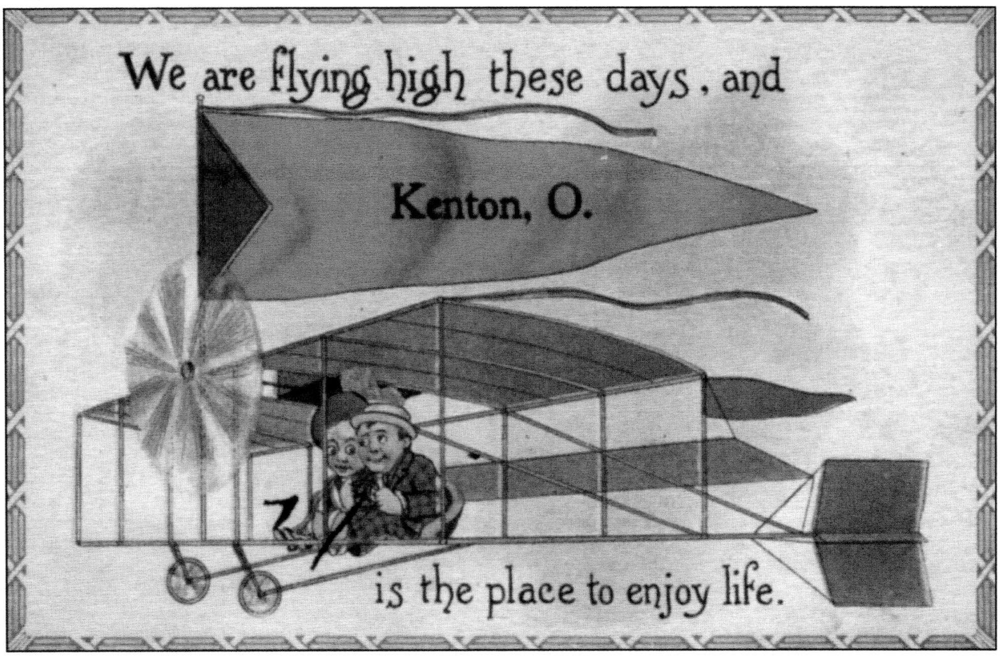

Using the Wright Brothers aircraft as inspiration, several publishers soon developed stock postcards to capitalize on air flight. This postcard was mailed only three years after the first airplane flew over Hardin County in September 1911. Very few residents had ever seen a flying machine, and they crowded open fields along the Erie Railroad for a glimpse of the airplane.

Two

PUBLIC BUILDINGS

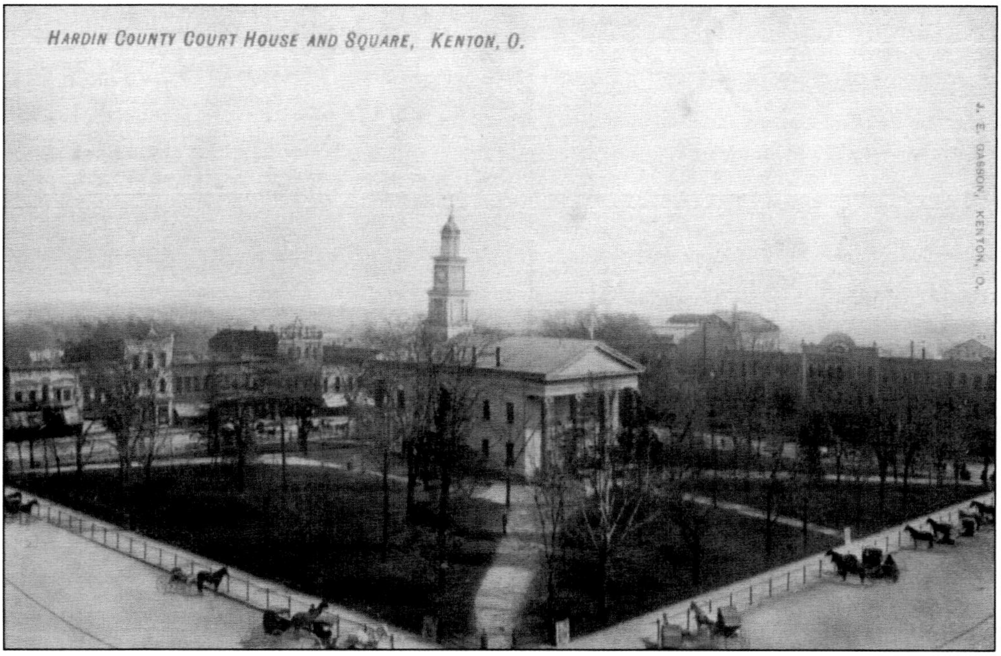

This is an aerial scene of the Hardin County Courthouse viewed from the northwest corner of the courthouse square. Hardin County was established in 1820 from the northern portion of Champaign County. An April 1906 *Kenton News-Republican* article promoted the release of James E. Gasson's new series of postcards, including this image, available at Gasson's Drug Store, the successor to Powell & Gasson's Big Drug Store.

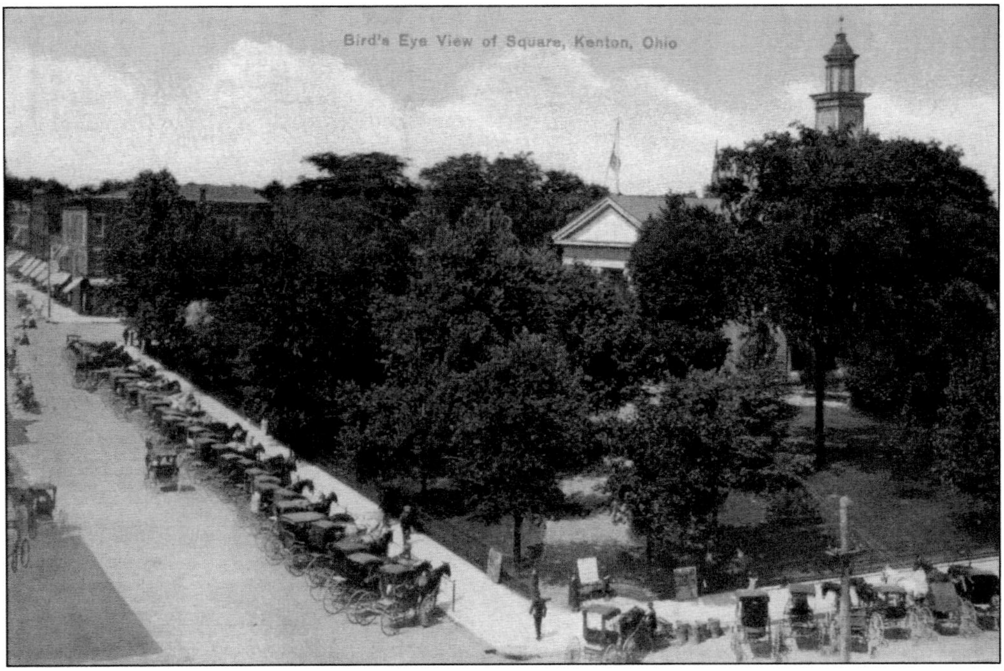

Hardin County's first courthouse, erected in 1835, was located on the east side of the courthouse square and burned in 1853. Following a public vote in April 1853, the second courthouse was constructed in the center of the square in 1854, creating a scenic courthouse park. The "big watch," Benjamin Garrettson's jewelry store sign, is visible in the upper left of the card.

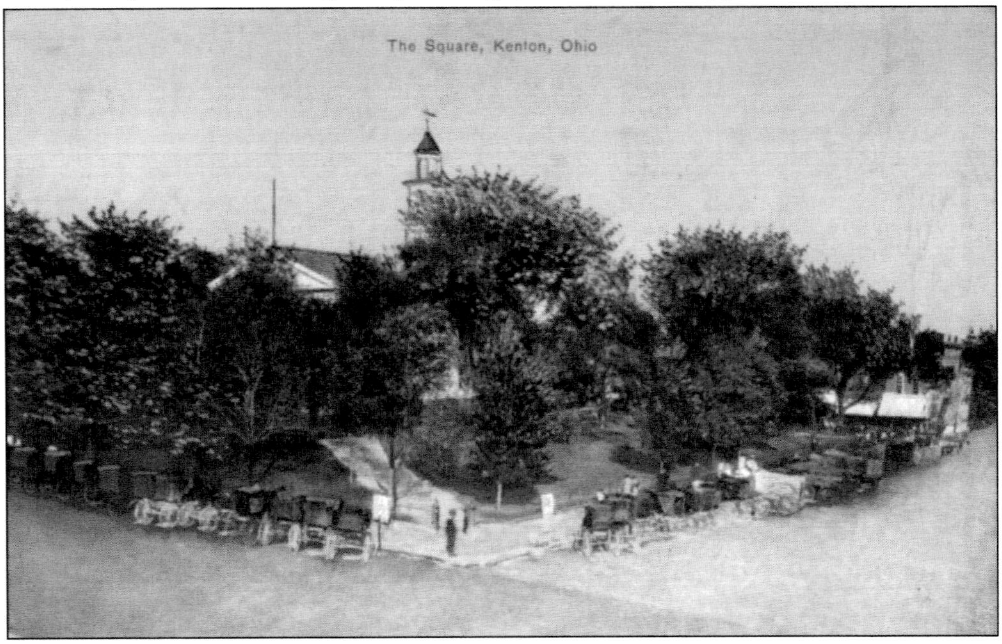

Between 1853 and 1854, the east-facing second Hardin County Courthouse was erected in the Grecian Temple style at a cost of $17,200. Future president James A. Garfield and presidential nominee William Jennings Bryan each made speeches at the courthouse. William Snodgrass published this image from around 1910 that was later resold by Wharton's Antiques Shop.

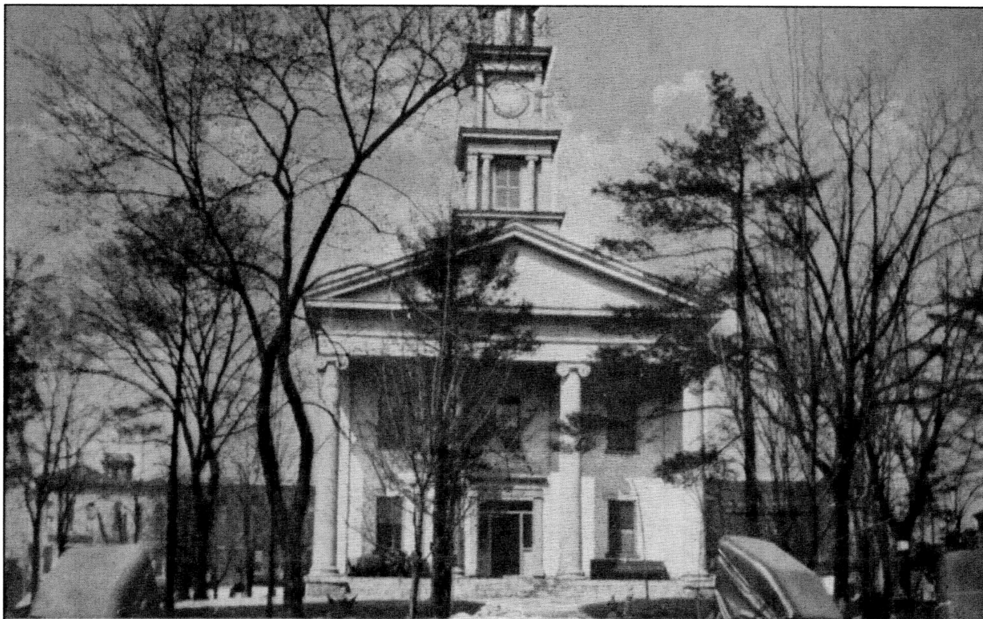

Hardin County Court House, Kenton, Ohio.

This is the east facade of the courthouse, as it looked about 1906, seven years before it was torn down. Portions of the limestone columns were placed throughout the county by the Hardin County chapter of the Daughters of the American Revolution in 1913 to mark the north-south route of Hull's Trail. Gen. William Hull led a company of men on a march toward Detroit during the War of 1812.

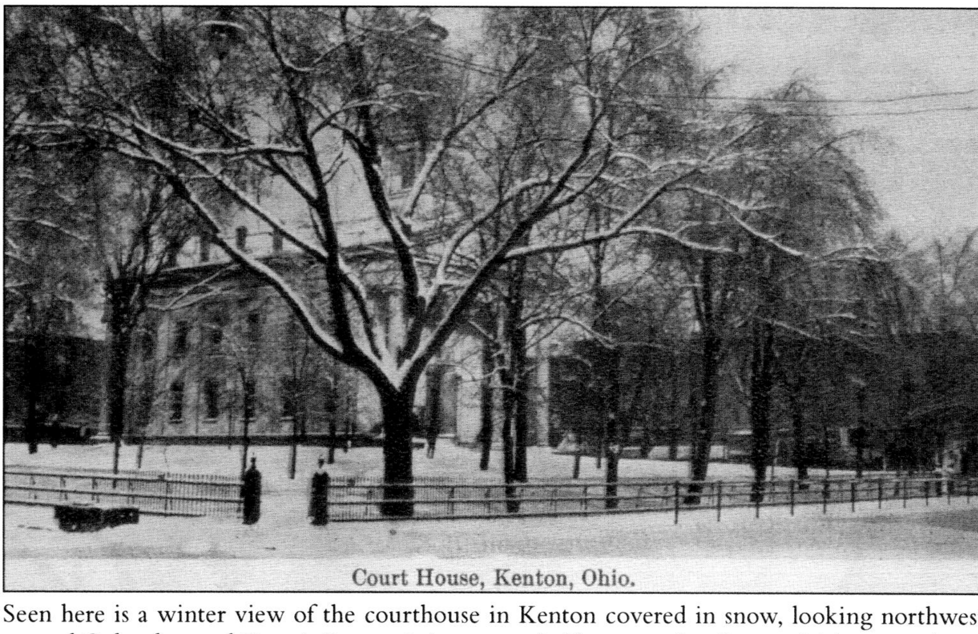

Court House, Kenton, Ohio.

Seen here is a winter view of the courthouse in Kenton covered in snow, looking northwest toward Columbus and Detroit Streets. It is surrounded by a wooden fence, which was replaced by one from the Champion Iron Fence Company in 1880 for $2,800. The electric lights were installed during the early 1900s. Many of the brick buildings visible in the background have survived and still house local businesses.

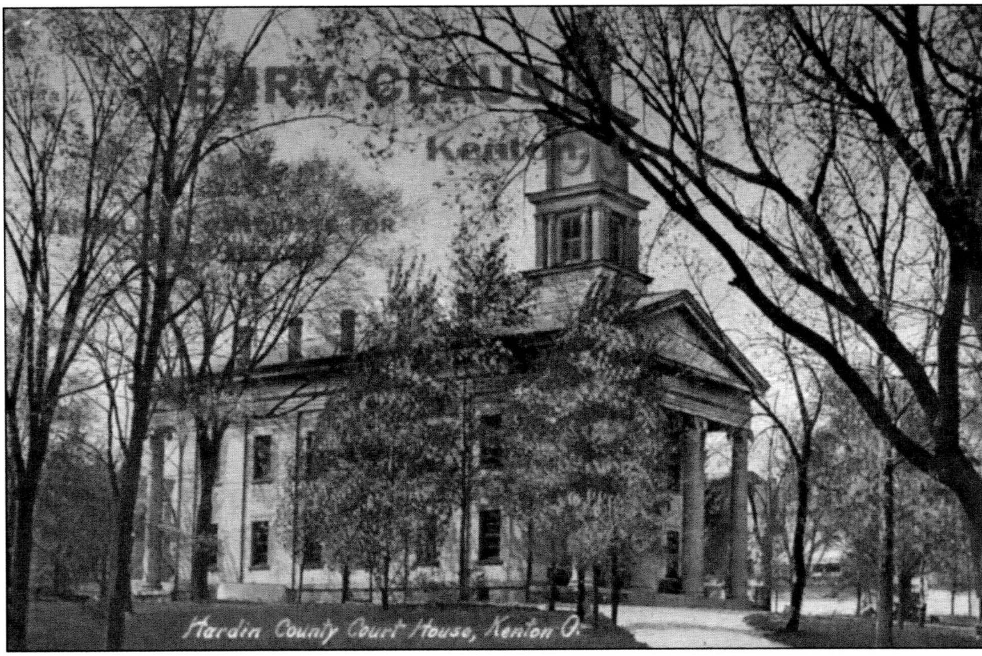

Using the Hardin County Courthouse as a backdrop, Henry Claus, an assistant cashier with the Kenton Savings Bank, advertised his political ambitions. He ran as the Republican candidate for county auditor in 1912. Despite his efforts, Claus was unsuccessful in his attempt to be elected, losing to Ulrich J. Pfeiffer (3,090 to 2,609).

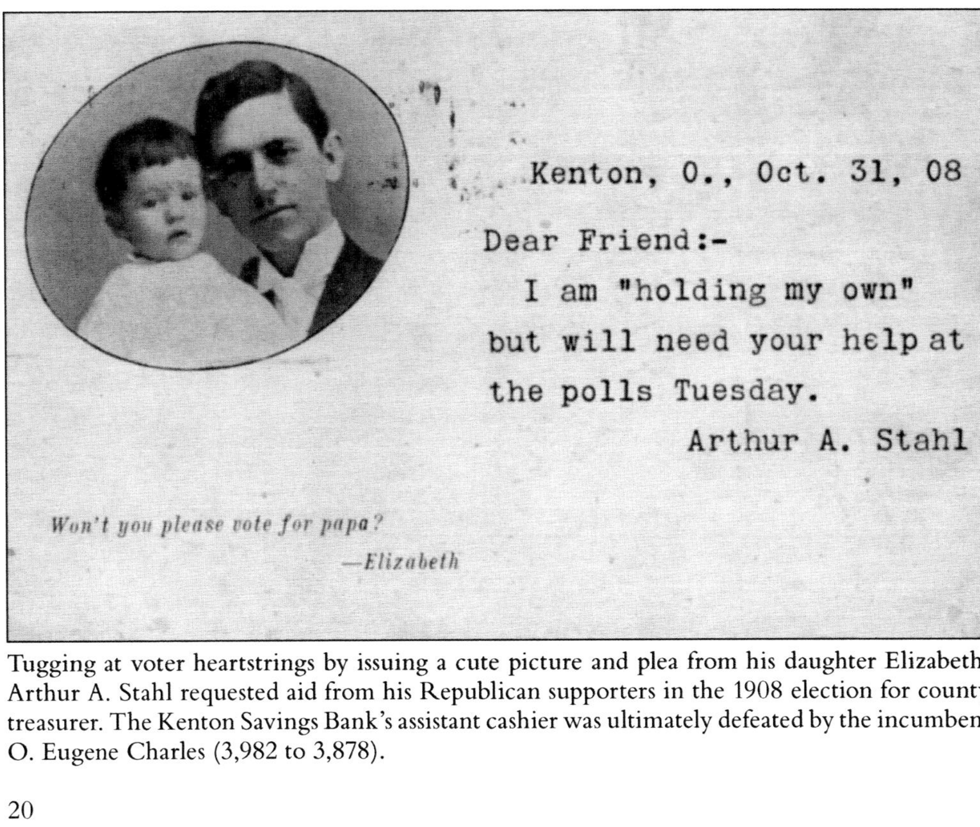

Tugging at voter heartstrings by issuing a cute picture and plea from his daughter Elizabeth, Arthur A. Stahl requested aid from his Republican supporters in the 1908 election for county treasurer. The Kenton Savings Bank's assistant cashier was ultimately defeated by the incumbent O. Eugene Charles (3,982 to 3,878).

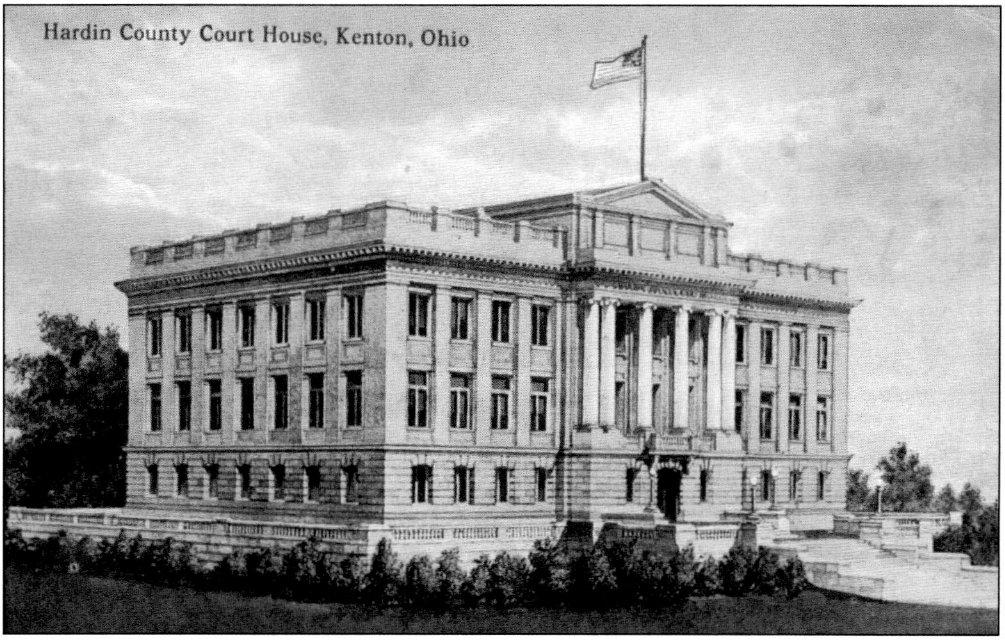

The cornerstone of the third Hardin County Courthouse was laid with much fanfare in 1913. The Neoclassical Revival building was dedicated in May 1915. The $275,000 building featured marble floors, skylights, and murals on the third floor. The bell from the second courthouse was saved and now greets visitors to the current courthouse.

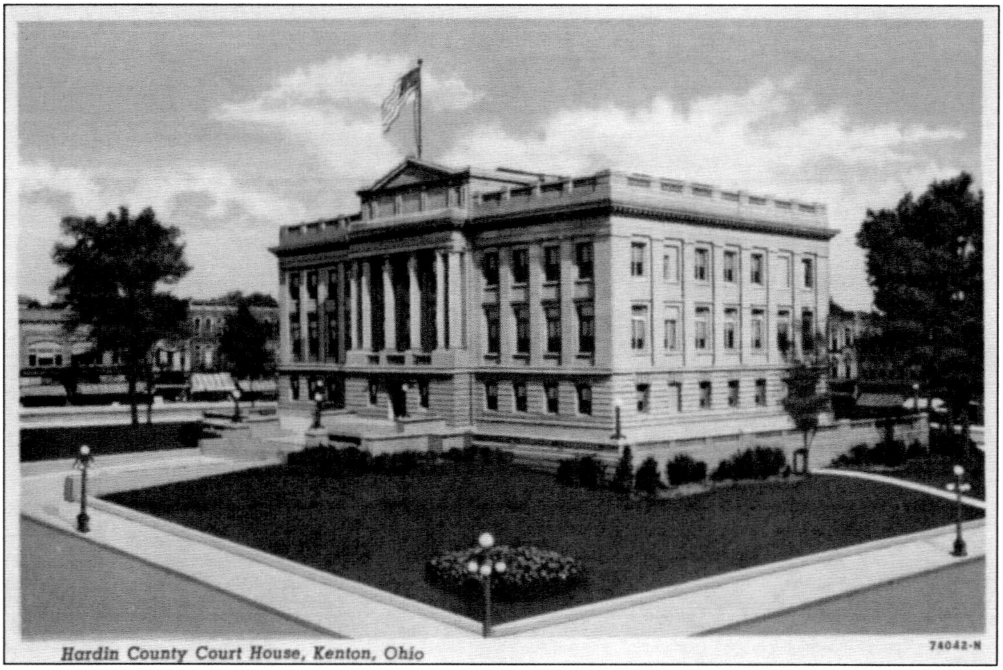

The Kenton News Agency produced this postcard of the third Hardin County Courthouse in the 1930s. The company was located in the Kenton Theatre building on West Franklin Street. The Sullivan Block on West Columbus Street can be seen to the extreme left of the card. Some versions of this card by other publishers list it incorrectly as the Harding County Courthouse.

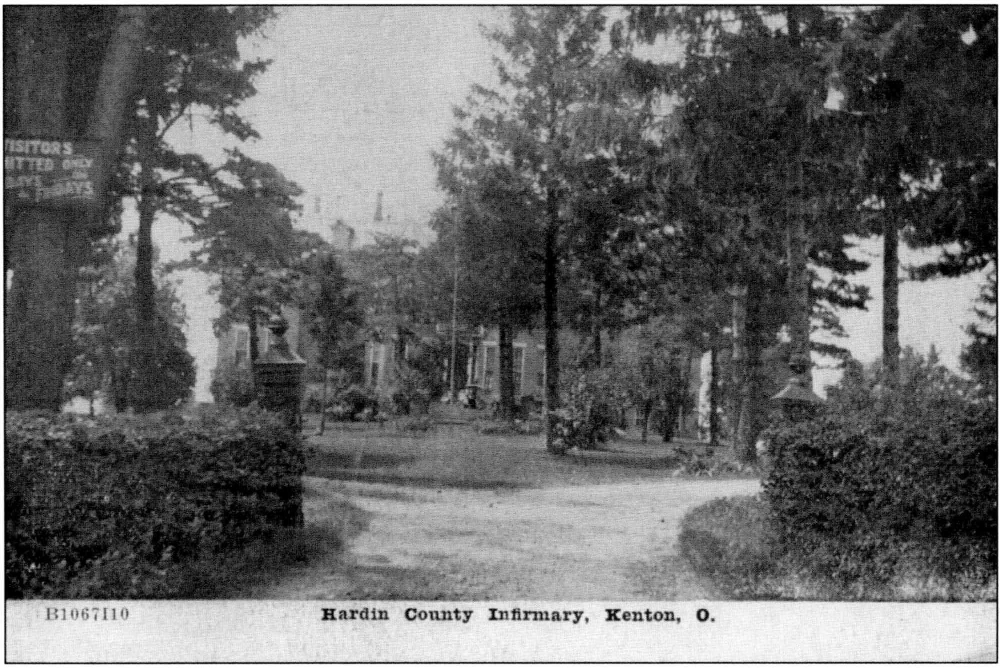

The Hardin County infirmary, planned since the 1850s, finally opened in January 1871 and served the public until 1954 when the main building, seen here about 1908, was replaced by the Hardin County Home. Today, the property is operated by the county commissioners as the Hardin Hills Health Center.

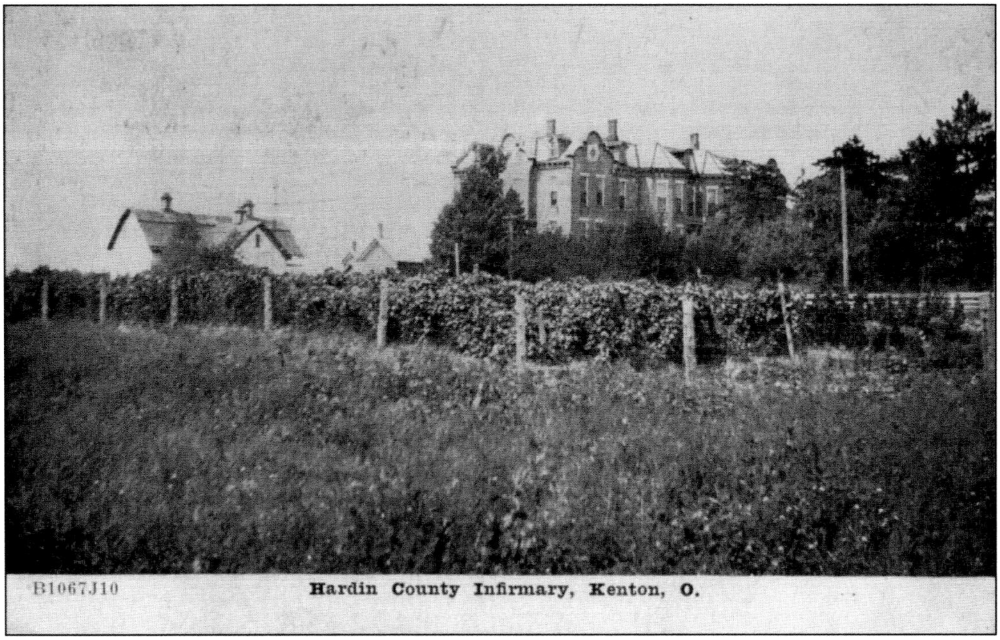

The Hardin County Infirmary was erected just west of Kenton on the Lima Pike (State Route 309). The 40-room main building, carriage house, and farm were constructed from 1869 to 1870 at a cost of $46,000. The working farm in the rear included a cattle barn, hog pens, chicken coop, smokehouse, woodshed, and bakery.

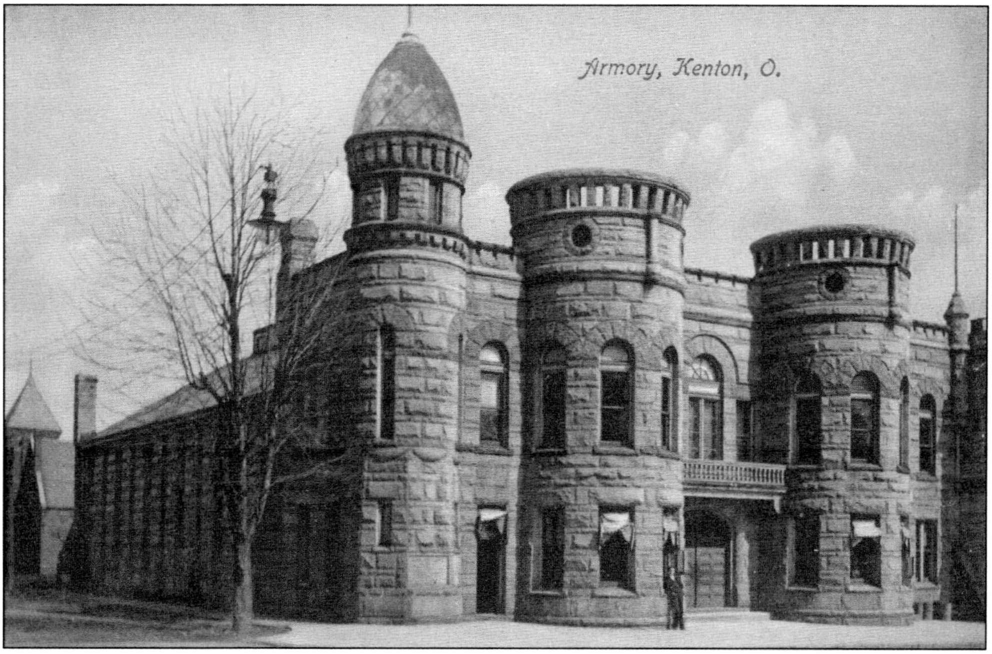

The Hardin County Armory, located at the corner of North Main and East Carroll Streets in Kenton, was constructed in the Romanesque style at a cost of $22,000. Ohio governor William McKinley attended the laying of the cornerstone in August 1894 and dedication in April 1895. The First Baptist Church can be seen to the left rear of the building.

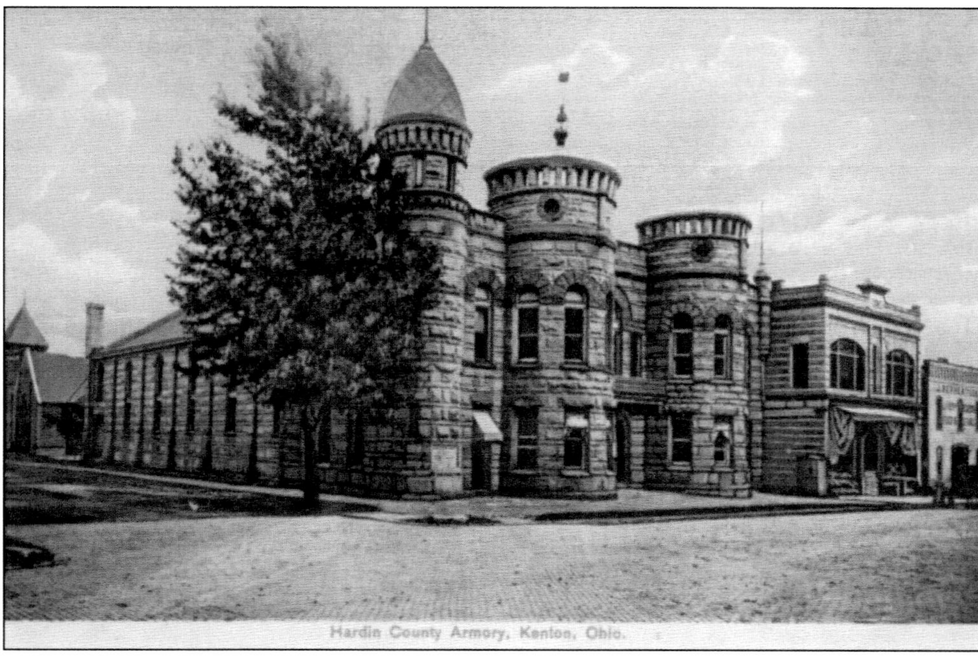

The armory has served as courthouse annex, temporary schoolhouse, wedding chapel, and reception hall. It also hosted numerous dances and athletic activities. A fire in 1947 caused severe damage to the roof and interior. During the early 1990s, the building was restored to its former glory. The Reppert & Sons Livery is to the far right.

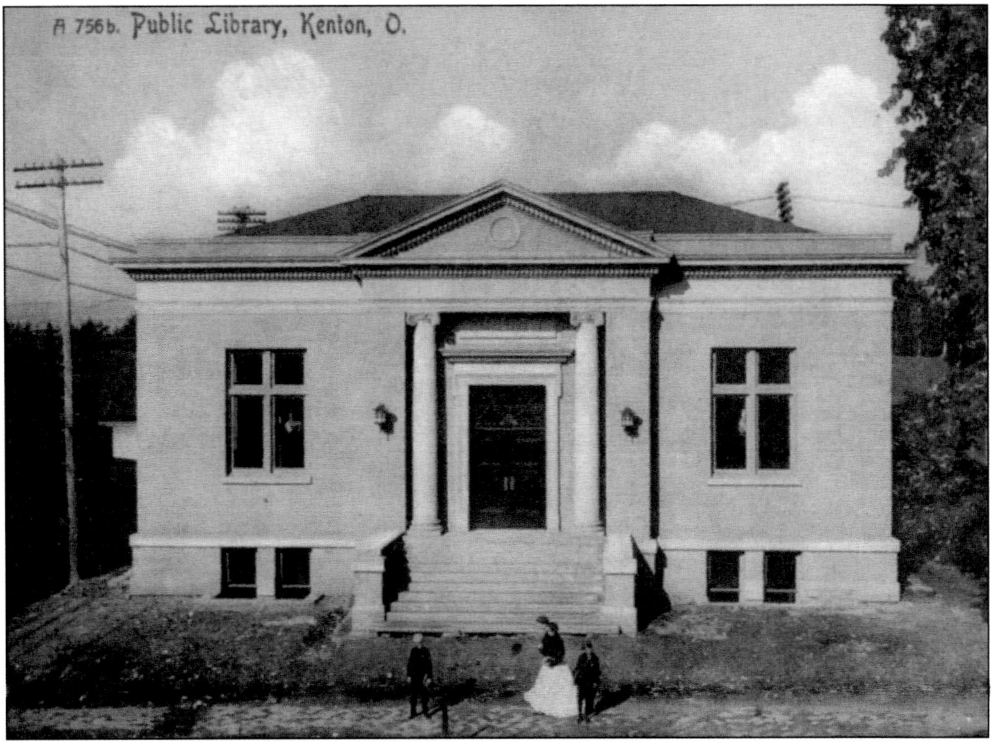

The Kenton Library Association formed in 1853 and opened its first lending library in an upstairs room in the Pfeiffer Block on the corner of North Main and East Columbus Streets in 1886. A $20,000 donation from the Carnegie Foundation allowed the organization to move into the new Carnegie Library Building on North Detroit Street in 1905.

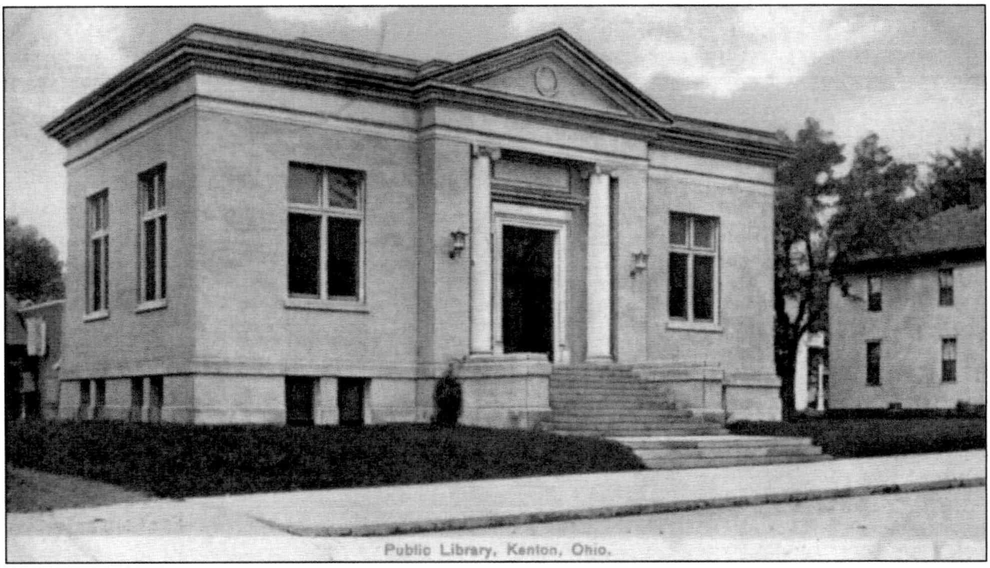

The Hardin County District Library moved to East Columbus Street on the site of the former Ellis Junior High School in 1968. In 1977, the facility was renamed for local benefactor Mary Lou Johnson. The house to the right of the library was torn down and replaced by a service station that now houses Mount Victory Meats.

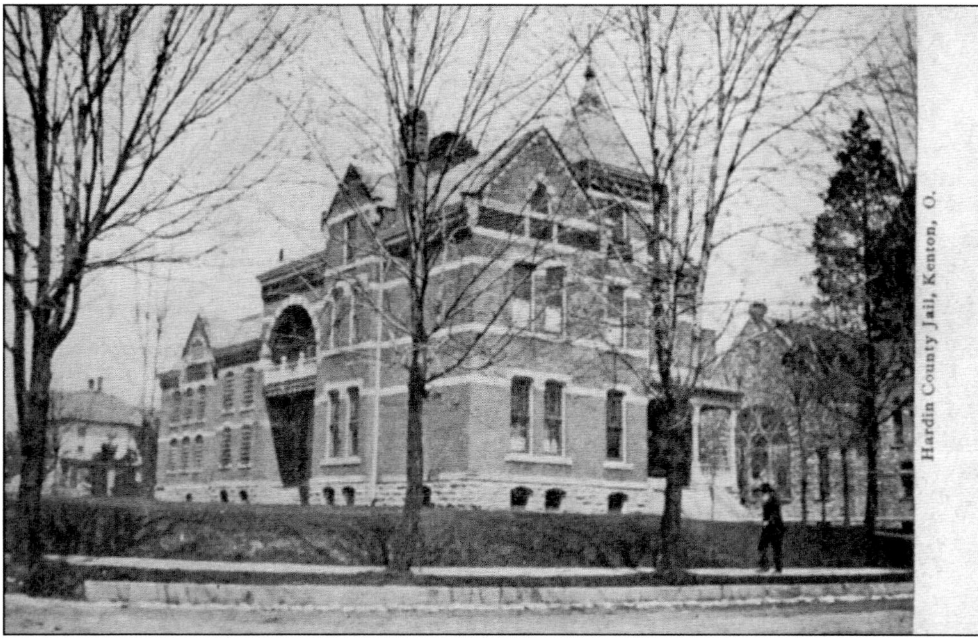

Hardin County's third jail was built on East Carroll Street in 1886 to replace the 1855 jail on the same site. There were 16 cells on each floor and an apartment in the front for the sheriff's family. The facility ceased housing inmates following construction of the Multi-County Correctional Center near Marion. In 2008, the sheriff's department moved into the remodeled Jacob Parrott Armory on South Main Street.

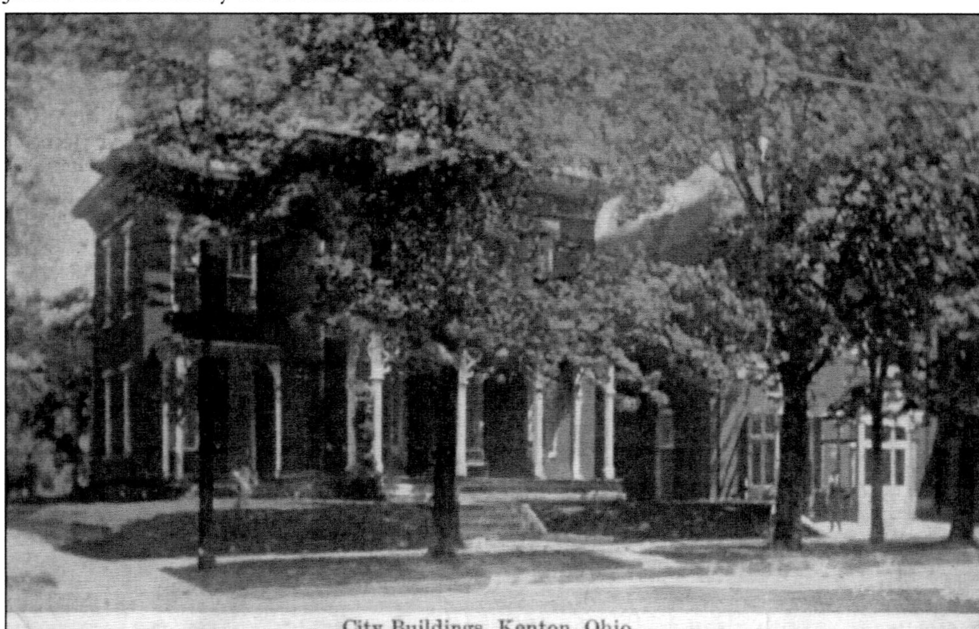

A building was constructed on North Main Street (south of the Price Funeral Home) in 1870 to house the town hall, engine house, and city jail. In 1907, the James White house, on the corner of West Columbus and North Market Streets, was purchased and remodeled to accommodate the new Kenton City Building, seen here about 1910.

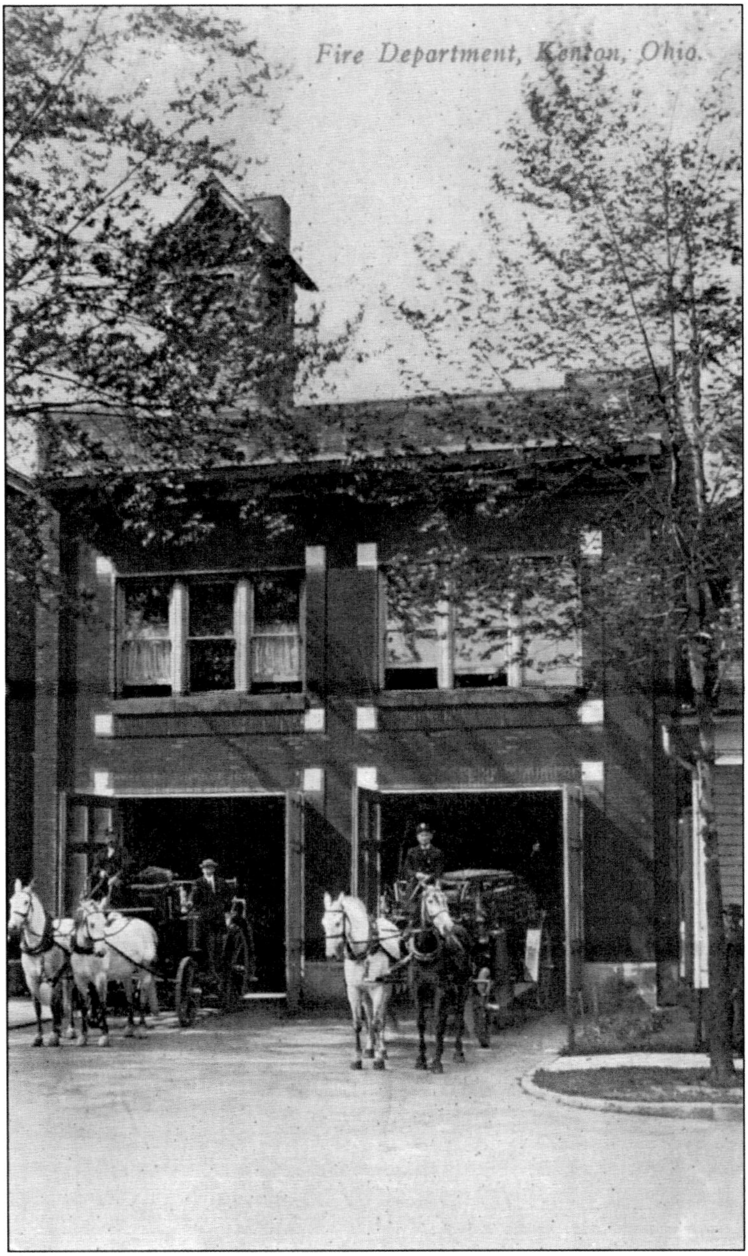

The Kenton Fire Department can trace its history to the first purchase of firefighting apparatus in July 1850. The original hook and ladder company was formed in March 1853 following the courthouse fire. The Reindeer Fire Company No. 2 was organized in January 1859 and quartered in a temporary engine house until a new station was built in 1870. The Star Hook and Ladder Company was organized about 1870. The competing Simon Kenton Steam Engine Company was formed in July 1872. Upon outgrowing the North Main Street station, the department purchased the former Ross home on West Columbus Street to erect a new engine house. The station, seen here about 1910, was constructed in 1907 for $9,000 and occupied until 1984. In 1985, the Kenton Fire Department moved into a much larger station on South Main Street, which cost $350,000 to erect.

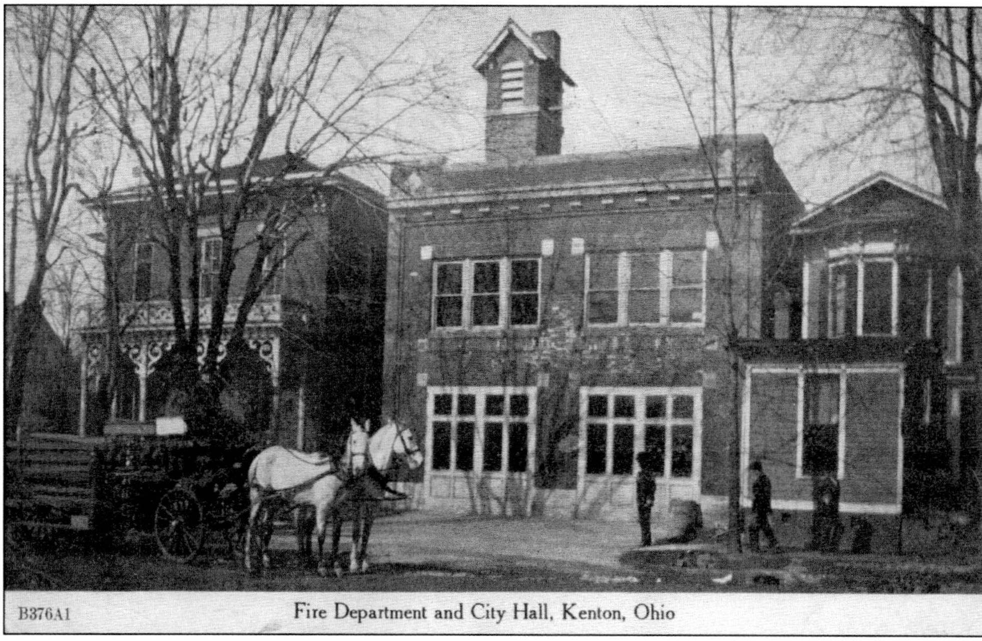

One of Kenton's horse-drawn engines poses about 1908 in front of the Kenton City Hall and Fire Station on West Columbus Street. Kenton's first hand-powered pumper, the Reindeer Fire Engine, was purchased in 1858. The first horse-drawn fire apparatus, Simon Kenton No. 1, was purchased in 1872, and the department's first motorized fire truck was purchased in November 1920.

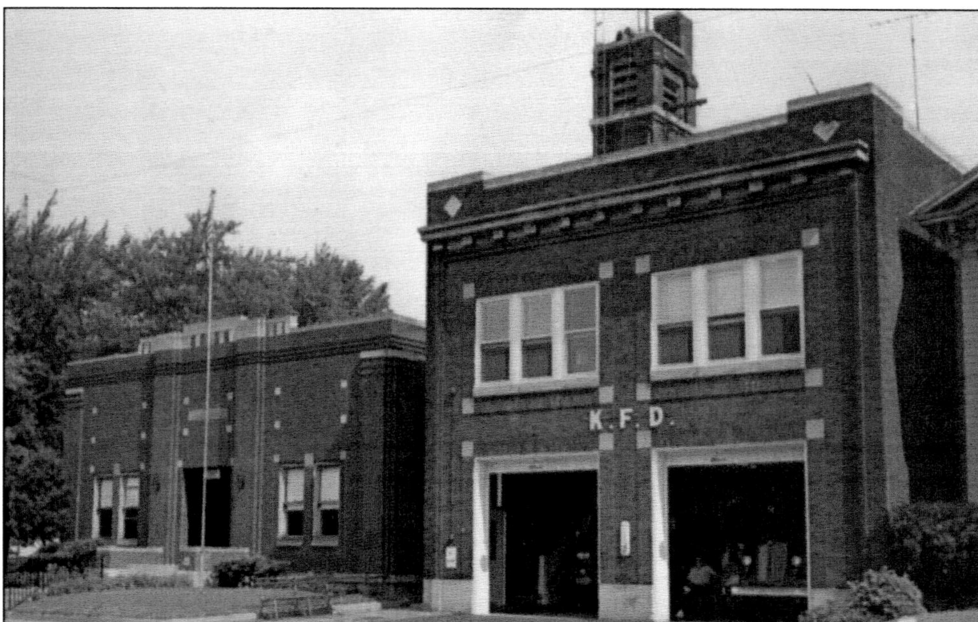

The Kenton City Building, seen here about 1970, was constructed in 1937 and contained the city jail in the rear. The Kenton city offices moved into the Kenton Municipal Building on West Franklin Street in 1991, abandoning this structure; it now houses a private business. Erected in 1907, the engine house next door opened in February 1908 and was razed in 1984.

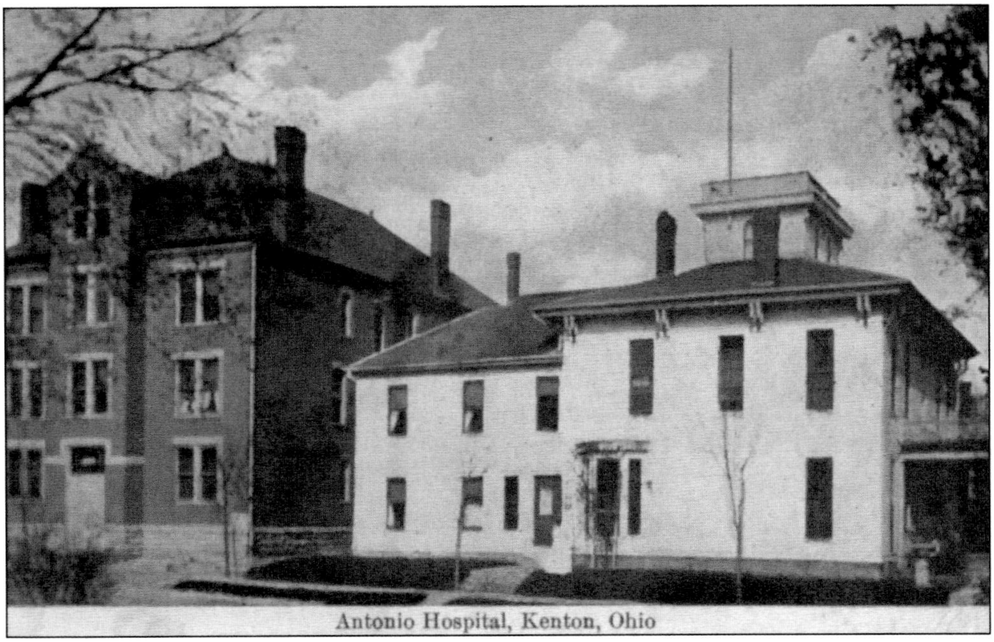

Rev. Anthony Siebenfoercher opened the San Antonio Hospital, known originally as Saint Mark's Hospital, with the Sisters of Charity in April 1897. The 1900 wood and 1907 brick additions are seen to the left of the former Moore Boarding House, which was converted into the hospital. The sisters also operated their school of nursing here from 1910 until 1918.

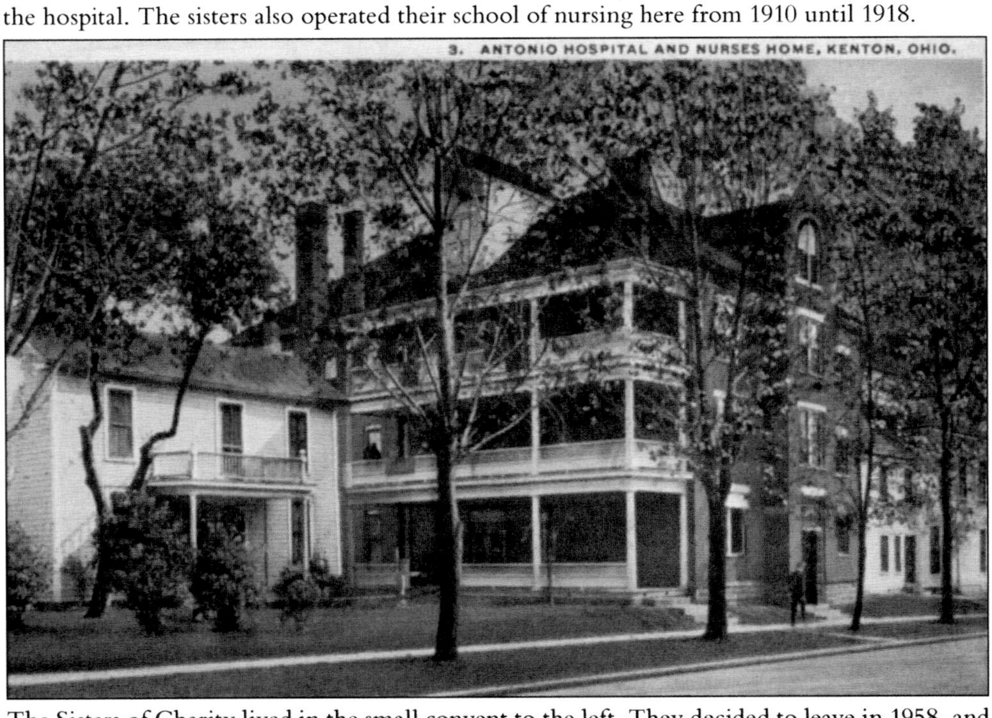

The Sisters of Charity lived in the small convent to the left. They decided to leave in 1958, and the institution was closed in 1964. Shortly afterwards, San Antonio Hospital was sold to the Hardin Memorial Hospital Company. In September 1971, the hospital was sold to a group that reopened the complex as the Corinthian Nursing Home.

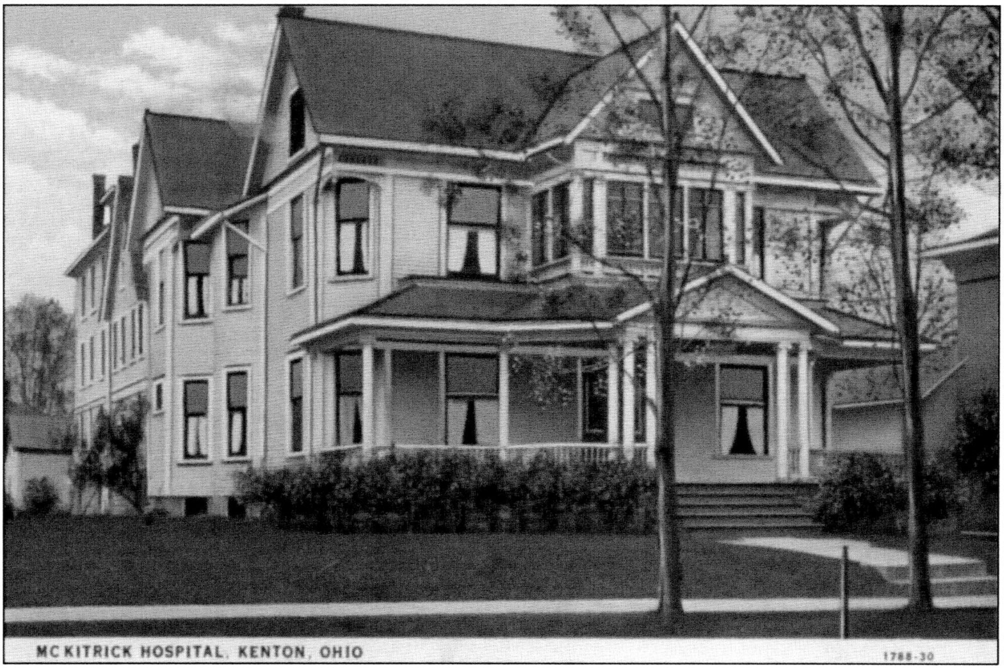

Dr. Austin S. McKitrick, one of Kenton's leading physicians, opened Hardin County's first public hospital in January 1918. He purchased and renovated the former Henry Price residence on North Detroit Street. It was renovated several times until it contained 21 rooms. The third floor housed an early nurse's school during the 1920s.

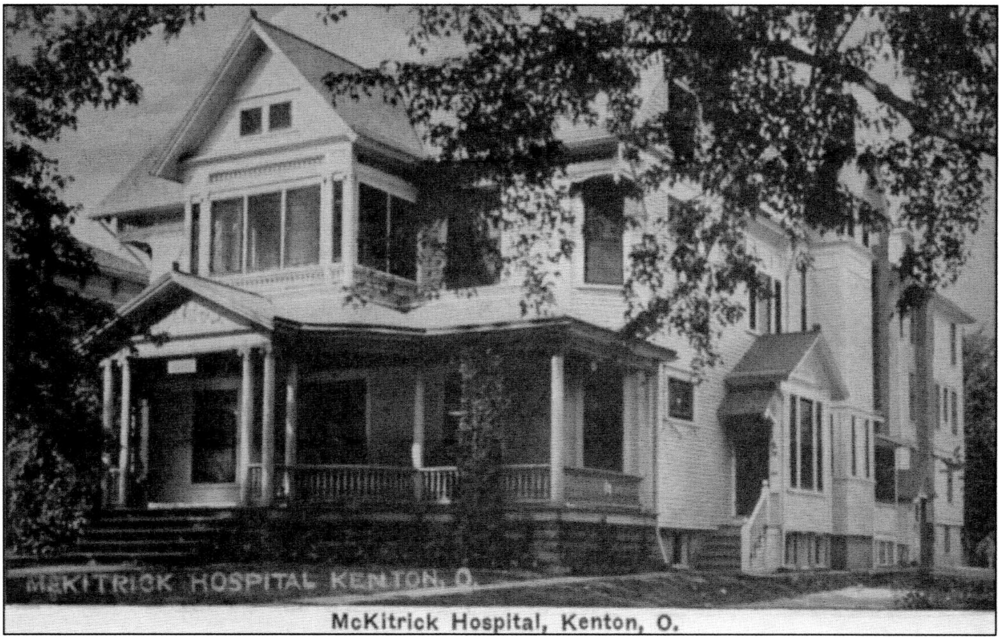

Gail H. Kurtz mailed this postcard to her friend Carrie Clinger, a patient in the hospital, during August 1943 as a souvenir of her stay. The McKitrick Hospital Company operated the institution from 1923 until Hardin Memorial Hospital opened. The hospital transferred its last patient in 1952 before officially closing. The building now operates as the Whitley Apartments.

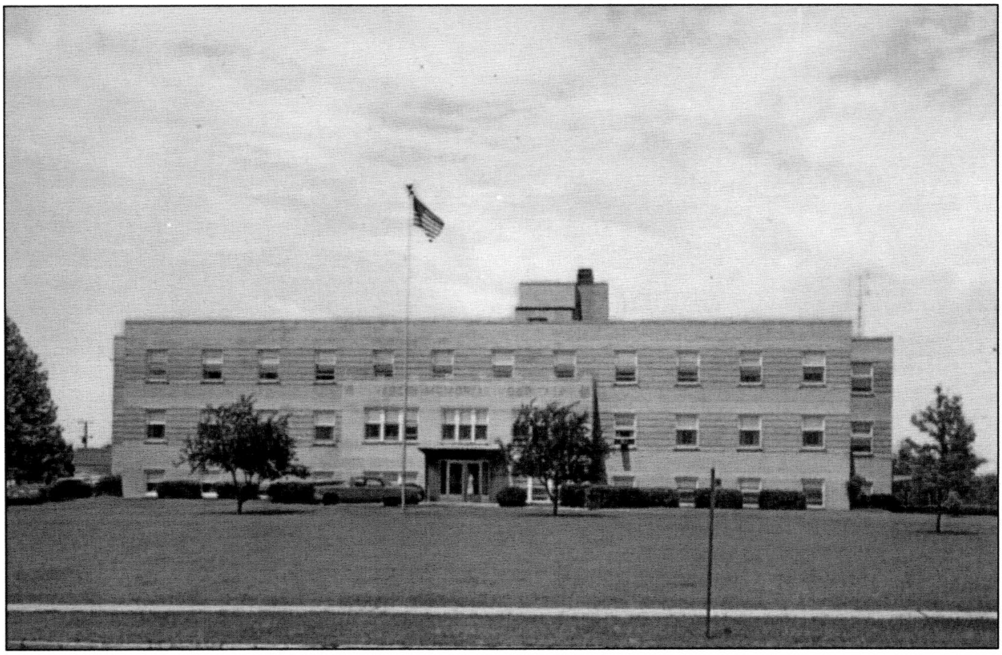

Plans for replacing the aging McKitrick Hospital began in the mid-1940s. Hardin Memorial Hospital opened east of town along Franklin Street in February 1952. While the building, photographed about 1965, was undergoing expansion in 1971, the company sold the San Antonio Hospital complex. It remains the only hospital in Hardin County.

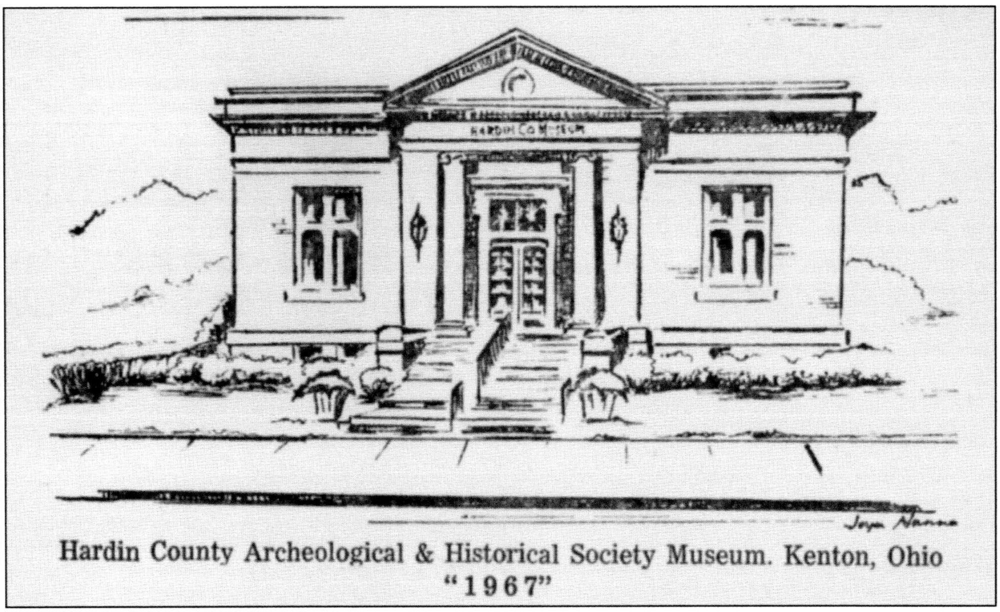

Hardin County's Archaeological and Historical Society Museum occupied the former library building from 1967 until 1983 when the Sullivan-Johnson Museum on North Main Street opened during the county's sesquicentennial. The abandoned building was restored in the 1990s and now houses Kenton Dental Care.

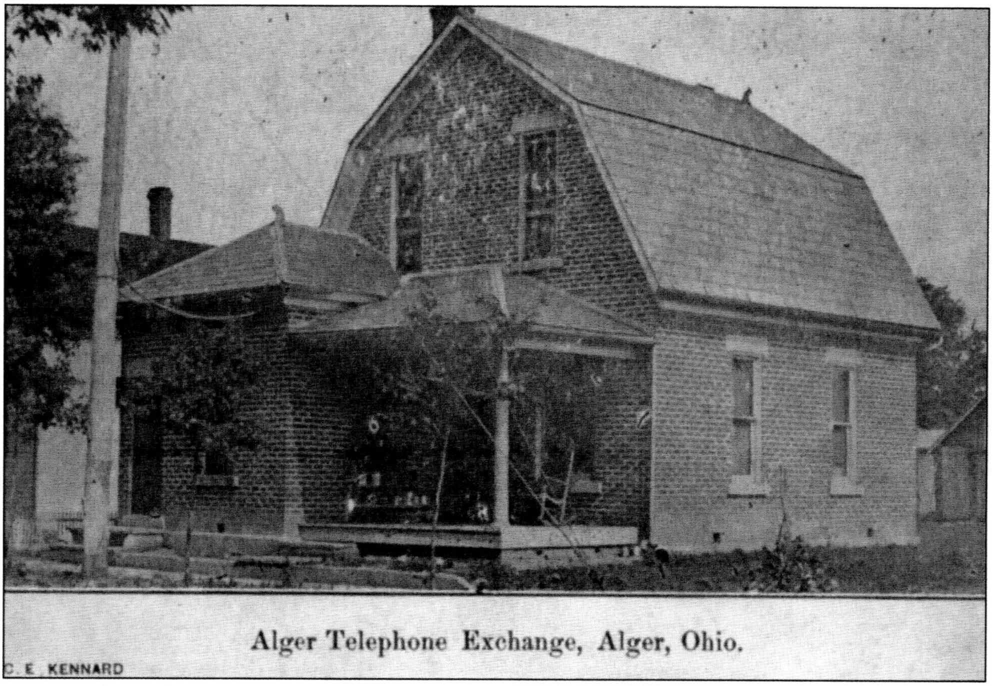

During the early 1900s, telephone service was beginning to take root in Hardin County. Construction of the Alger Telephone Exchange allowed parties along the Scioto Marsh to call nearby cities and railroads, resulting in easier shipping and increased productivity. In March 1907, the Ada Telephone Exchange Company purchased the Alger and McGuffey exchanges.

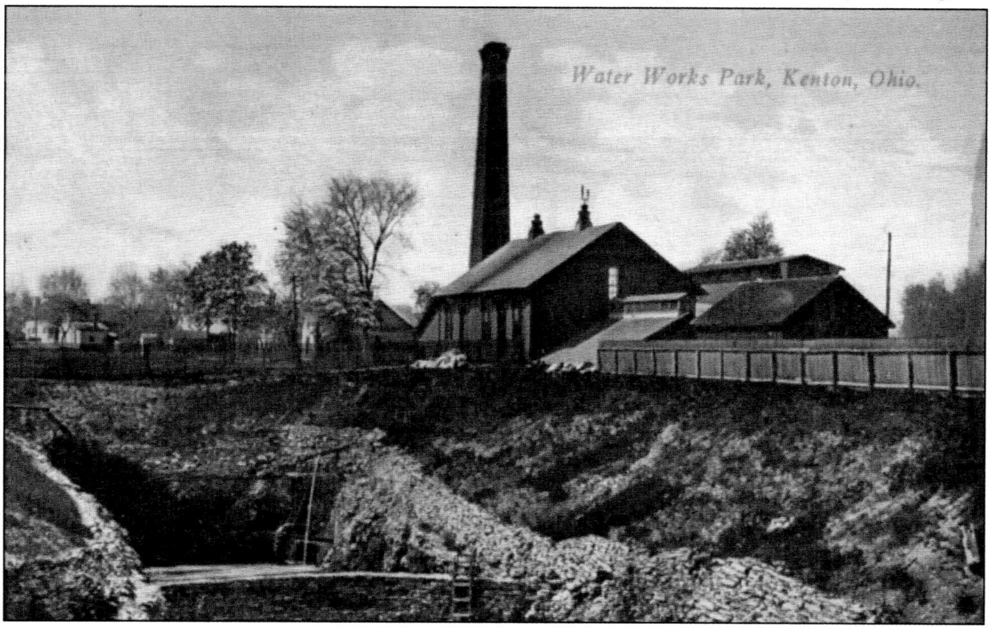

The Kenton Water Works Company was established in 1881. Kenton purchased the company in 1887 and erected a water treatment plant in 1933. A baseball diamond (Water Works Park) was developed in the 1890s between the Scioto River and the structure. The field also hosted football games before Robinson Field was completed in 1936.

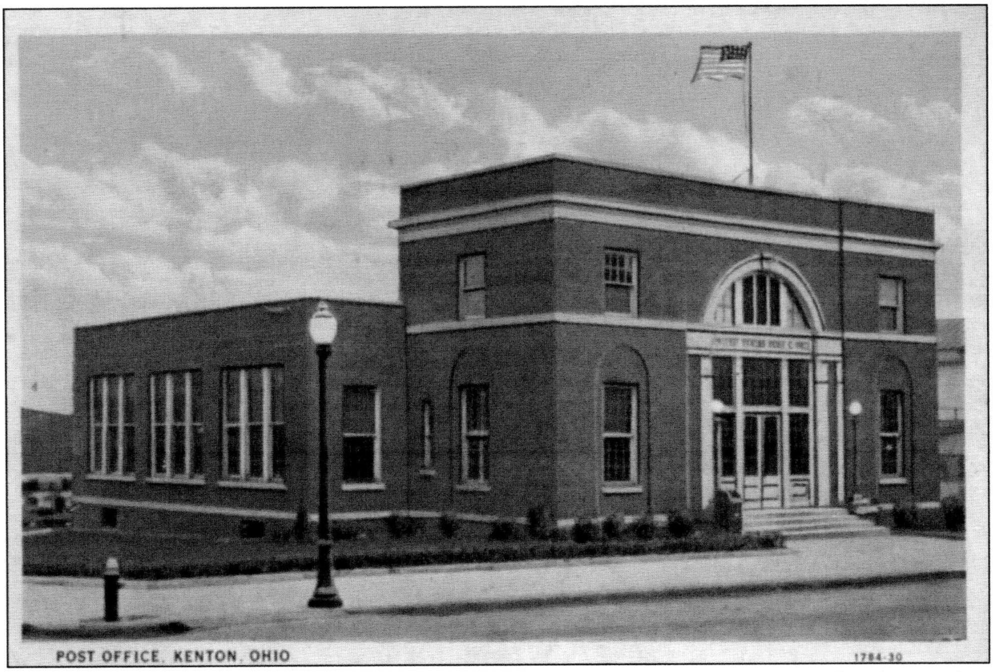

The McArthur Post Office, established in 1832 at Fort McArthur, was renamed and moved to Kenton the next year. The office spent time in several locations around the courthouse square and a short period in the Furney Building. The current Kenton Post Office on West Franklin Street was constructed in 1925 and dedicated in February 1926.

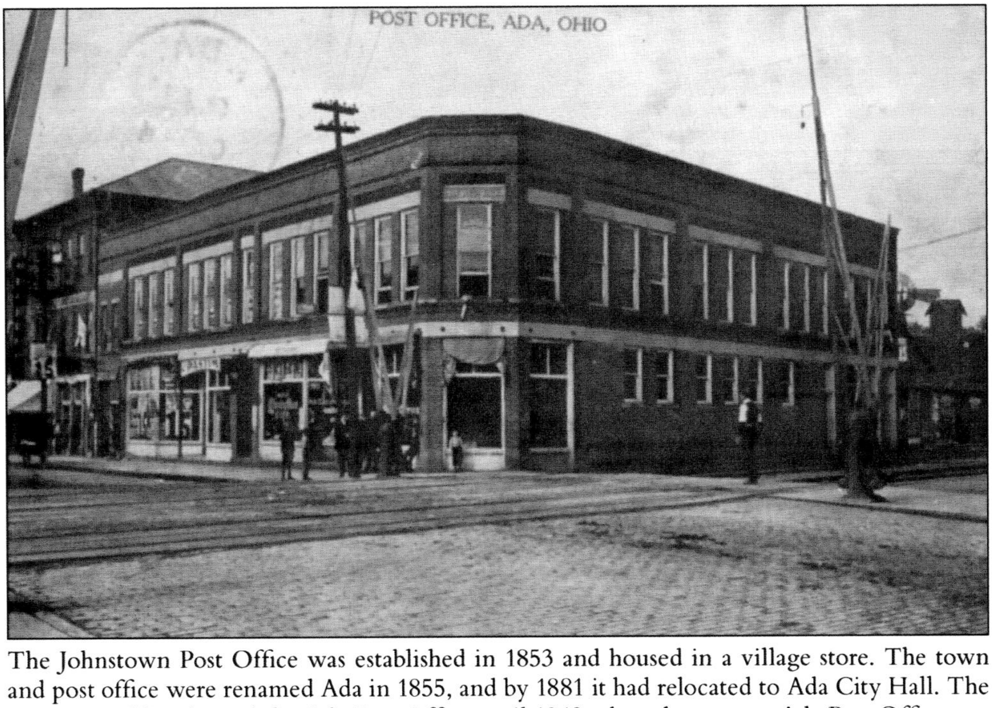

The Johnstown Post Office was established in 1853 and housed in a village store. The town and post office were renamed Ada in 1855, and by 1881 it had relocated to Ada City Hall. The Brewer Building hosted the Ada Post Office until 1942 when the current Ada Post Office was constructed on South Main Street.

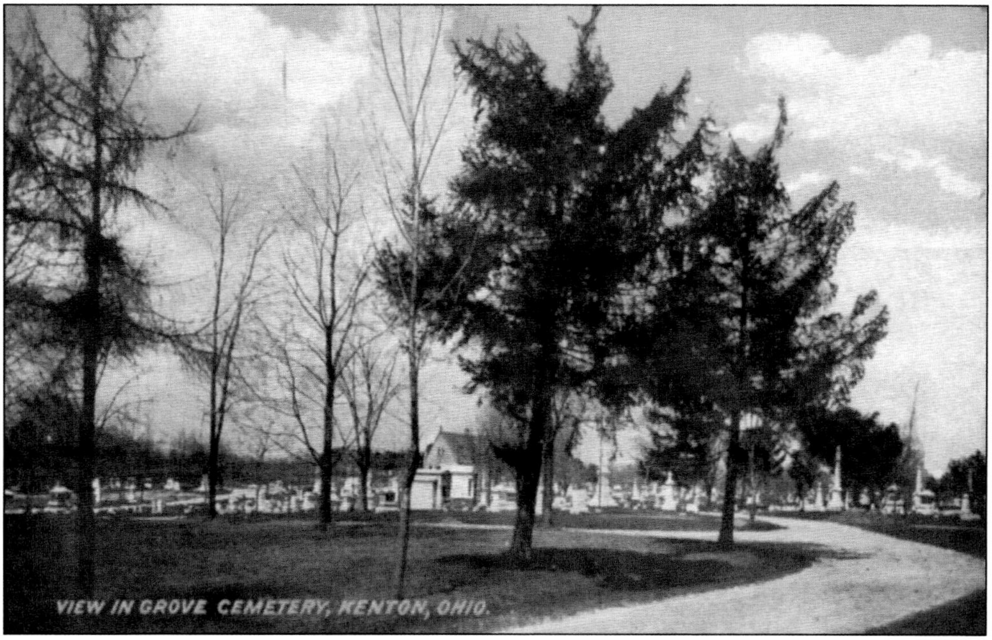

Kenton's original cemetery was platted northeast of town in 1833 but was never used. The Grove Cemetery Association was established in August 1854 and sold its first plots in October. The City of Kenton took control in 1874 and erected the chapel and vault in 1894. Other early burial grounds were the Methodist Cemetery (Columbus and Carroll Streets), Pioneer Cemetery (Franklin Street), and Saint Mary's Catholic Cemetery (Cemetery Road).

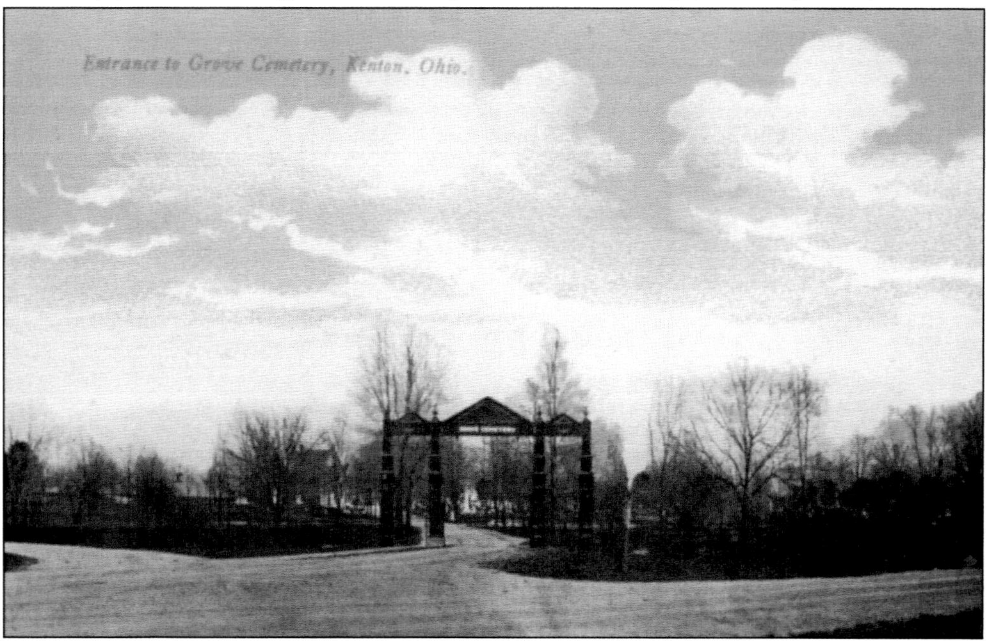

The original Grove Cemetery entrance, viewed here from East Franklin Street (Harding Highway) in about 1910, featured this cast-iron gate produced by the Champion Iron Fence Company. The gate was reportedly torn down during a scrap-metal drive in the 1940s. A mausoleum was erected north of the cemetery along Cemetery Road (Jacob Parrott Boulevard) in 1919.

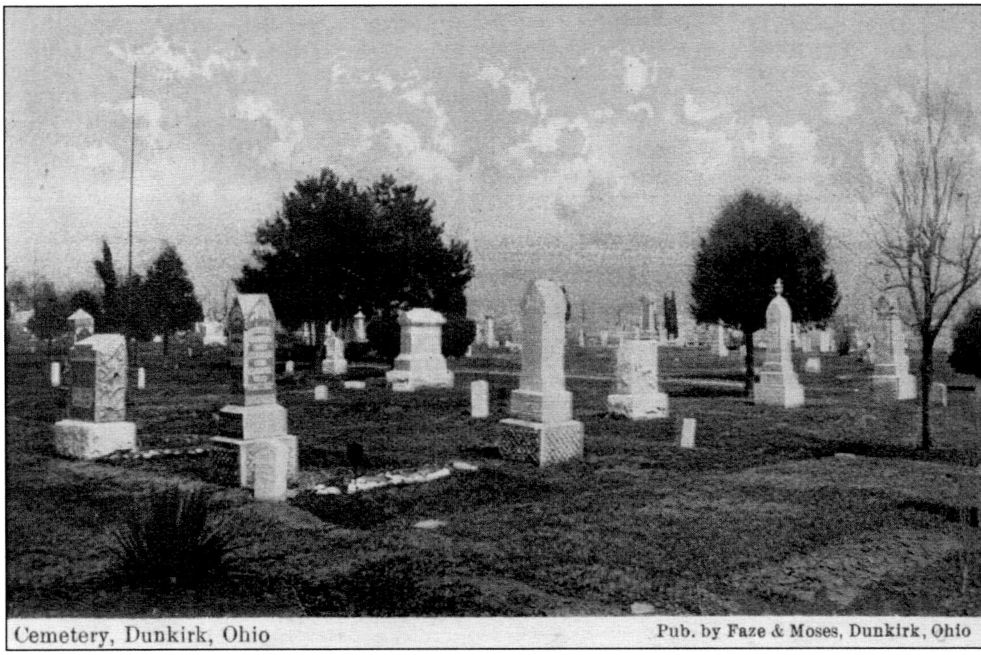

The Faze & Moses dry goods store published this view of Dunkirk Cemetery in 1910. The cemetery began as a family plot located on the farm of Levi Bodley. Its first recorded internment was an unknown local worker in 1835. Following the burial of his wife, Bodley donated the land to the Blanchard Township Trustees for use as a public burying ground.

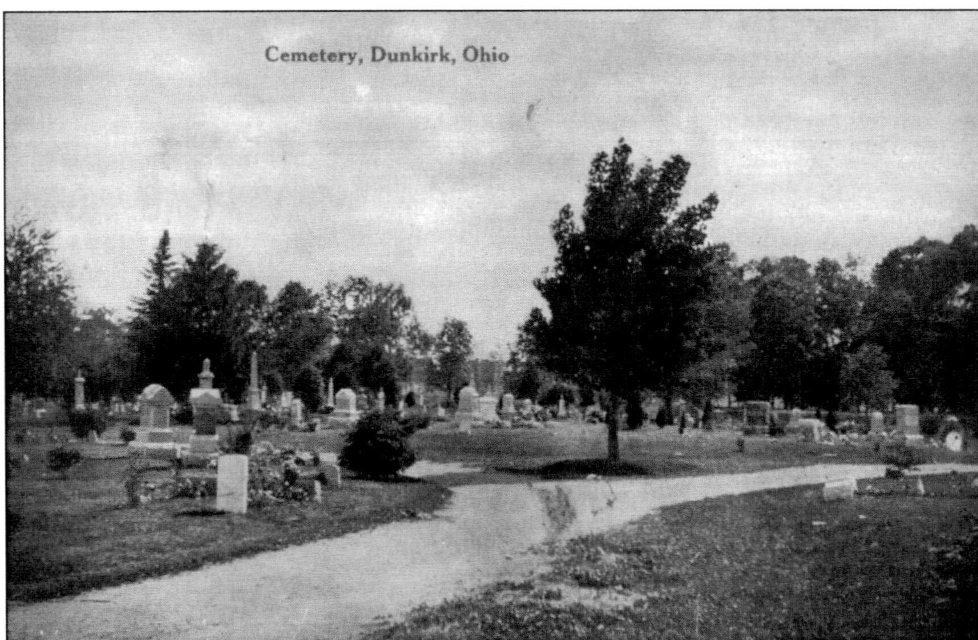

This is the Dunkirk Cemetery, located south of town along State Route 68, as it looked about 1910. A mausoleum was constructed on the property in 1903. Additional lands were donated by the cemetery's neighbors in 1968, increasing the total size to a little over 20 acres.

Three

Street Scenes

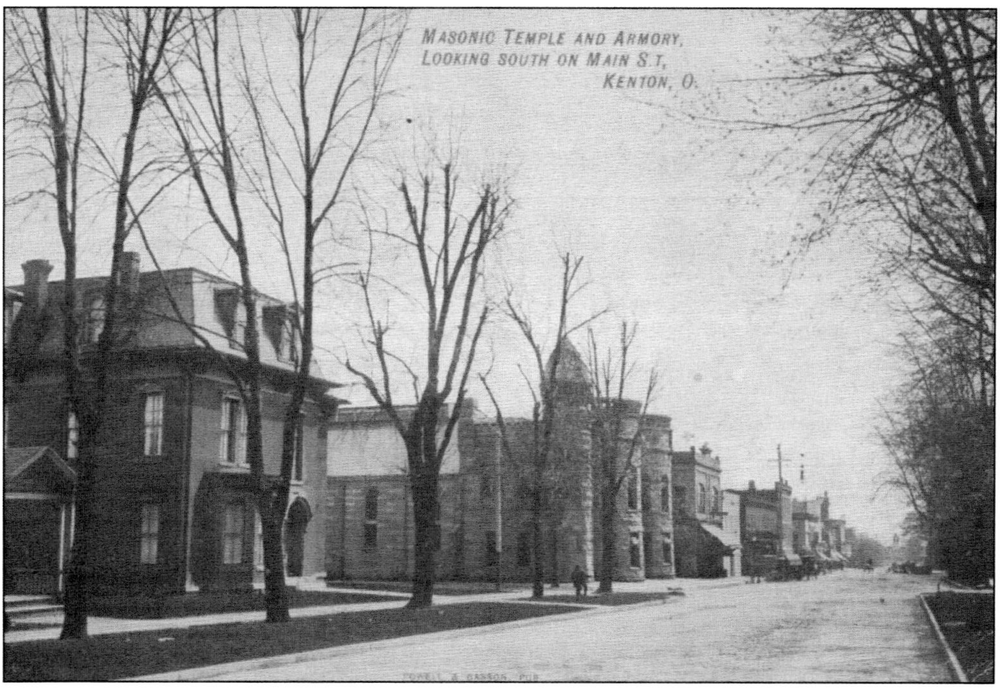

Powell & Gasson's Big Drug Store published this c. 1905 view of North Main Street facing south toward downtown Kenton from a vantage point near the front of Daniel Sullivan's home. The Masonic Temple and Hardin County Armory are visible on opposite sides of East Carroll Street. The South School is visible at the end of the street.

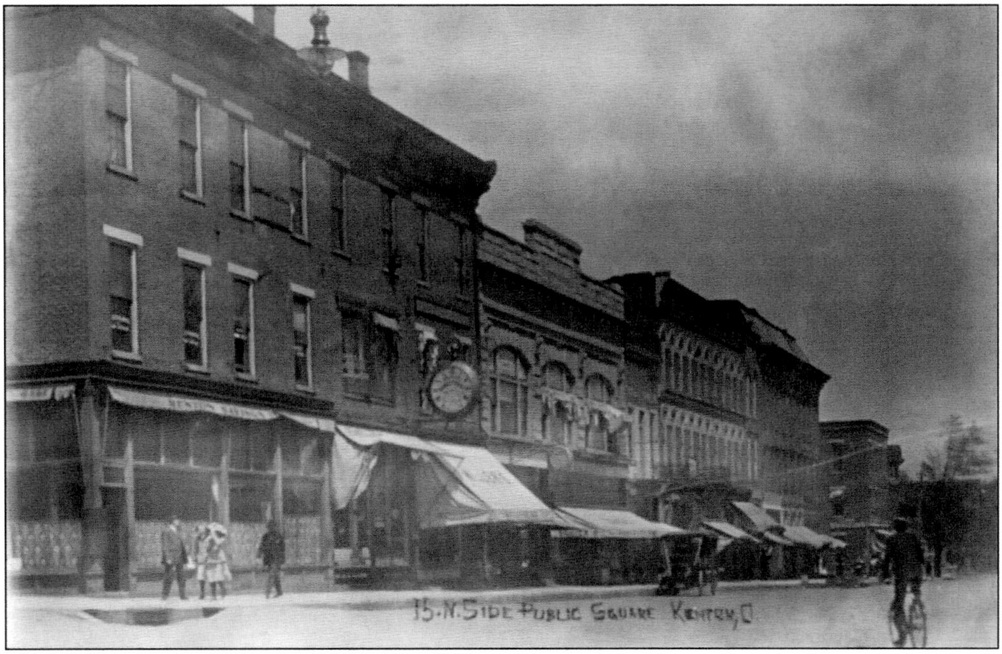

Seen here is a Real Photo postcard mailed to Canada in 1911 showing the north side of the public square. Some of the storefronts visible on the street include Kenton Savings Bank, Miller's Footwear, Schick's Dry Goods, Stinson's Jewelry Store, and Kellogg's Grocery. The building in the center of the block was constructed by saddler Daniel Sullivan, whose name also adorns the local museum.

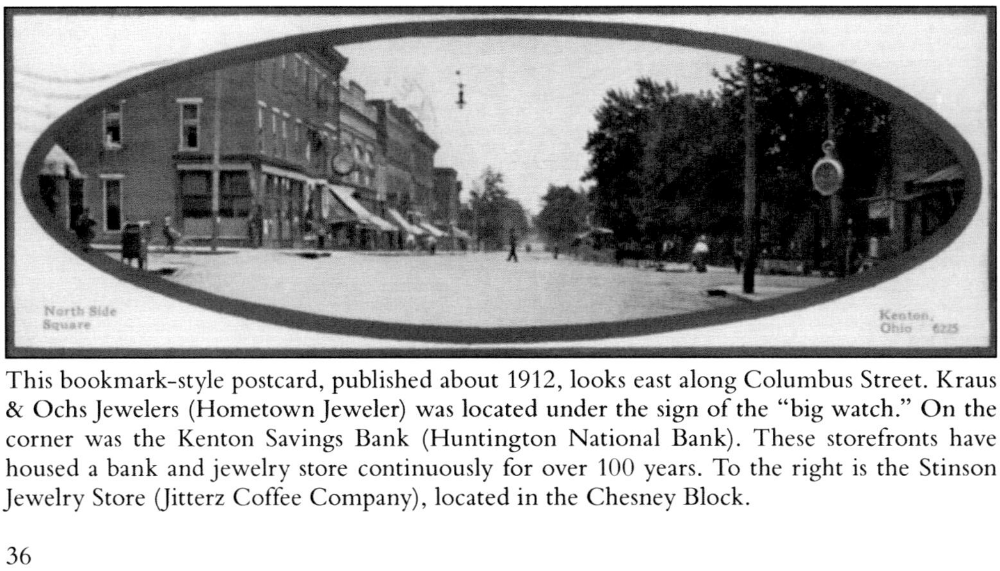

This bookmark-style postcard, published about 1912, looks east along Columbus Street. Kraus & Ochs Jewelers (Hometown Jeweler) was located under the sign of the "big watch." On the corner was the Kenton Savings Bank (Huntington National Bank). These storefronts have housed a bank and jewelry store continuously for over 100 years. To the right is the Stinson Jewelry Store (Jitterz Coffee Company), located in the Chesney Block.

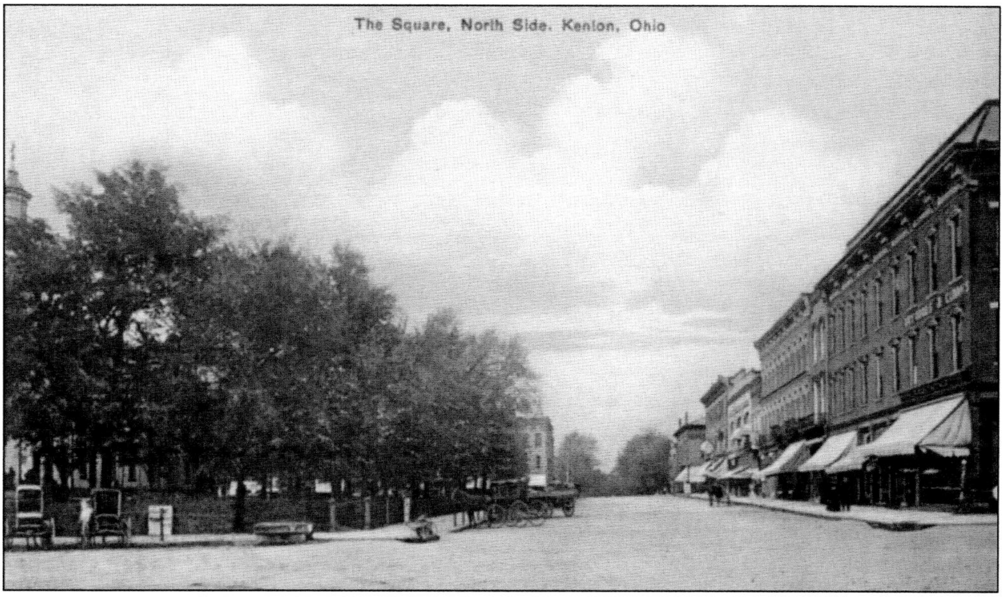

This postcard facing west along Columbus Street from its intersection with Main Street was published by William Snodgrass around 1910. The courthouse and steeple can be seen through the trees to the left. The J.S. Armitage & Company dry goods store (Professional Building) is in the right corner. The Norse & Caine dry goods store and Kraus and Ochs' sign are visible at the far end of the street.

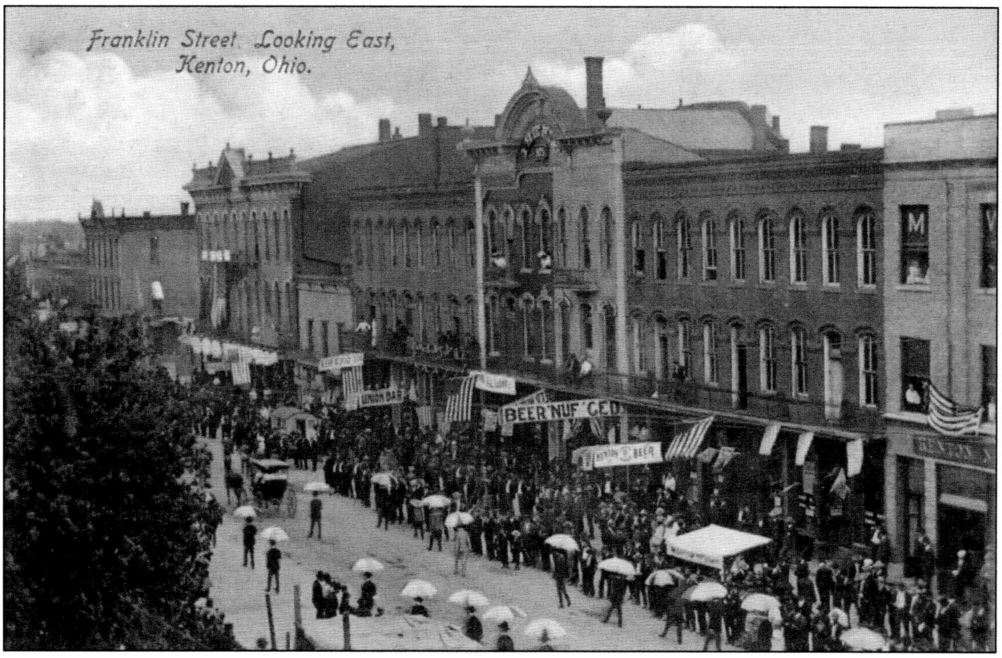

Revelers watch an eastbound parade on Franklin Street from the sidewalk and balconies above the numerous saloons located along the south side of the courthouse square. Dickenson's Grand Opera House, located on the east end of the block, was erected in 1863 and burned in 1932. The Kenton National Bank was organized in 1886 and moved into the corner of the Ahlefeld Block in 1904.

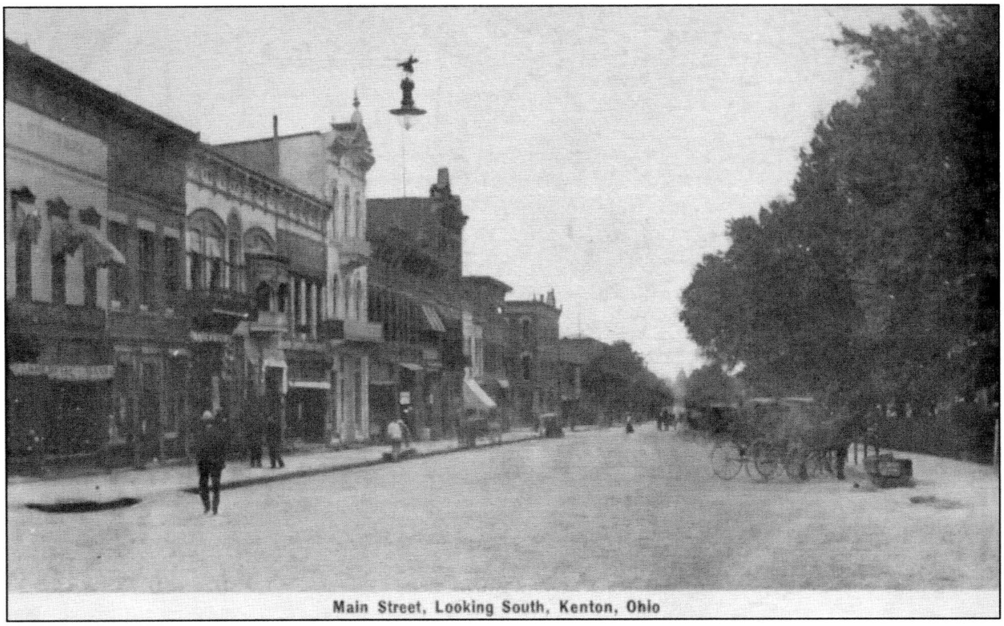

The east side of Kenton's courthouse square features some of the oldest surviving buildings in the downtown area. The taller buildings seen underneath the streetlight are the Price Block (1875), City Block (1878), and the Odd Fellows Block (1878). The Pfeiffer Block to the left housed the Commercial Bank downstairs and the public library on the second floor.

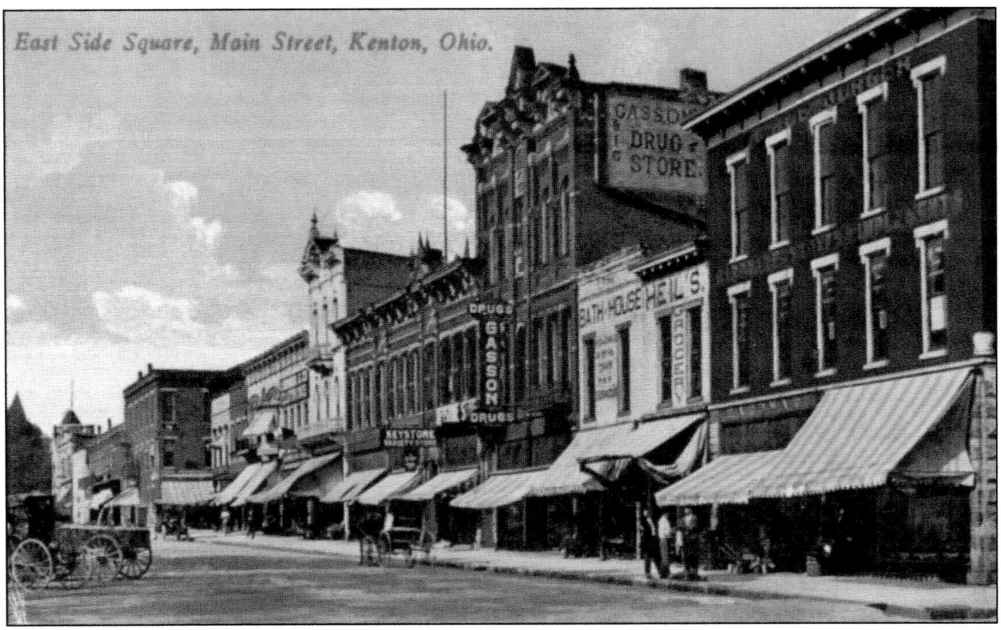

Main Street, home to Gasson's Drug Store, is viewed here north toward Columbus Street from the intersection with East Franklin Street in 1910. Numerous postcards of Kenton were published in the early 1900s by James E. Gasson. William W. Durbin established the original headquarters of the International Brotherhood of Magicians on this block in 1926.

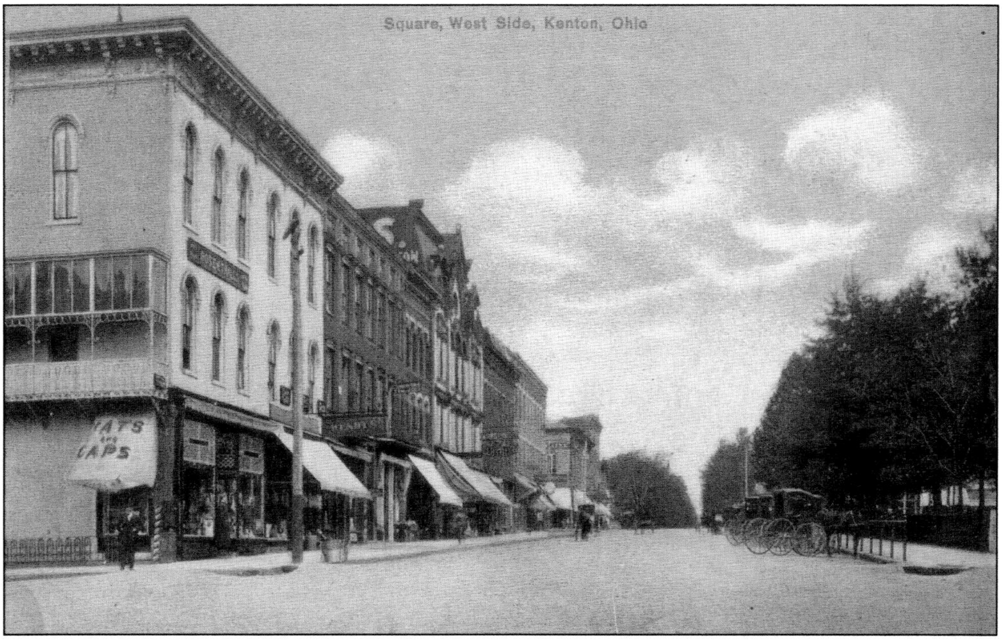

William Snodgrass published this view of the west side of the courthouse square about 1910. The Brunson Block on the corner, occupied by Rosenthall's Clothing Store, now houses B.R. Brunson's Restaurant. The Nourse & Caine dry goods store (Finders Keepers) is visible at the far end of the street.

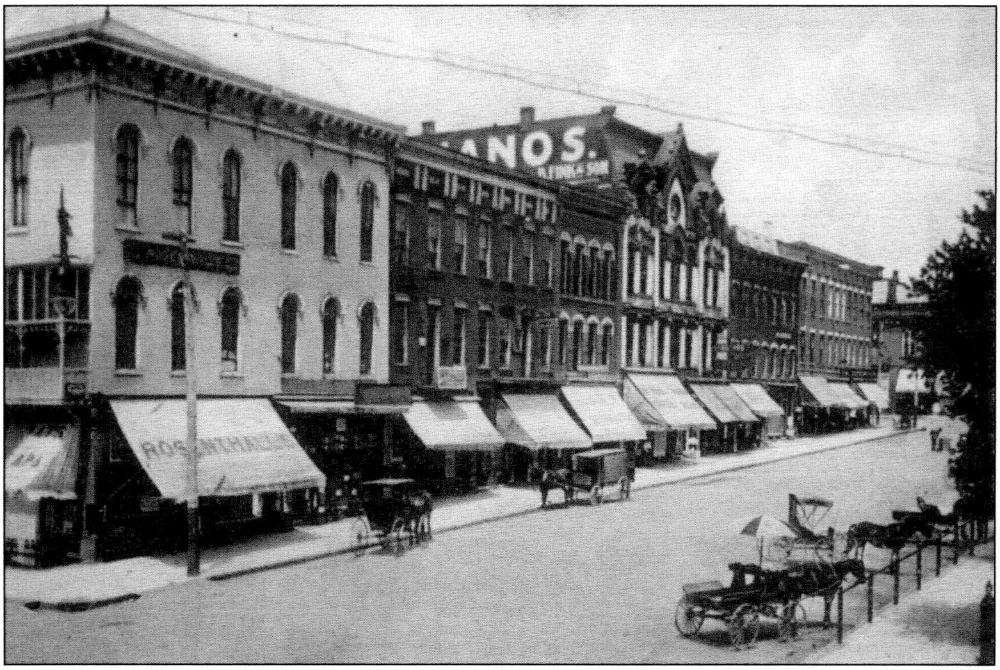

This 1910 view of Detroit Street faces north toward Columbus Street. The three-story Masonic Block in the center was built in 1877 by Benedict Fink and John A. Shectala. In 1886, Charles B. Fink joined his father in the B. Fink & Son dry goods and music store. By 1915, Albert C. Fink had opened a separate piano store.

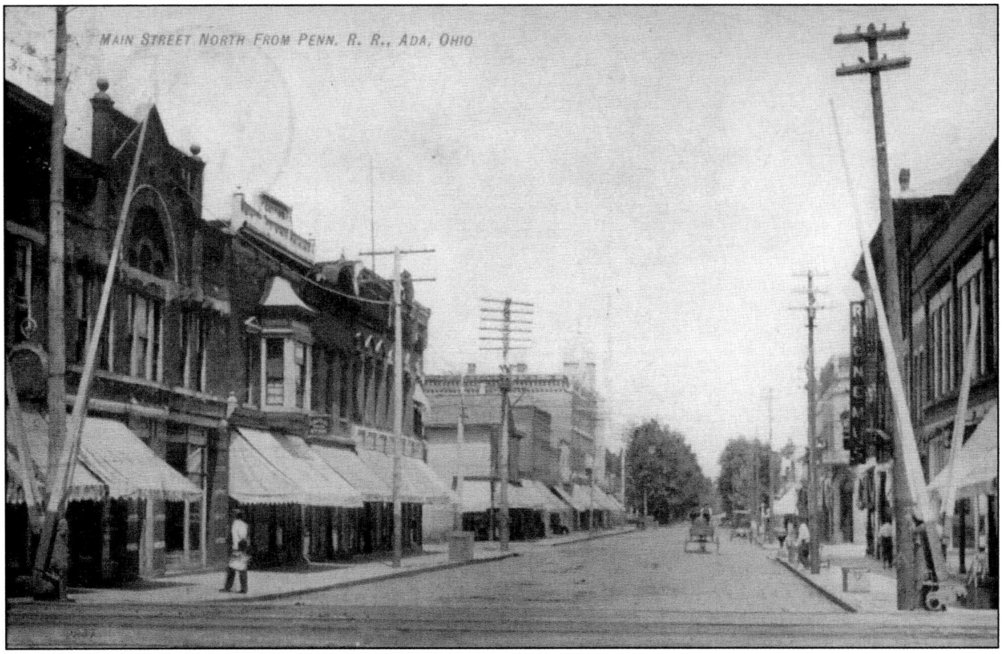

Ada's North Main Street business district in 1912 included the Central Drug Store, Liberty Bank, Cunningham & Sons dry goods, Arthur C. Church's jewelry store, and Rhonemus Clothing Store. The arrival of the railroad led to Ada's rise to prominence in northwestern Hardin County, which, in turn, served as the death knell for nearby Huntersville.

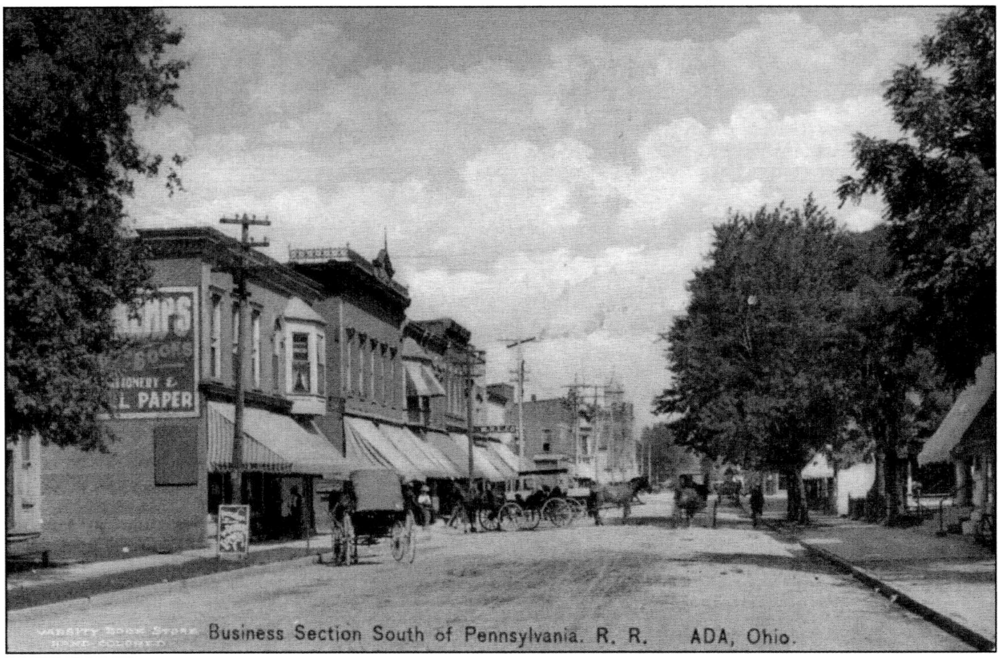

Ada's Varsity Book Store published this image of South Main Street looking north toward the Pennsylvania Railroad tracks in 1912. The competing Kemp Drug Store is seen on the left side of the street. The Electric Shoe Shop across the street specialized in horseshoing and harness repairing. The Methodist Episcopal Church steeple can be seen in the distance.

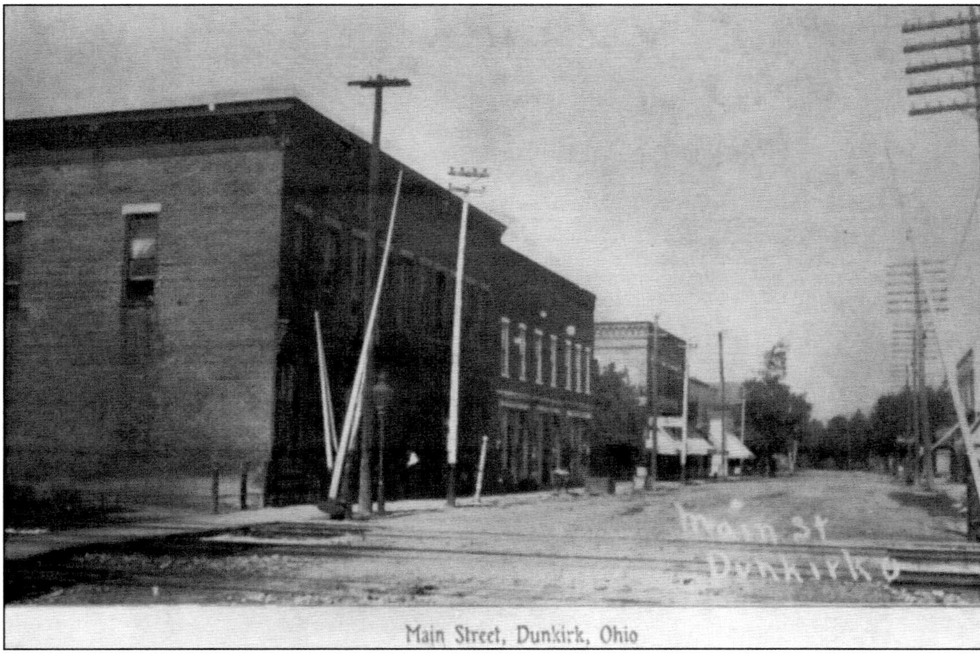

This is Dunkirk's Main Street (State Route 68) looking north from the Pennsylvania Railroad tracks prior to paving of the street. On May 21, 1903, a fire destroyed several of the buildings north of the tracks. Subsequent fires and demolitions have left few of the early buildings downtown.

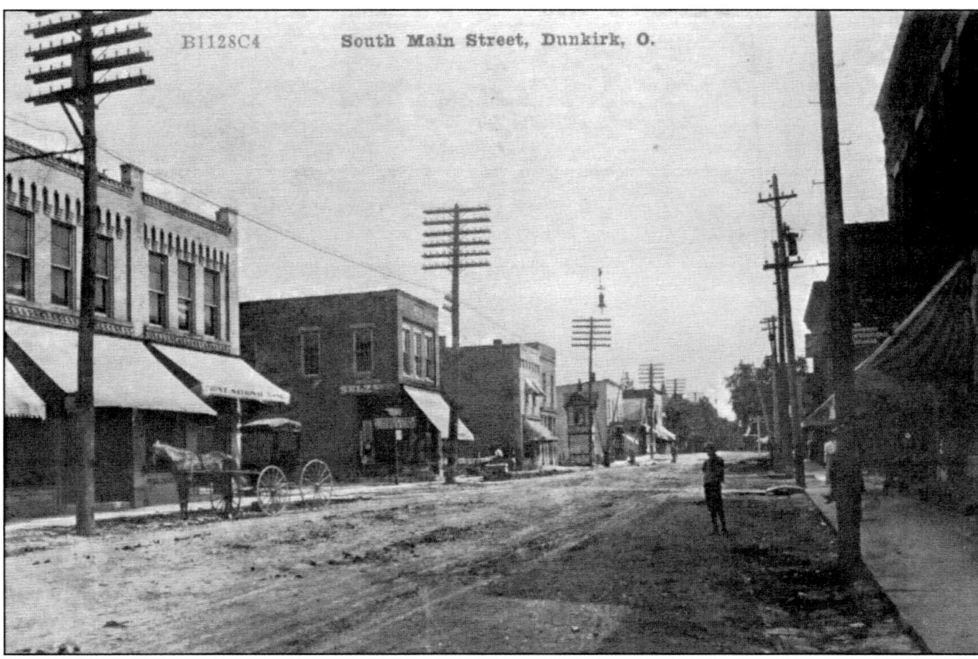

The horse and buggy is hitched in front of the First National Bank. The bank, established in 1903, erected the building at the corner of Main and Wayne Streets. In 1933, it failed but reopened as a branch of the Kenton Savings Bank in August 1940 and is now the First Citizens National Bank.

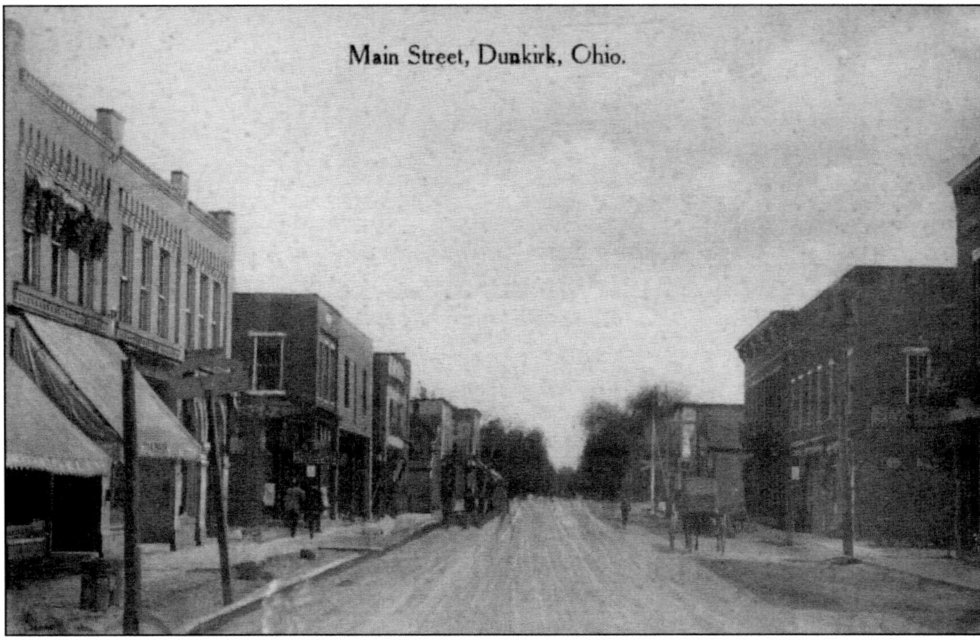

Harold F. Bowers' Drug Store in Dunkirk published this c. 1910 image of the downtown area before electrical poles were installed. Situated in Washington Township, the town was platted by county surveyor Robert D. Millar in April 1852 and incorporated in 1867. In 1905, the town featured two competing depots on opposite sides of the railroad tracks.

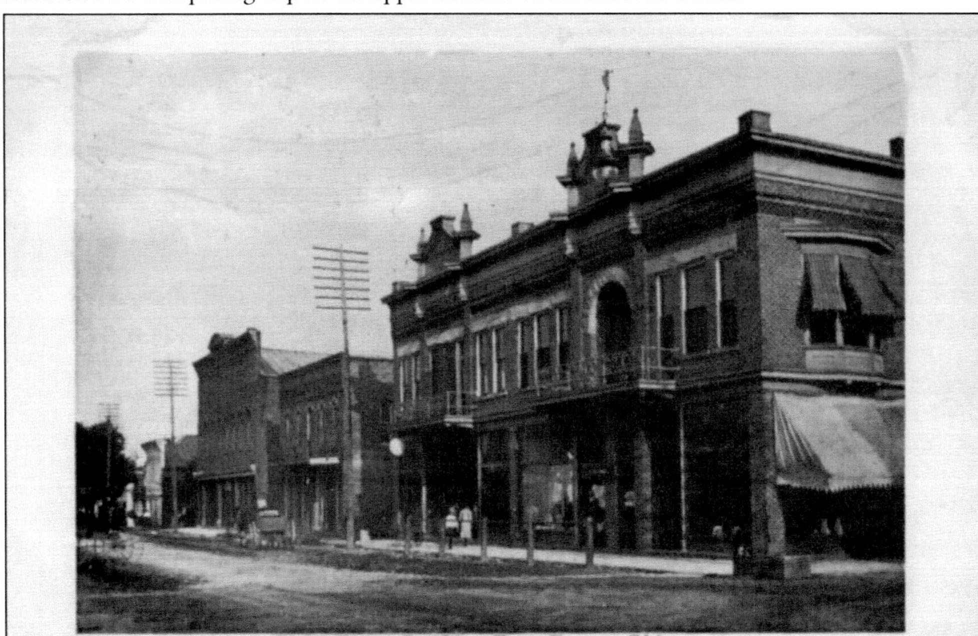

This view of Forest's Lima Street, looking east from the railroad tracks, was published about 1910. Forest was laid out and platted by John A. Gormley in 1855 and incorporated in 1865. Originally overshadowed by nearby Patterson, the town grew substantially around the intersection of the Pittsburg, Fort Wayne & Chicago Railroad with the Mad River & Lake Erie Railroad.

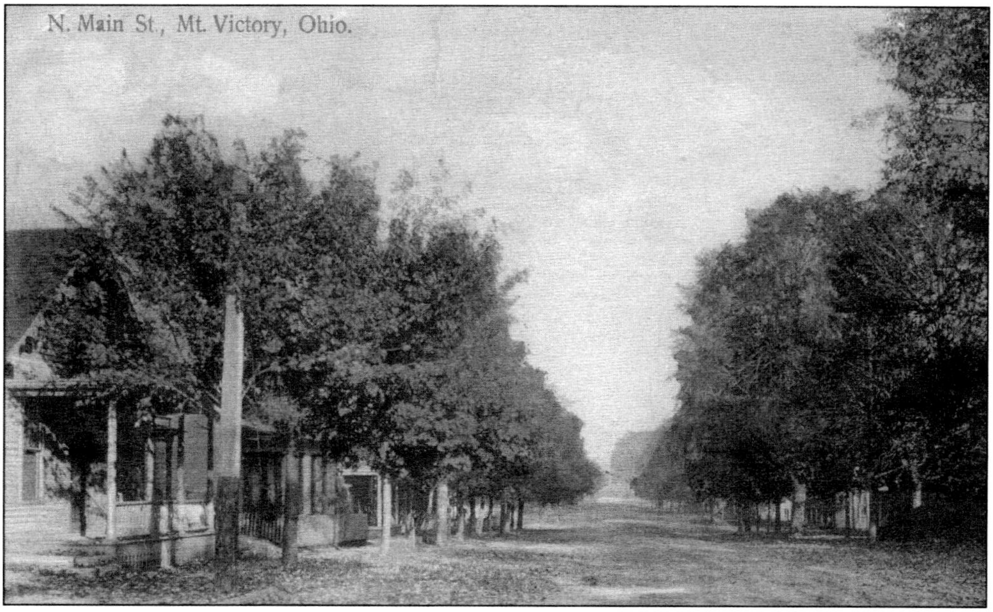

Seen here is an early residential view of North Main Street in Mount Victory (State Route 31) published about 1910. The town was founded by Ezra Dille and platted in 1851. Following a devastating fire in the 1890s, the east side of Main Street was rebuilt from brick in the early 1900s. Many of the buildings downtown have been restored and operate as antique, craft, and specialty shops.

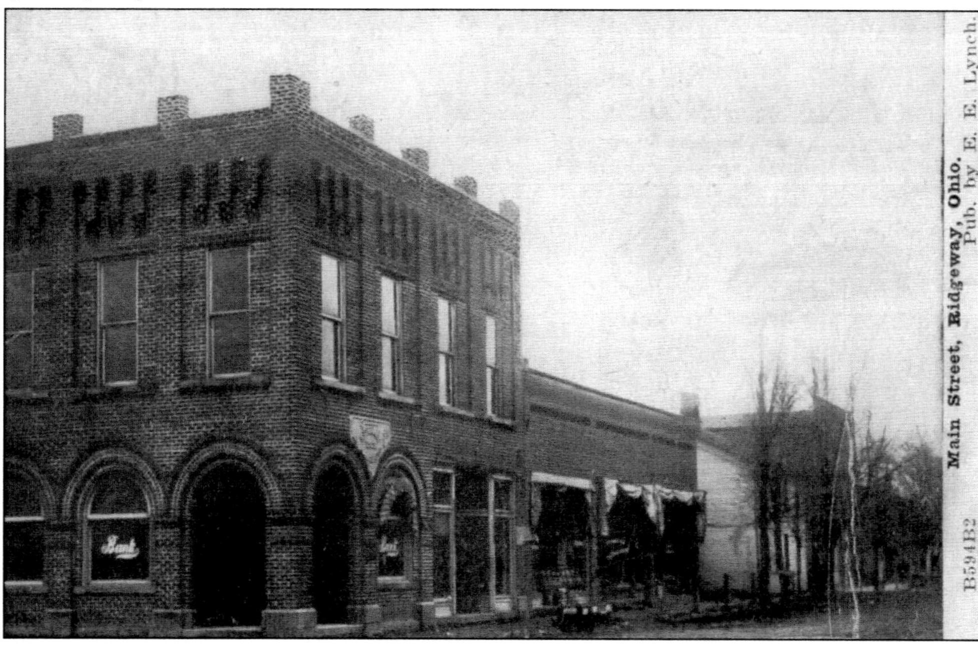

Ridgeway was incorporated in 1858 under the name West Ridgeway. The brick structure on the corner was erected in 1903 by the Ridgeway Savings Bank. The upstairs was home to the Ridgeway Opera House, which hosted civic, school, and church activities. This 1911 postcard was published by Dr. Elmer Ellsworth Lynch, a local physician who operated a drugstore in the town from 1901 until about 1915.

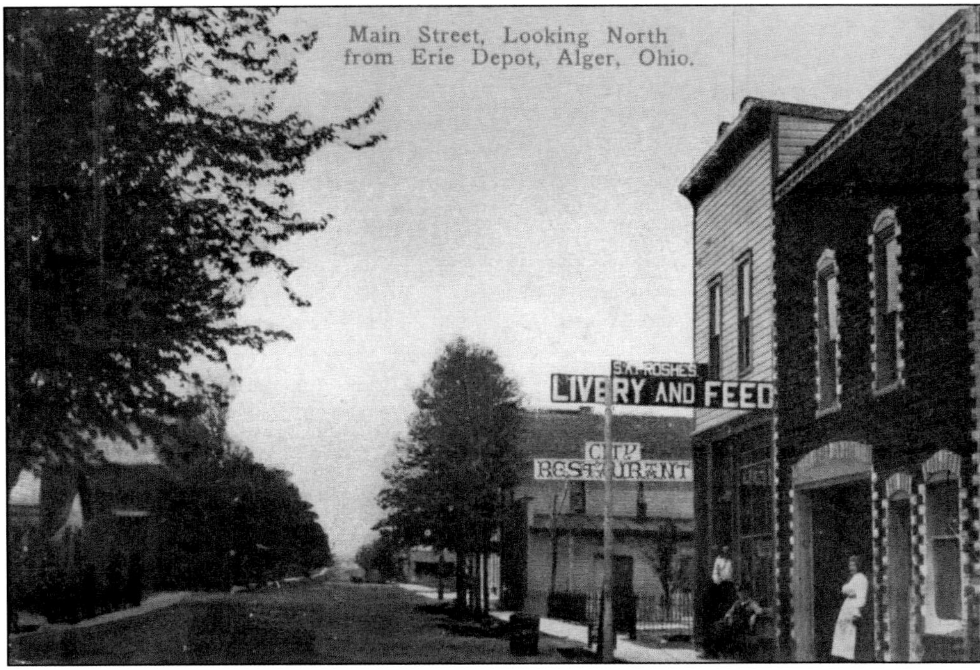

Originally known as Preston Station, Jagger was platted in 1882 along the Chicago & Atlantic Railroad and incorporated in 1896. The name was changed to honor Michigan governor Russell A. Alger, who was born in Ohio. In 1909, much of the downtown, including the hotel and livery, was destroyed by fire.

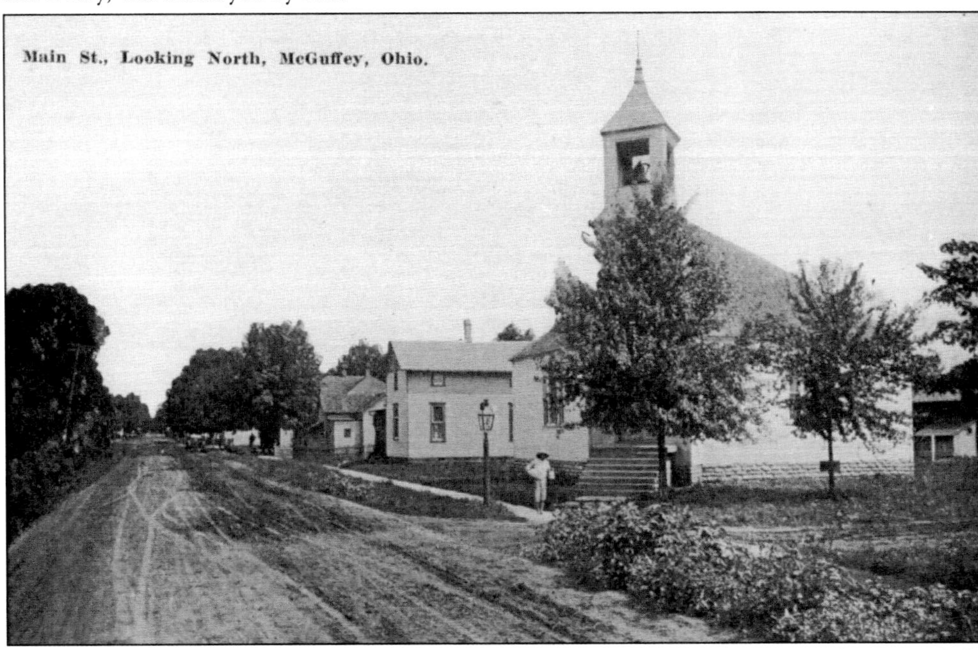

This early view of McGuffey's Main Street as it winds past one of the local churches toward the marshes was published by James W. Bowen about 1910. Bowen operated a grocery and general store in McGuffey from November 1904 until about 1915. In 1914, he purchased 19 acres of marshland from the Scioto Land Company to try his luck at onion farming.

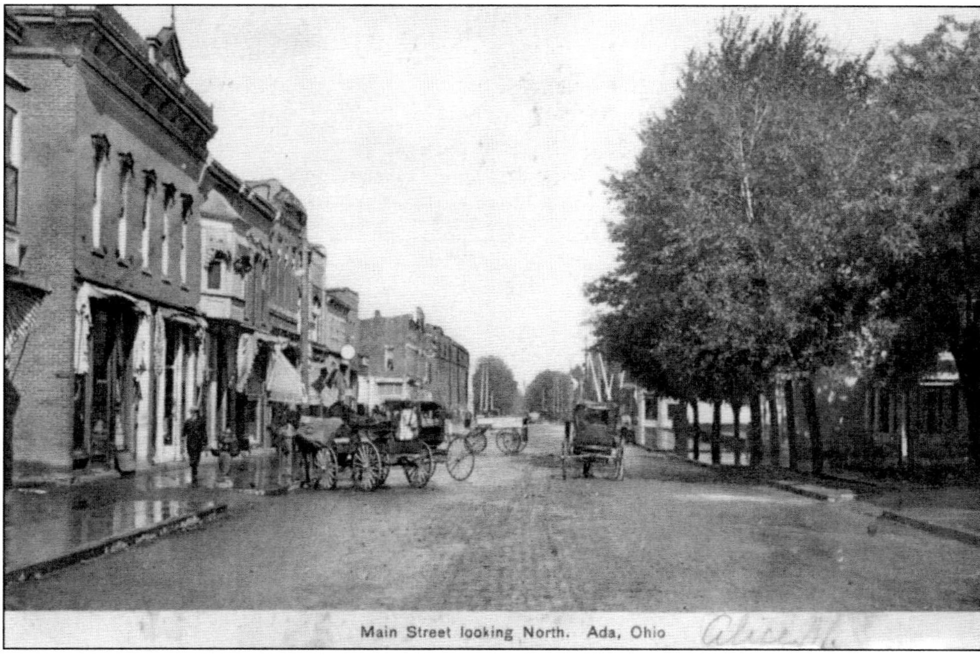

Charles R. Wilson, proprietor of the Varsity Book Store, published this 1907 image of downtown Ada looking north toward the Pennsylvania Railroad tracks. The picture shows the recently paved street shortly after a rainstorm. The area alongside the tracks, behind the trees on the right, is now Ada's Railroad Park.

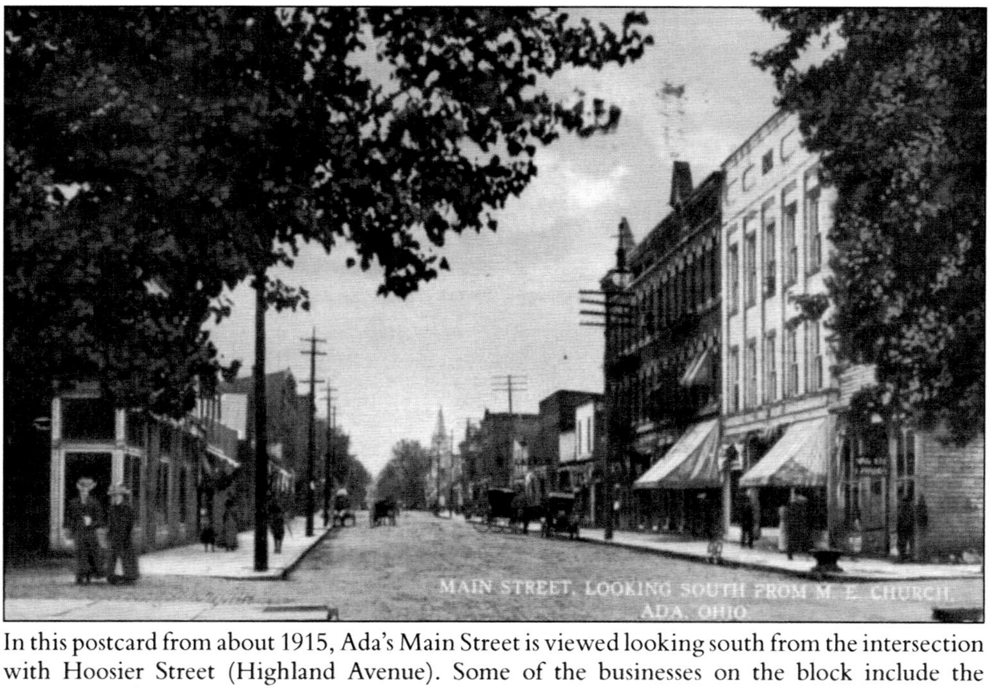

In this postcard from about 1915, Ada's Main Street is viewed looking south from the intersection with Hoosier Street (Highland Avenue). Some of the businesses on the block include the Young Hotel, Rhonemus Clothing Store, Conner Brothers Grocery, Lyle's Millinery Shop, and the Stemple Meat Market. The steeple of the First Presbyterian Church can be seen in the distance.

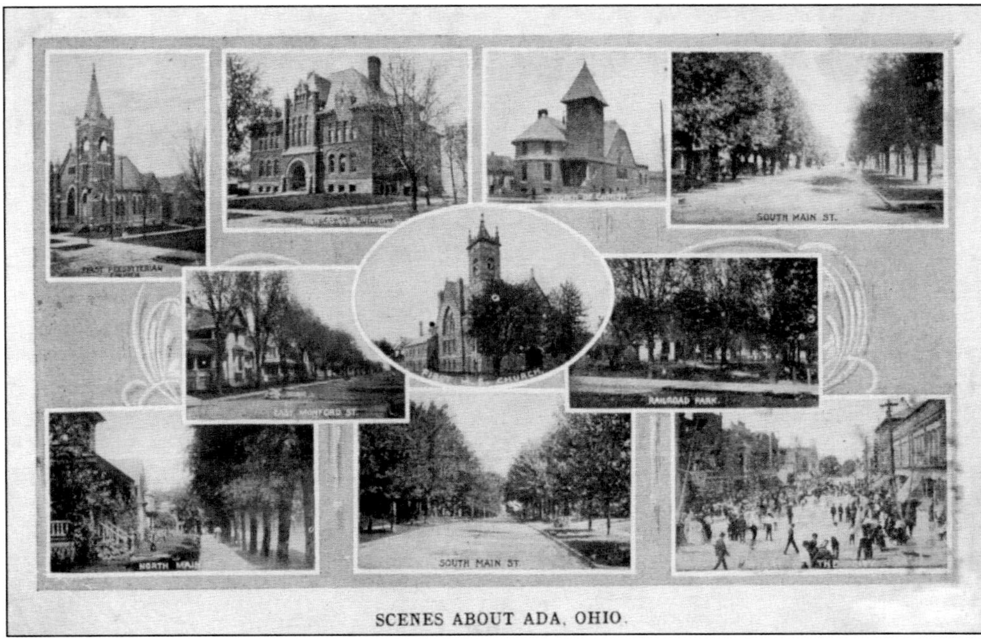

This 1909 postcard contains images of city streets, churches, and prominent buildings in Ada, which was settled in 1853 as Johnstown. In order to avoid confusion with another town, the village was renamed in 1855 by Thomas Kelly, a postmaster from Washington, DC, for his favorite sister. The railroad changed the name from Johnston's Station to Ada in 1867.

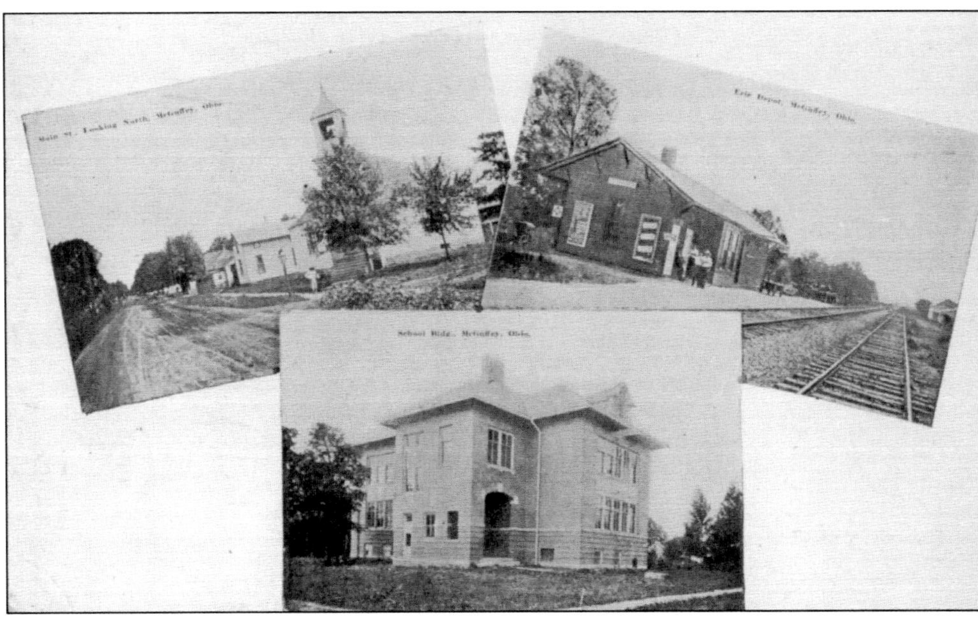

James W. Bowen published this postcard around 1915 as part of a set that included the three smaller images as separate postcards. McGuffey was platted in 1890 and incorporated in 1896. The Chicago & Erie Railroad Depot was built to accommodate workers and for easier shipment of the many vegetables grown in the Scioto Marsh. The McGuffey School building was constructed in 1908 for $18,000.

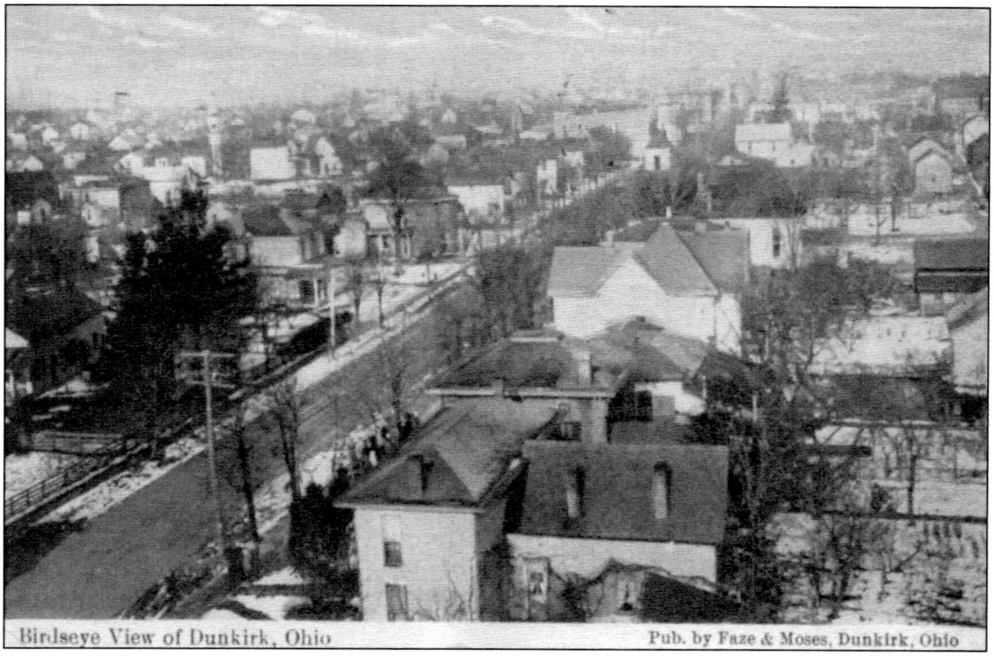

Nelson F. Faze and Charles W. Moses, owners of the Faze & Moses dry goods store, published this aerial view of Dunkirk looking roughly north along Main Street about 1909. The steeple of the Wesley Methodist Episcopal Church on West (Buckeye) Street can be seen in the upper left. The image was probably taken from the steeple of the Methodist Episcopal Church on South Main Street.

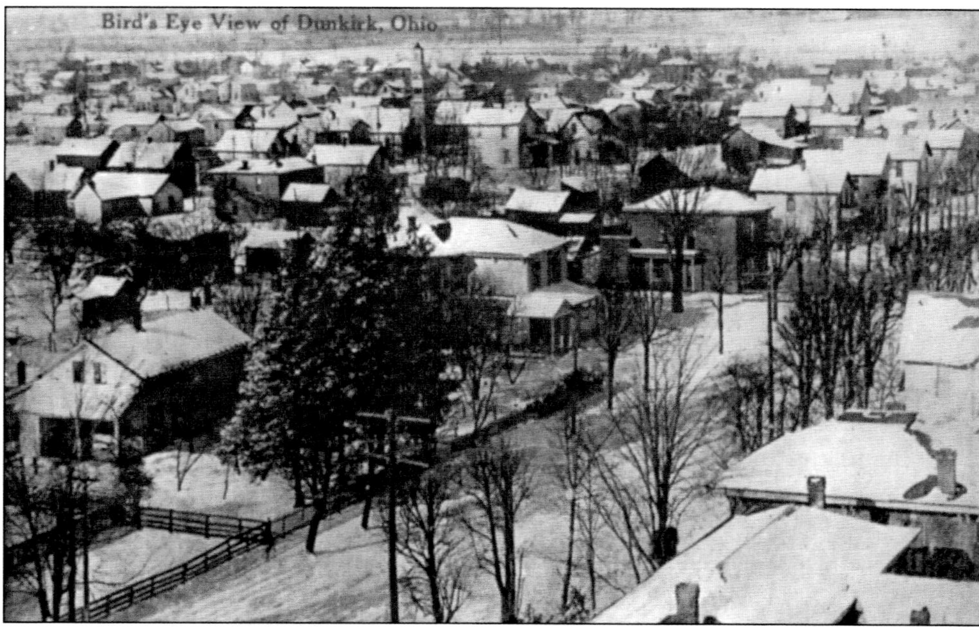

Here is a view of Dunkirk from above published by Thomas & Company of Findlay, Ohio, around 1910. The image was captured looking northwest across Lincoln Way (Main Street) during winter. Findlay is located about 13 miles north of Dunkirk in Hancock County. The Wesley Methodist Episcopal Church is visible in the background.

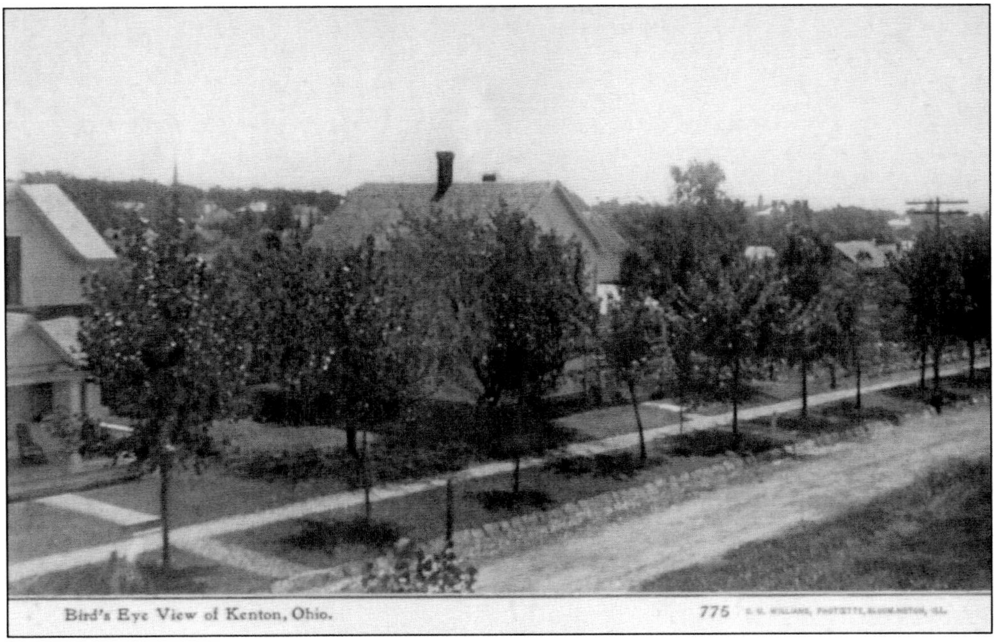

This is a bird's-eye view showing the outskirts of Kenton about 1909. The postcard was sold by the House of McCoy, which was located on West Franklin Street. Dr. John A. Rogers opened the first drugstore in Kenton in 1845. James N. McCoy launched the second drugstore in 1860 and was later joined by his sons Robert and Wilbert.

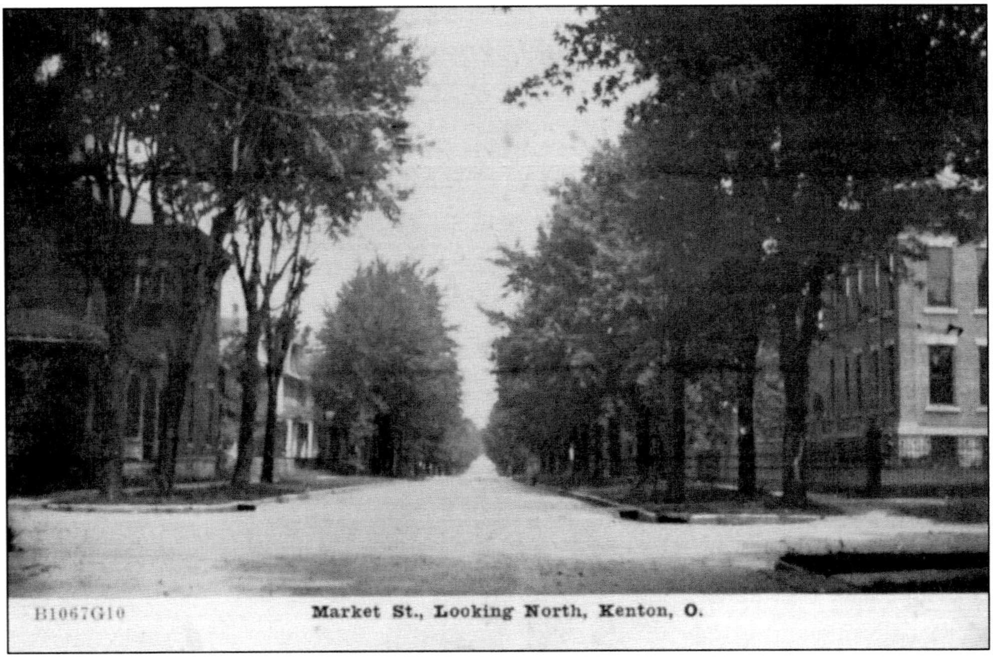

The Kenton Central Grammar School is seen to the right in this 1908 image of the North Market and West Carroll Streets intersection. North Market Street received its name from the early markets and shops located at the southern terminus of the road near the railroad tracks. The Brecheisen Bottling Works was located across the street from the school.

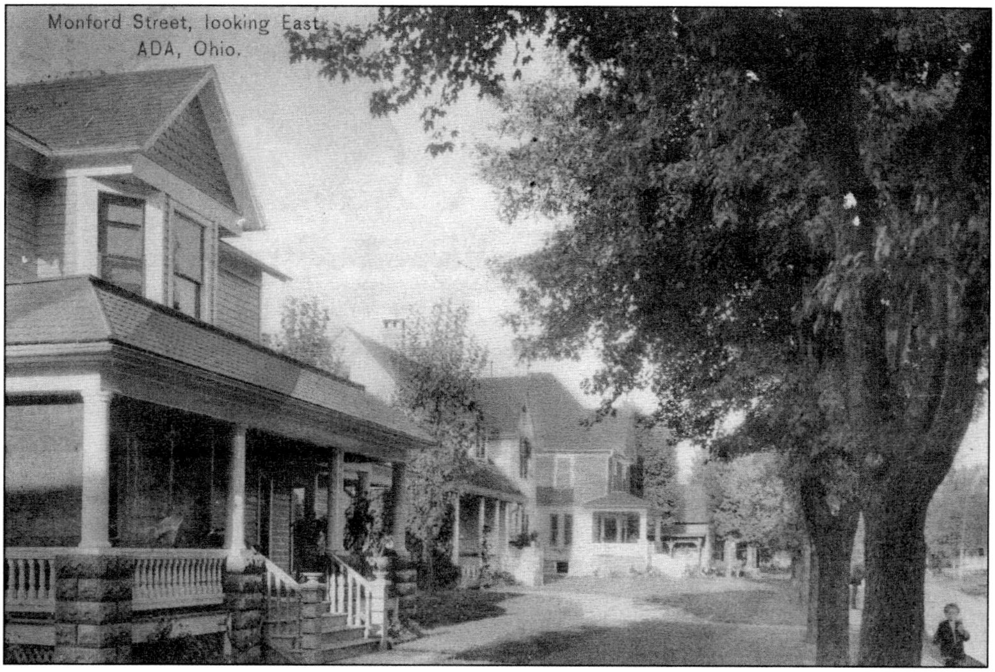

The Varsity Book Store published this 1910 image of Montford Street in Ada. The street was named after a Mr. Montford, a railroad contractor when the Ohio & Indiana Railroad extended the line through Ada in 1853. The first two blocks of East Montford Street were paved in 1908.

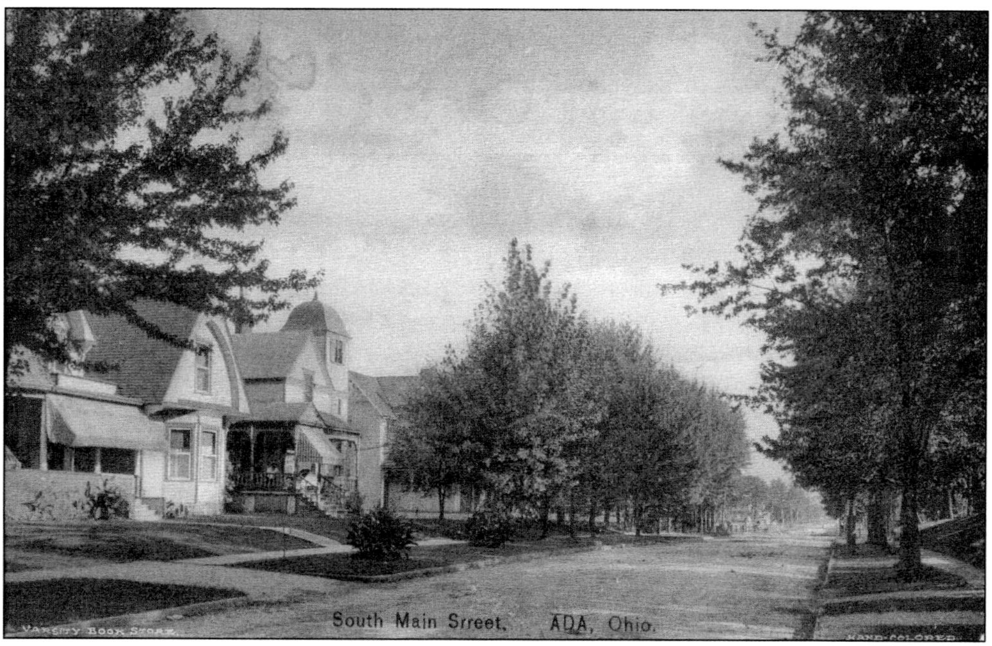

This 1910 image of South Main Street's residential section was published by the Varsity Book Store. The street was originally named Margaret Street in honor of the wife of early resident Samuel M. Johnson. Its name was changed by city ordinance in July 1872, and in 1905 the street was the first in Ada to be paved its entire length.

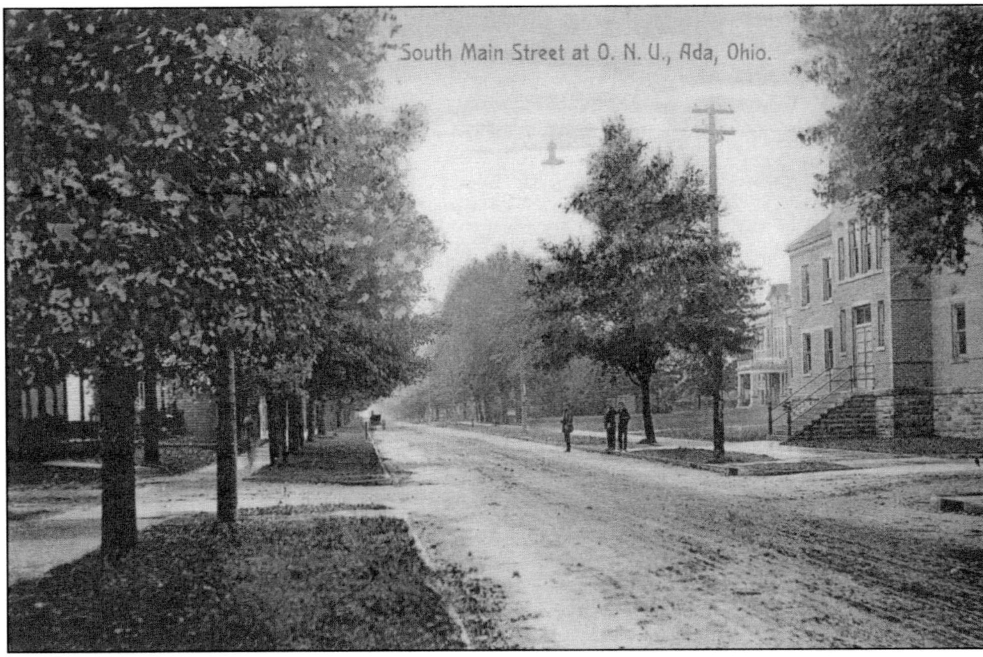

Dana E. Welsh's Central Drug Store produced this vintage image of South Main Street as it runs in front of Ohio Northern University about 1910. Some of the early school buildings can be seen to the right of the gentlemen. The Northwestern Ohio Normal School, established by Dr. Henry S. Lehr, opened in August 1871.

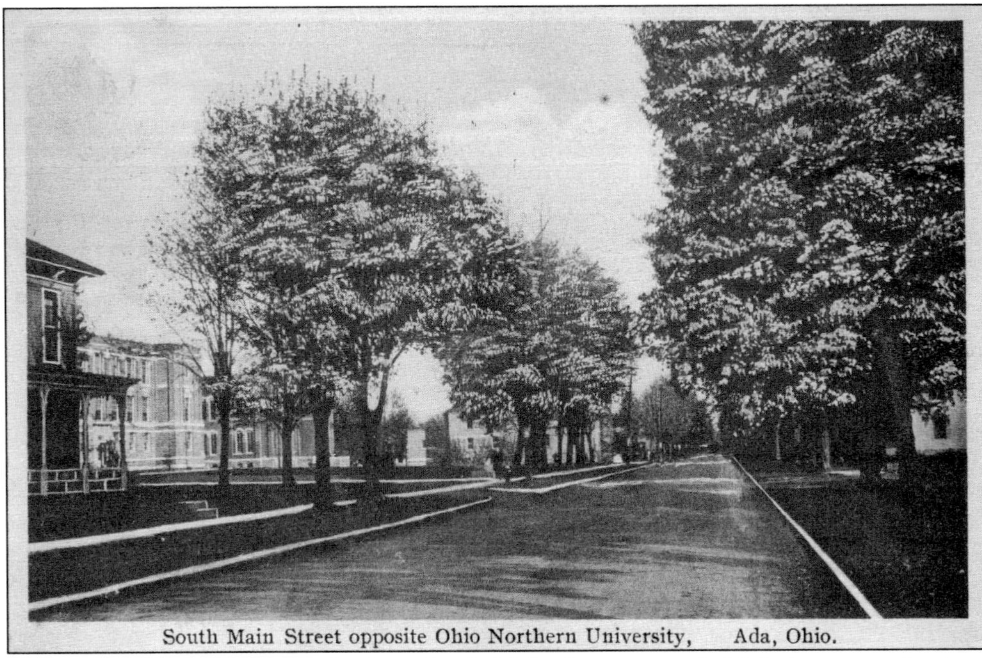

This 1917 postcard looks north along South Main Street toward Ada's downtown business district from the intersection with Normal (West College) Street. Ohio Northern University's Lehr Memorial, Hill Memorial, and Brown Memorial Chapel can be seen to the left. The university has expanded several times and now encompasses a large portion of western Ada.

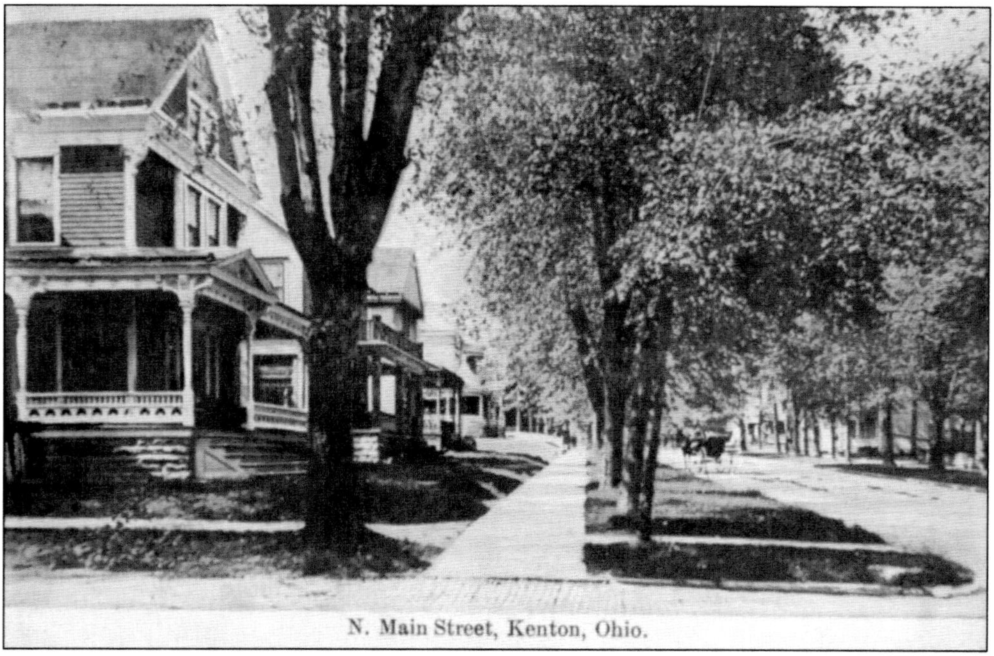

Most of these Victorian-era homes, viewed from the intersection at Carroll Street, survive along North Main Street in Kenton. Daniel Sullivan, a saddler and harness maker, built the fourth house on the left in 1896. His granddaughter Mary Lou Johnson left the home to the public, and it opened as the Sullivan-Johnson Museum in 1983.

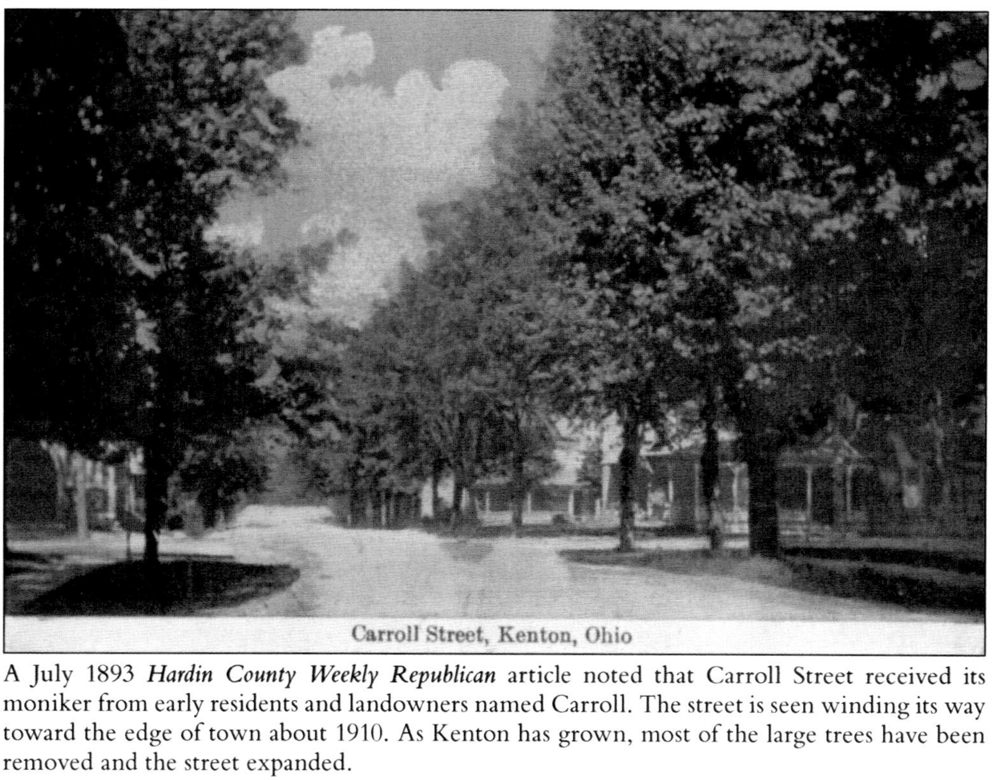

A July 1893 ***Hardin County Weekly Republican*** article noted that Carroll Street received its moniker from early residents and landowners named Carroll. The street is seen winding its way toward the edge of town about 1910. As Kenton has grown, most of the large trees have been removed and the street expanded.

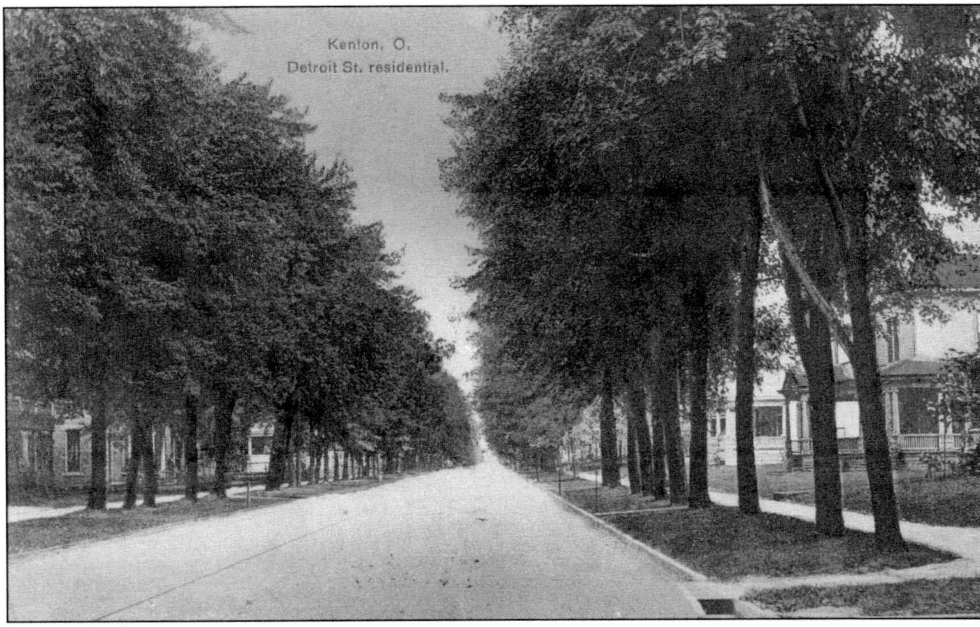

According to the July 1893 *Hardin County Weekly Republican* article, Detroit Street received its name due to the simple fact that it followed the early trails north to Toledo, Ohio, and, eventually, Detroit, Michigan. Today, it is known as State Route 68. Numerous Victorian homes were constructed along the street, and the area was listed in the National Register of Historic Places in 1985.

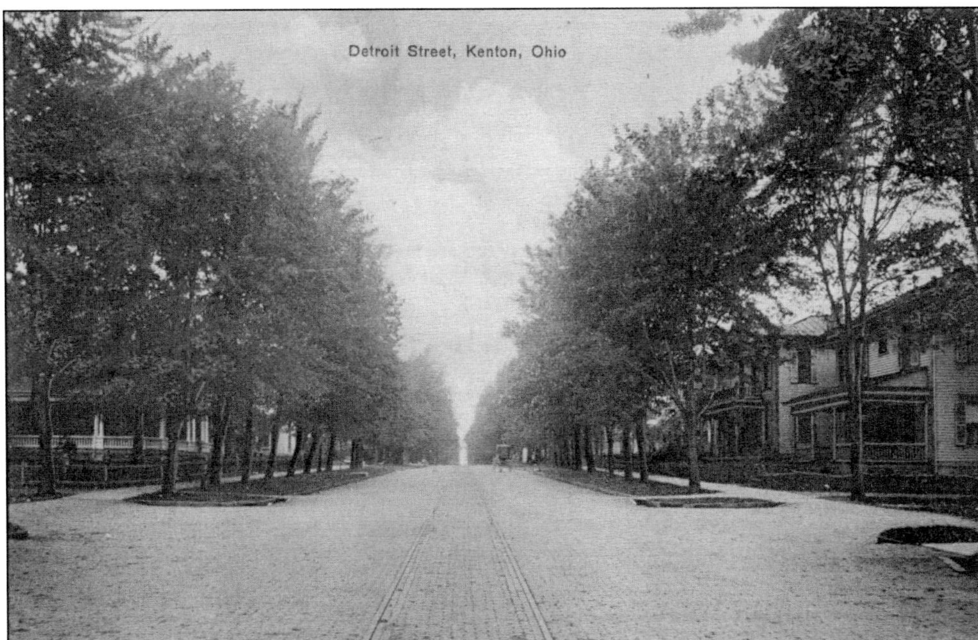

This postcard of North Detroit Street was published around 1905 by William W. Snodgrass, owner of the Snodgrass Drug Store in downtown Kenton. Note the railroad tracks that are visible in the center of the street. An interurban electric railway was planned and promoted from 1906 to about 1915, but it never became fully operational.

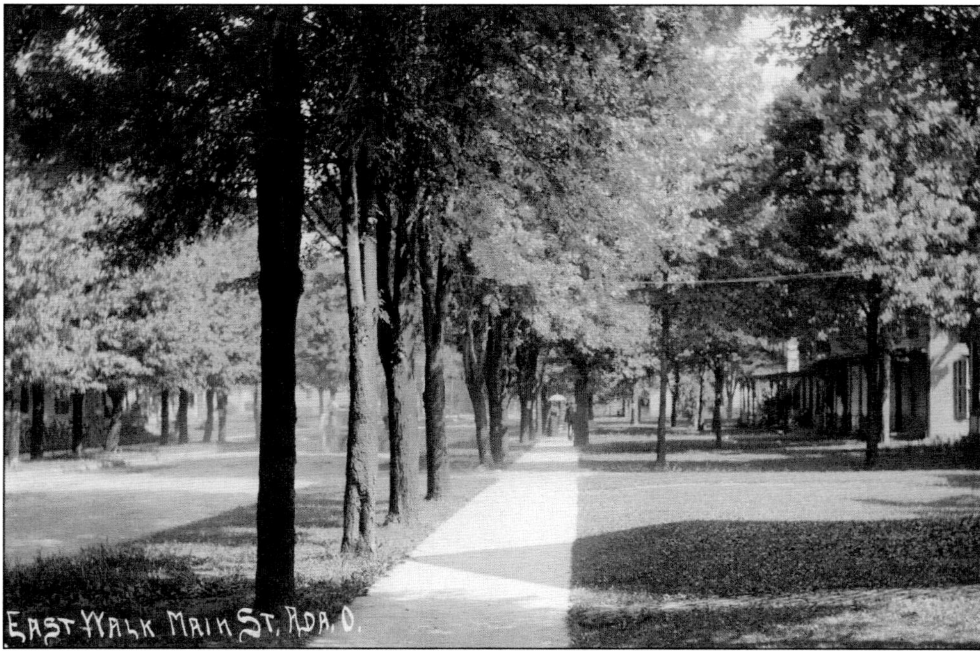

This Real Photo postcard of the sidewalk along Ada's Main Street was produced about 1906. Local photographers such as Martin V. Gilbert, Albert W. Clutter, and Clara Paeszler captured numerous people, places, buildings, and events, and then offered them for sale to the public as alternatives to the hand-tinted stock postcards available in the early 1900s.

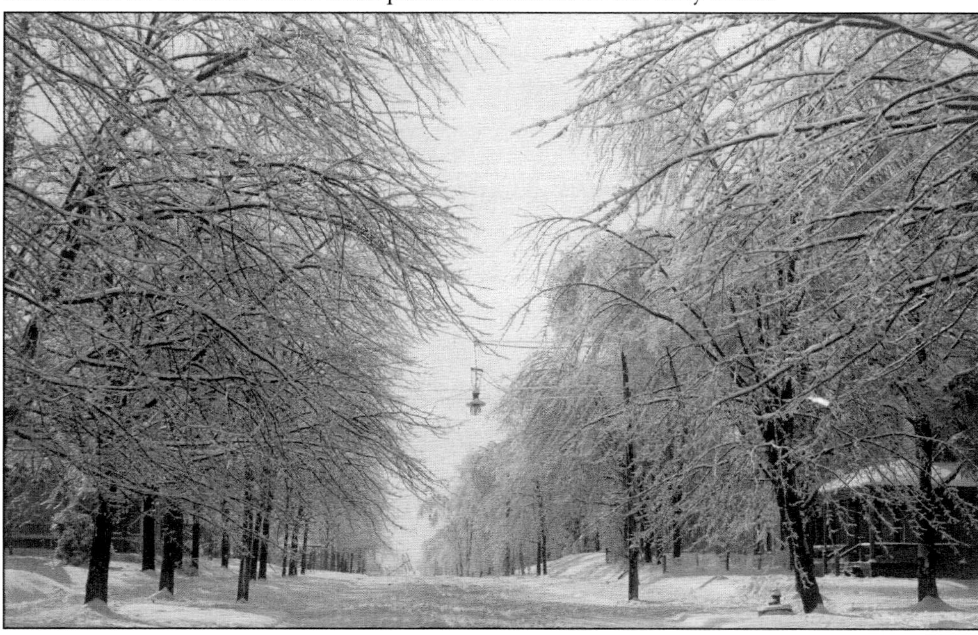

Seen here is a Real Photo postcard of Ada published in 1909. The photographer captured the serenity of the bustling city following the winter storm of February 17 and 18. One of the power poles can be seen lying on its side at the end of the street. In January 1918, Hardin County experienced a large snowstorm that reportedly dumped over a foot of snow near Dunkirk in less than a day.

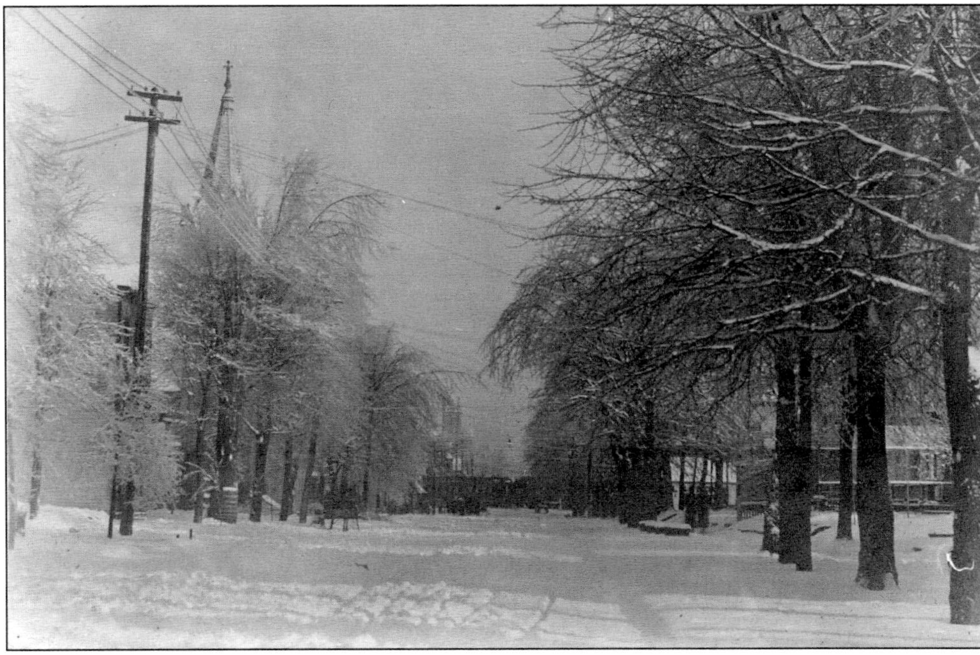

This photograph of Ada facing north along South Main Street was taken following the winter storm of February 1909. A Pennsylvania Railroad passenger train can be seen crossing the road in the center of town. The First Presbyterian Church is visible to the left of the picture with the First Methodist Episcopal Church in the distance.

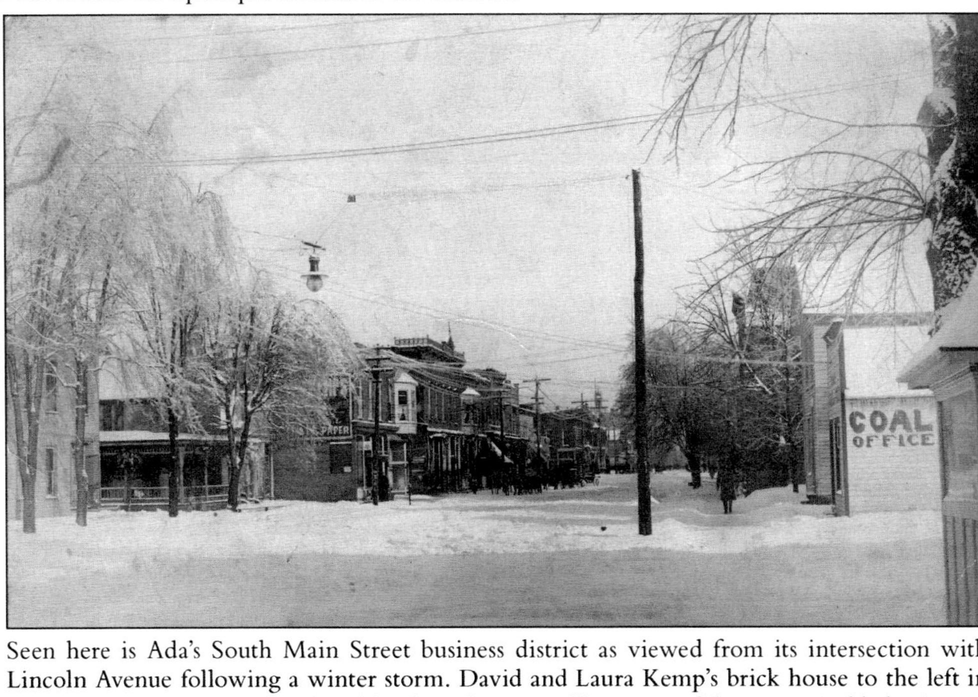

Seen here is Ada's South Main Street business district as viewed from its intersection with Lincoln Avenue following a winter storm. David and Laura Kemp's brick house to the left in the image was eventually replaced by the Ada Post Office. One of the recognizable businesses is the Kemp Drug Store, later Gardner's Drugstore, with its advertisement visible on the side of the building.

Four

LOCAL BUSINESSES

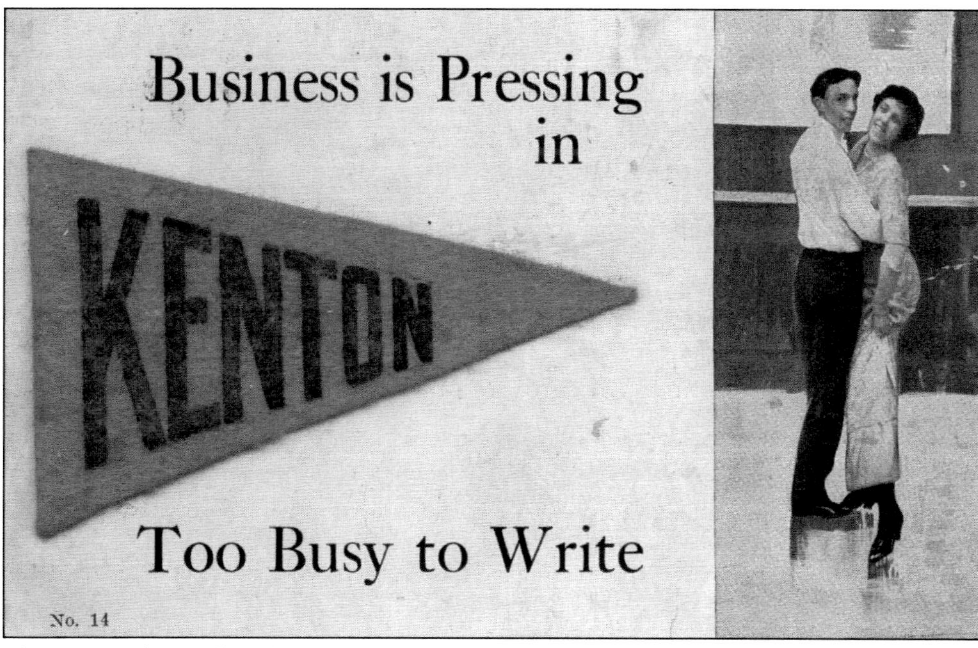

This is one of several stock postcards featuring felt pennants that promoted Kenton and other Hardin County towns in the early 1900s. A few of the numerous business interests in the county included agriculture, factories, foundries, furniture, banking, lumber, quarrying, construction, jewelry, optometry, printing, saloons, and dry goods, as well as footwear, drug, and clothing stores. Howland's 1879 Atlas of Hardin County listed over 45 different businesses and occupations.

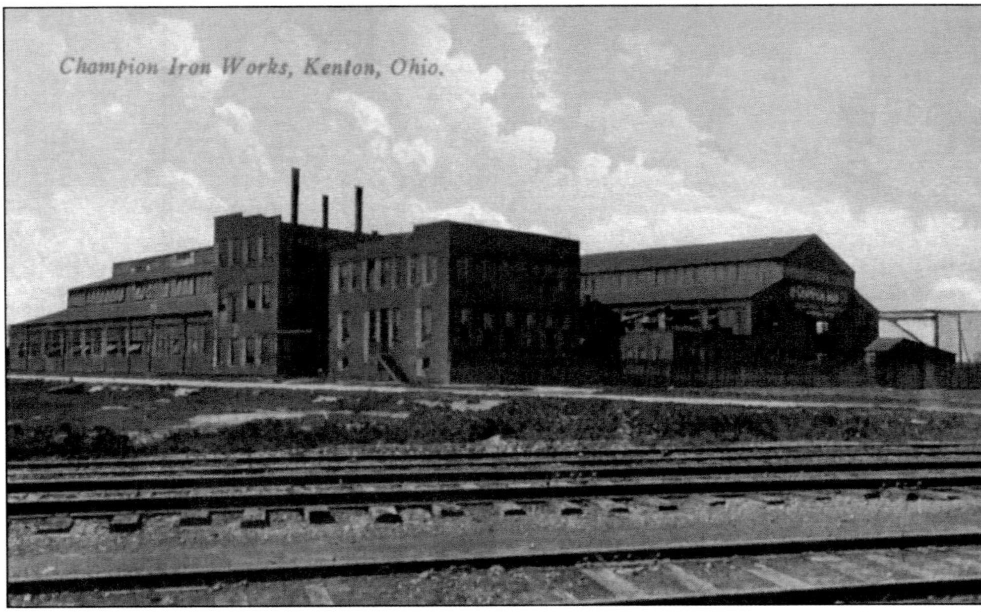

The Champion Iron Fence Company, established in 1875, produced fencing, jail cell, structural, and decorative ironwork. This facility, located south of Kenton, was constructed along the Erie Railroad in 1903 following the disastrous fire of April 1902 that destroyed its original factory on Columbus Street. Following a series of owners, including Philips & Davies, the complex closed and was abandoned by the 1990s.

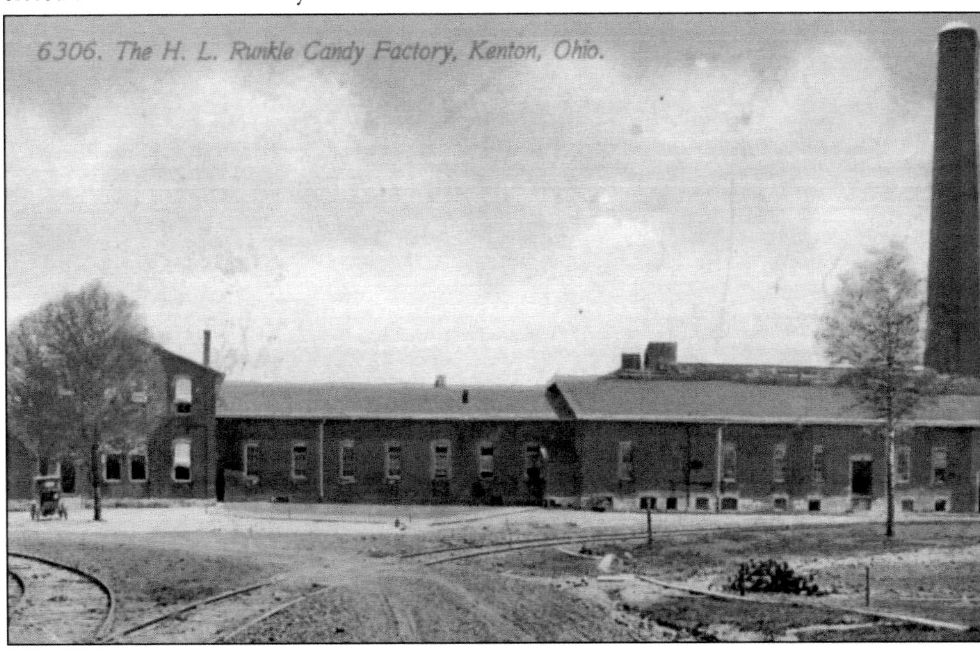

In 1899, Charles M. Roser and Henry L. Runkle started the Roser-Runkle Company on South Detroit Street in Kenton to produce candy, cakes, and cookies. Locals claim the Fig Newton cookie was invented here. The Runkle Candy Factory constructed this larger facility on South Wayne Street about 1910. Walter Johnson Jr. purchased the business in 1952. The Johnson Candy Company closed in the early 1980s.

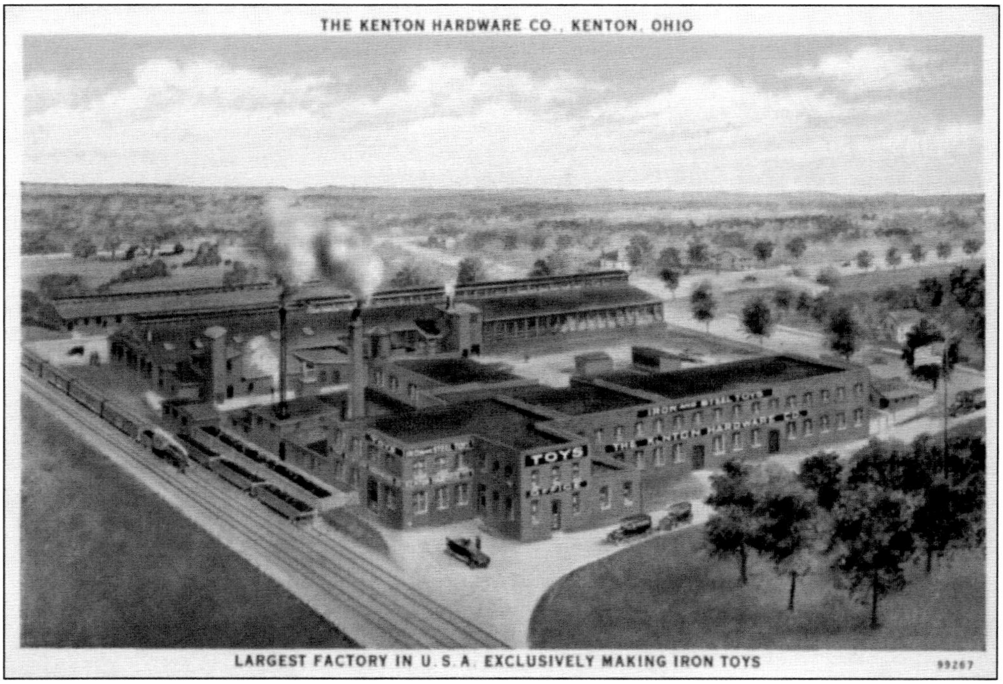

The Kenton Lock Manufacturing Company was established in 1890. Following the success of its Columbian Bank in 1893, the company offered a full line of banks and toys. The renamed Kenton Hardware Manufacturing Company operated as the nation's largest exclusive manufacturer of cast-iron toys until closing in 1952. Gene Autry toured the plant in August 1938. The Hardin County Historical Museum features a large exhibit of KentonToys.

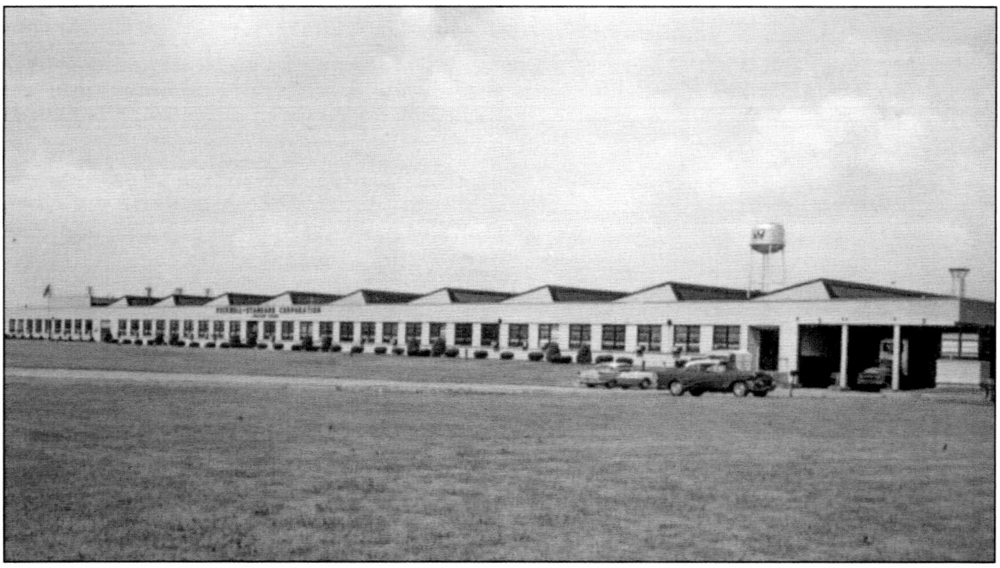

The Timken-Detroit Axle Company began production south of Kenton along State Route 68 in February 1949. The Rockwell Standard Corporation, photographed about 1965, manufactured axles, housings, hubs, brakes, and drums. The plant was renamed several times and expanded to encompass over 550,000 square feet. In 2004, Arvin-Meritor closed the facility, and it now sits empty.

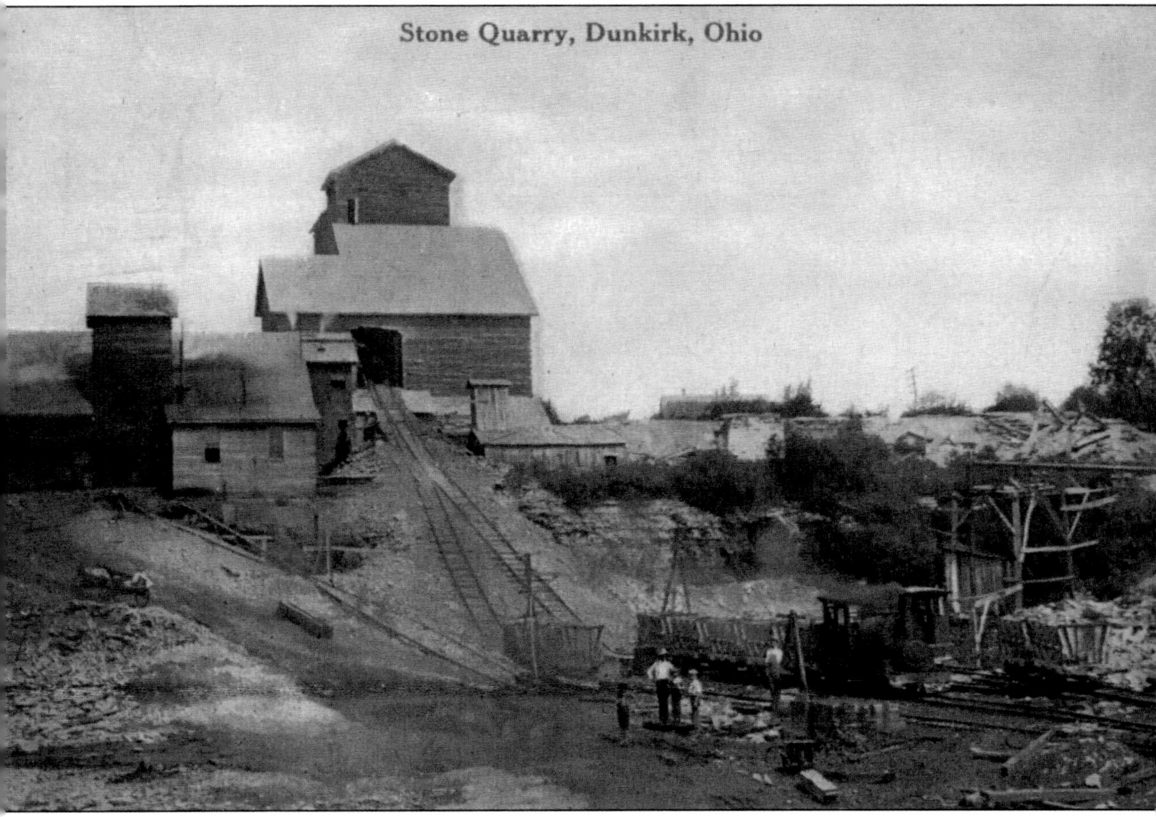

The glaciers that shaped northern Ohio during the last Ice Age left numerous pockets of gravel throughout Hardin County. Quarries were operated in or near Ada, Blanchard, Foraker, Forest, Hepburn, Kenton, Patterson, and Roundhead. The town of McVitty was established by the Big Four Railroad as a shipping station for the Herzog Stone Quarry. The Dunkirk Stone Quarry was started east of town in 1877. Hipple & Talbot purchased the business in 1883. Three years later, the Railway Stone & Ballast Company acquired a contract to provide ballast for the Pennsylvania Railroad. The stone was originally quarried by hand, and up to 60 railroad cars of stone were shipped each day. In 1900, Robert S. Bailey sold the 4.25-acre business to Charles L. Ireland, who transferred ownership to the France Brothers three years later. The Frances installed modern equipment, increasing productivity. By 1936, the operation had been dismantled, and the quarry was turned into a private lake.

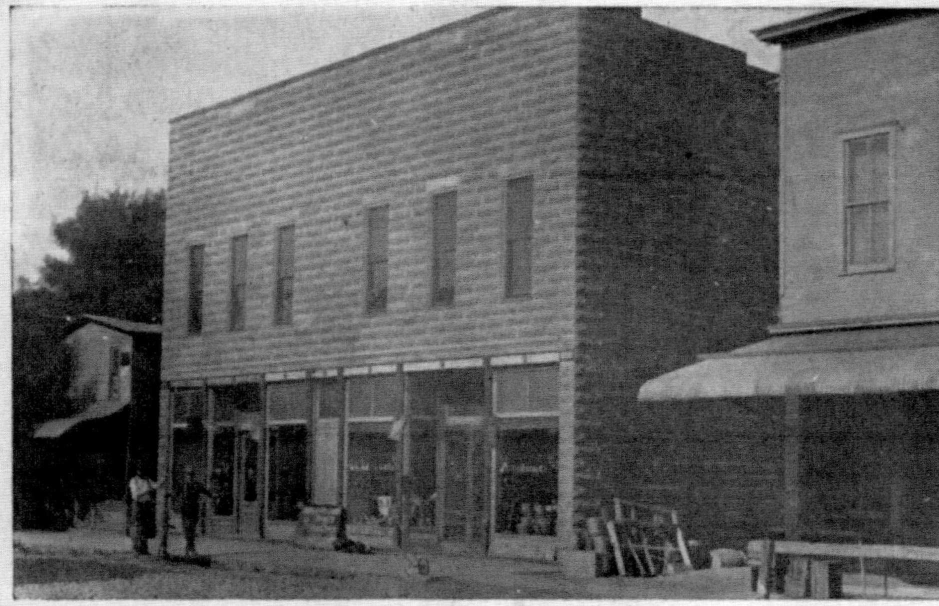

C. E. KENNARD'S HARDWARE STORE, ALGER, OHIO.

Charles E. Kennard's Hardware Store, seen here about 1910, dealt in hardware, stoves, agricultural implements, harnesses, wagons, and buggies. Kennard served as Alger's postmaster from 1905 to 1913 and operated the post office out of his store. The competing John W. Kirts Company offered a complete line of department store goods in Alger during the 1910s and 1920s.

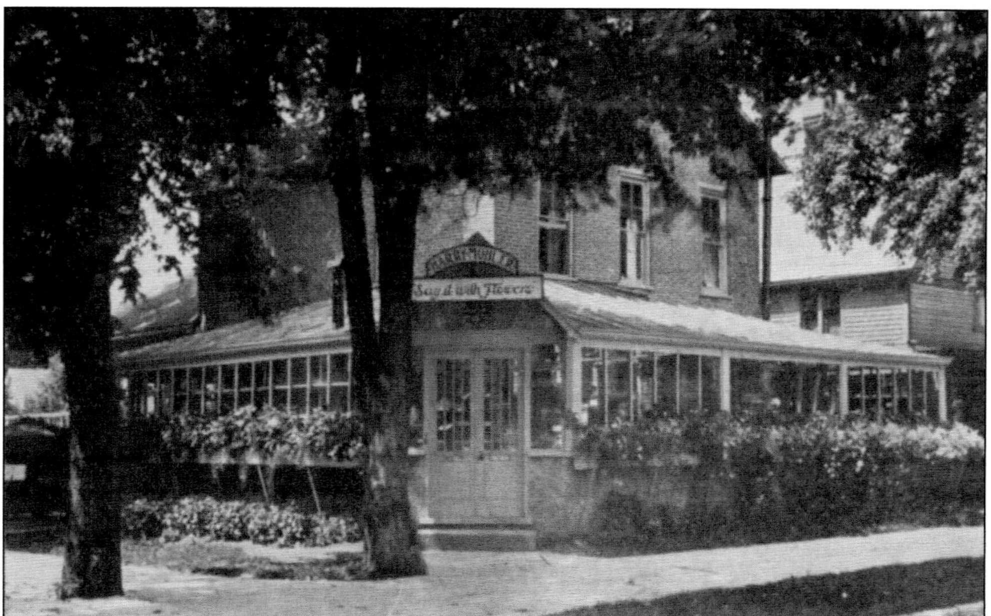

"SAY IT WITH FLOWERS"—MOHLER'S FLORAL SHOP, ADA, OHIO

Harry Mohler's Flower Shop at 137 South Main Street operated out of the former Kemp home (owners of the Kemp Drug Store). The Mohler family moved to Ada from Bluffton during the summer of 1924. The shop and greenhouse (in the rear) operated until about 1938 when the buildings were sold. They were razed in 1939 to make room for the current Ada Post Office.

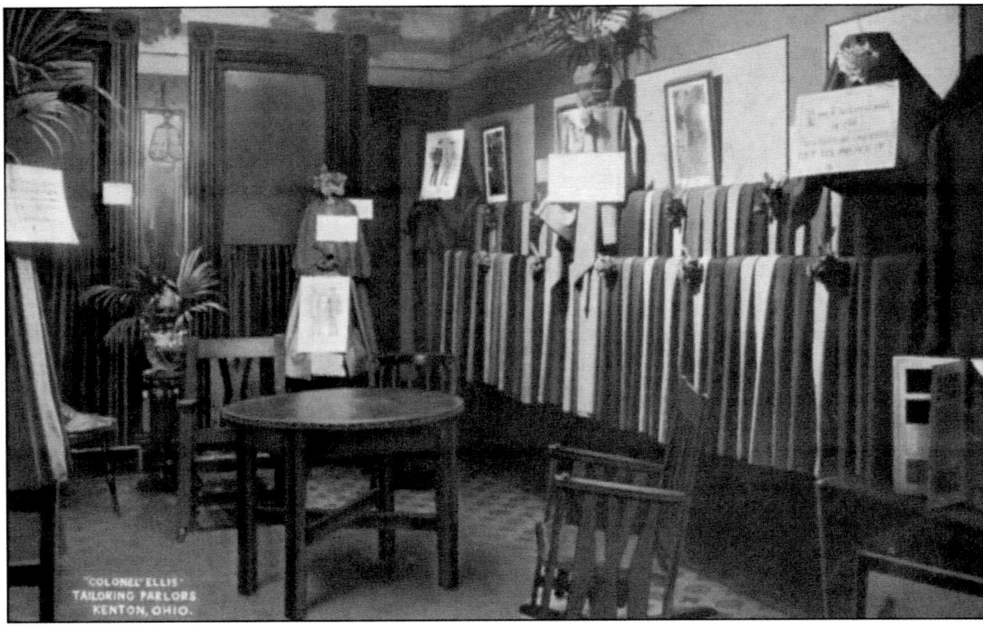

Among the numerous clothing stores and tailors that populated downtown Kenton was Carl "Colonel" Ellis's, which specialized in men's clothing. The interior of his tailoring parlor is seen here about 1912. After managing Rosenthall's Clothing Store, he opened his first shop on West Franklin Street about 1910. He moved to North Detroit Street around 1953, and his shop finally closed about 1975.

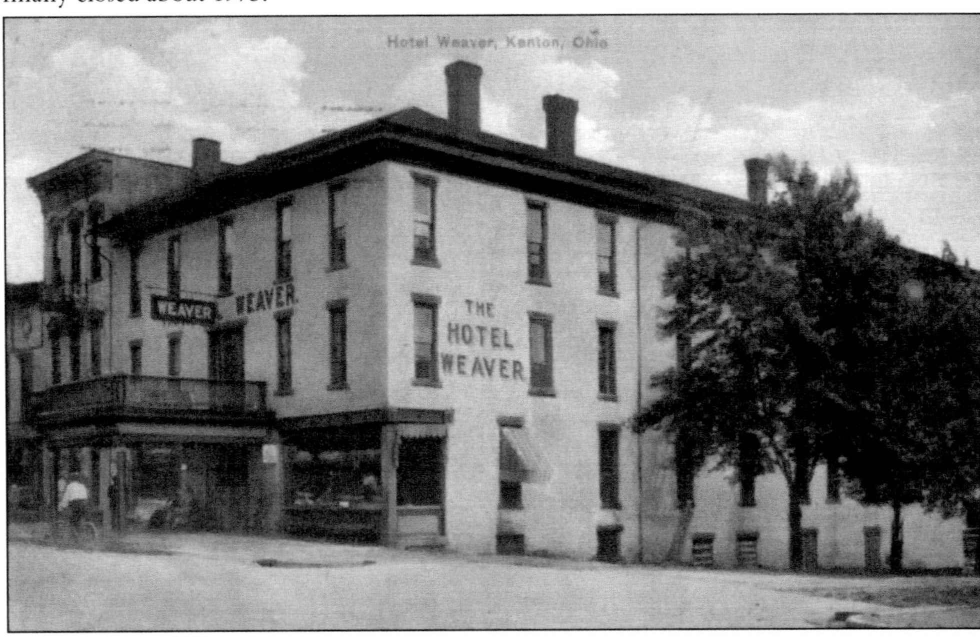

The two-story, brick Kenton Hotel was erected on West Franklin Street about 1847 by Benjamin Eglin. Henry Reese purchased the Union Hotel from Col. James Cantwell in 1865 and renamed it. Joseph C. Weaver purchased the Reese Hotel in 1904 and managed it until his death in 1923. Operated into the 1980s, the Weaver Hotel was razed and is currently a parking lot beside the Kenton Theater.

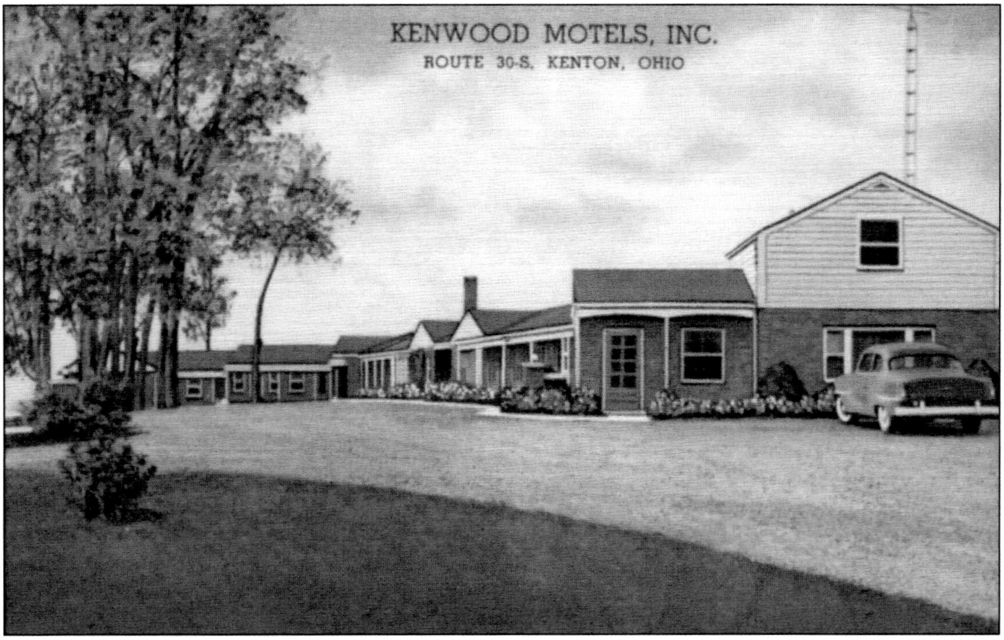

The Kenwood Motel, located east of Kenton on State Route 309, was built about 1950. This postcard shows the three-acre complex as it appeared during the 1950s. In 1963, Glenn and Ruth Price, operating as the Ulmer Company, purchased the Kenwood Motel. By the late 1960s, the 22-unit motel was advertising itself as AAA approved.

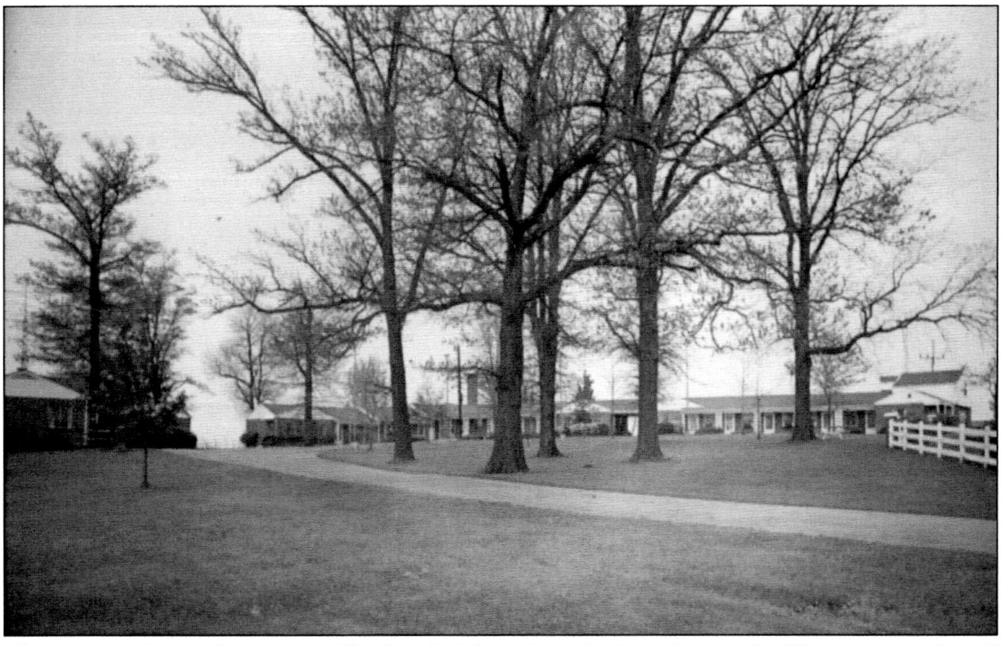

The Kenwood Motel, purchased by Reginald and Martha Jane Benson in 1974, promoted itself as "modern in every way" and listed its amenities on the back of this mid-1970s postcard. The 15-unit B&J Motel was constructed on the opposite side of Harding Highway about 1960. Amerihost Inn (Country Hearth Inn & Suites) erected Kenton's third motel on East Columbus Street in 1998.

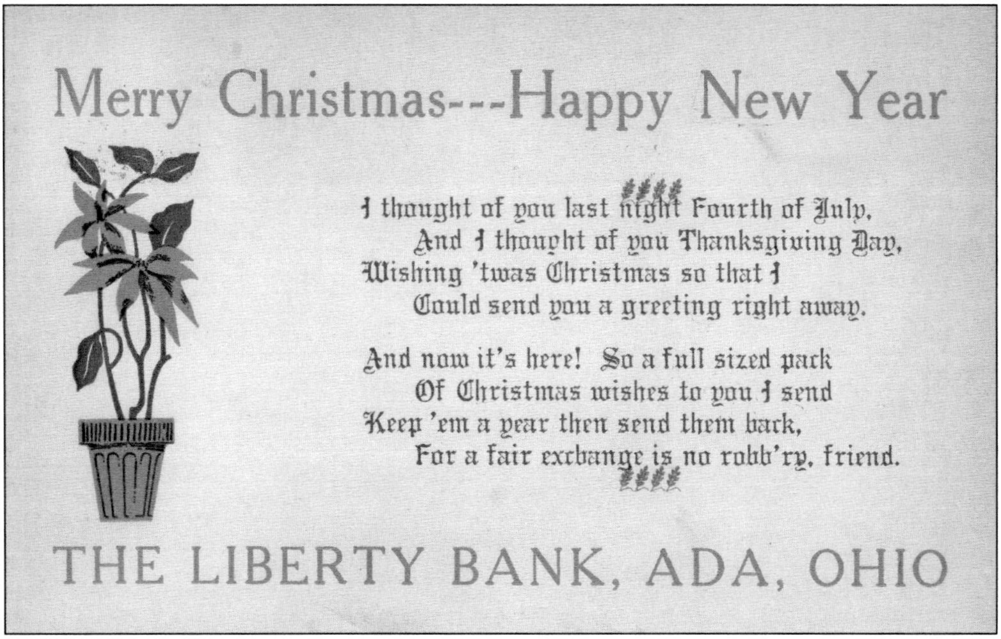

Christmas cards such as this one from the Liberty Bank in 1913 served as a simple thanks to loyal customers. The Liberty Bank was organized in April 1902 and opened its first branch on North Main Street. It moved to another location on Main Street in 1917 and merged with the First National Bank in 1958.

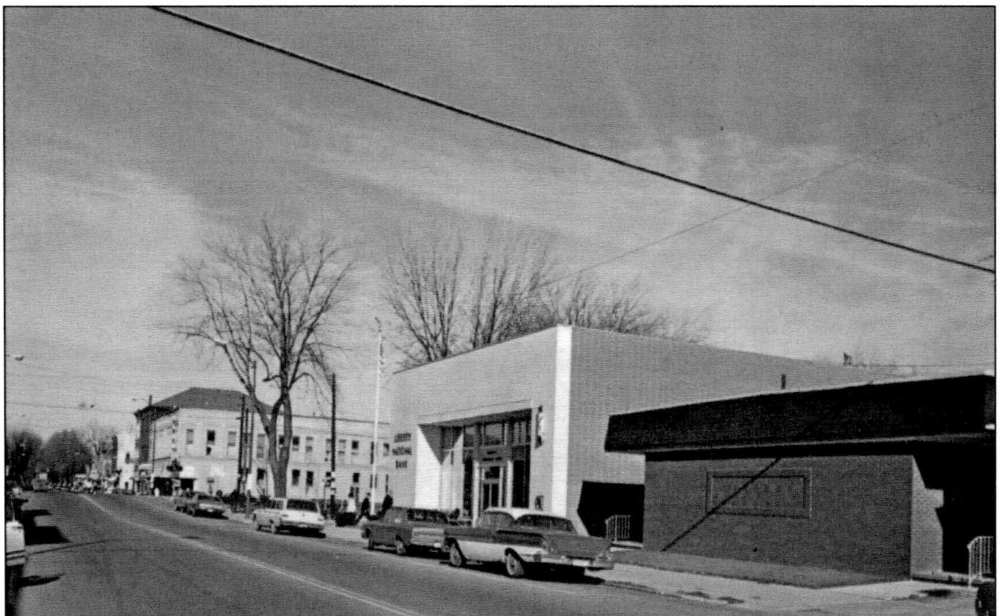

Pictured is the Liberty National Bank on South Main Street as it appeared about 1971. It traces its history from the Ada Savings Bank, organized in October 1893, to the First National Bank, which received its charter in June 1901. The bank is still located in this downtown building, constructed following the merger in 1958. Additional branches are located on East Franklin Street in downtown Kenton and in Bellefontaine.

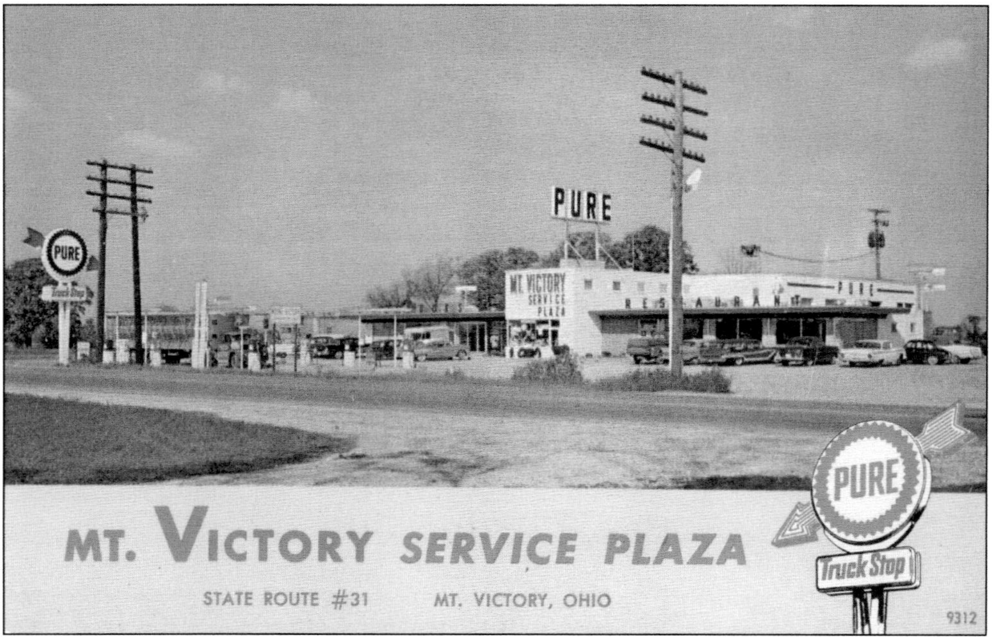

The Mount Victory Service Plaza grew out of the Elliot family cattle business in southern Hardin County. Around 1958, their shipping operations morphed into a truck stop, as seen here during the early 1960s. The complex included a gas station and 24-hour restaurant. A March 1971 fire destroyed much of the restaurant, which was remodeled and reopened by December.

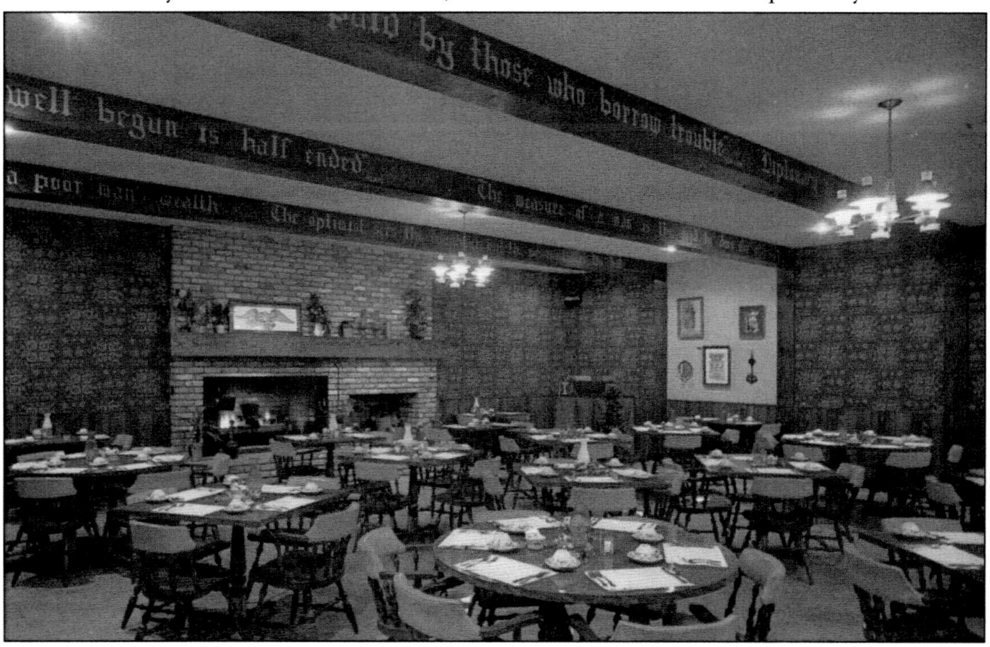

The Plaza Inn-Bakery Shop & Restaurant opened in June 1959 along State Route 31, south of Mount Victory. The award-winning restaurant opened with 42 seats and now features four dining rooms, including the Coach and Surry Room (seen here during the mid-1970s), a landing strip for fly-in diners, and a catering service, plus a miniature waterfall and gift shop in the lobby.

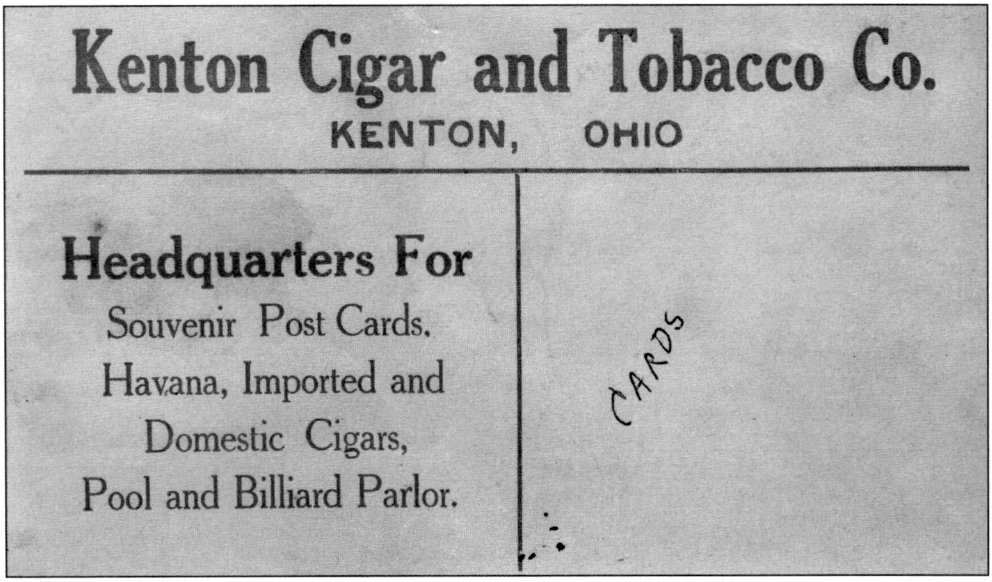

The Kenton Cigar & Tobacco Company on Franklin Street used this c. 1910 envelope to promote the sale of its postcards. Several other stores offered souvenir postcards, including the Snodgrass Drug Store, Furney & Son, House of McCoy, Wendt's, and Powell & Gasson's Big Drug Store in Kenton; Faze & Moses and Bowers Drug Store in Dunkirk; and the Central Drug Store and Varsity Book Store in Ada.

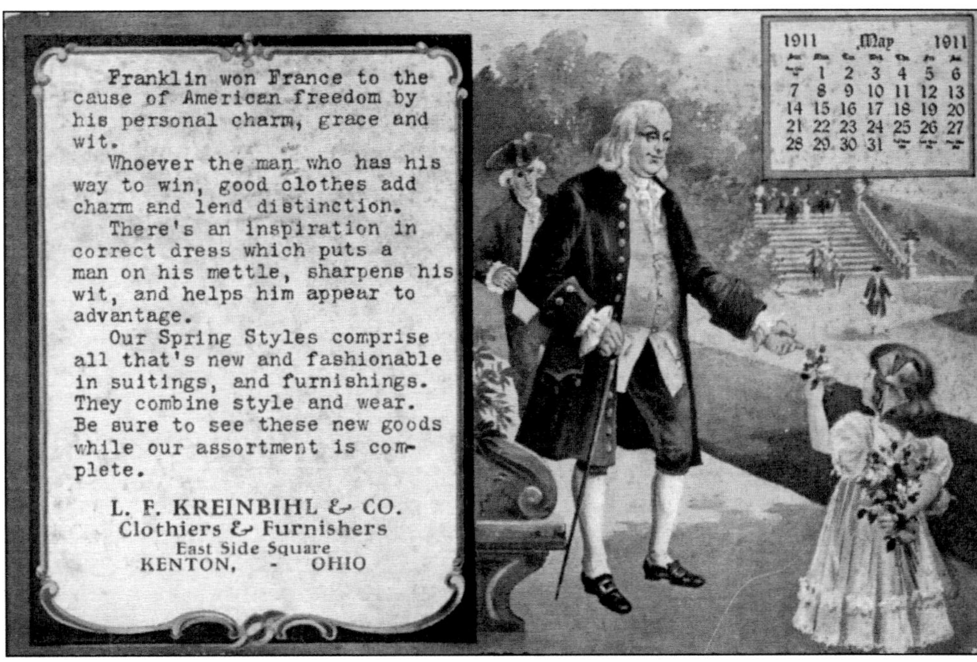

Louis and George Kreinbihl operated the L.F. Kreinbihl & Company clothing and furnishing store on North Main Street. Other clothing stores around the courthouse square during the 1910s included Thompson's Clothing, Conner Brothers, Globe Clothing Company, Rosenthall's, Mark's Clothing, Surprise Store, Morgenroth's, and Norse & Caine.

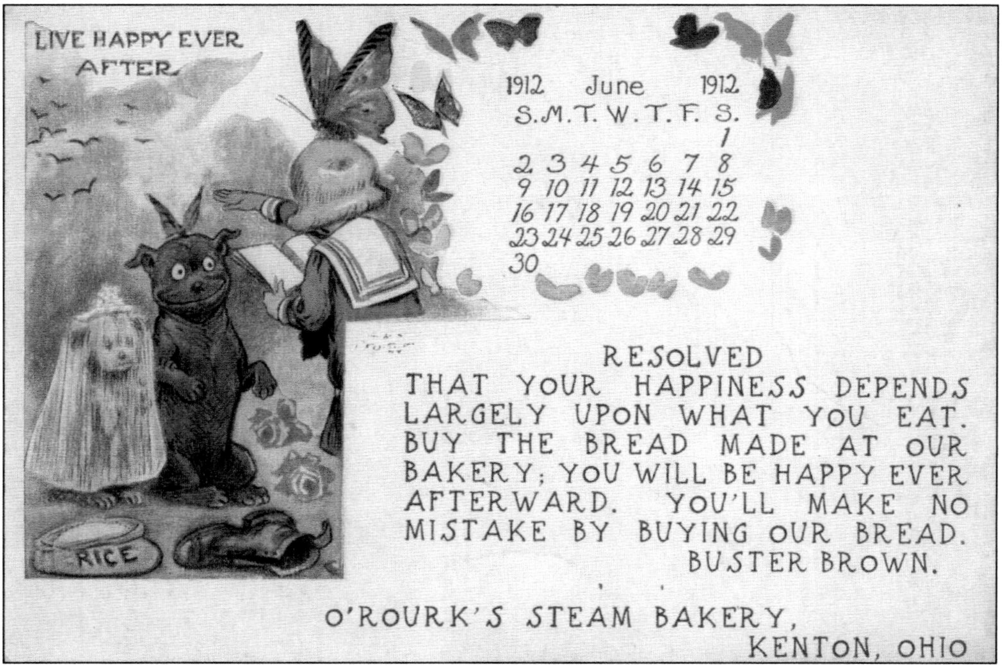

O'Rourk's Steam Bakery operated in Kenton from about 1905 until 1929. In 1911, Michael O'Rourk purchased a building at the intersection of South Main and Espy Street for the bakery. This oversized postcard from 1912 features Buster Brown and his dog Tige promoting the bakery's bread. An August 1906 *Kenton News-Republican* advertisement promoted O'Rourk's Bread with the tagline, "Is always good. Try It."

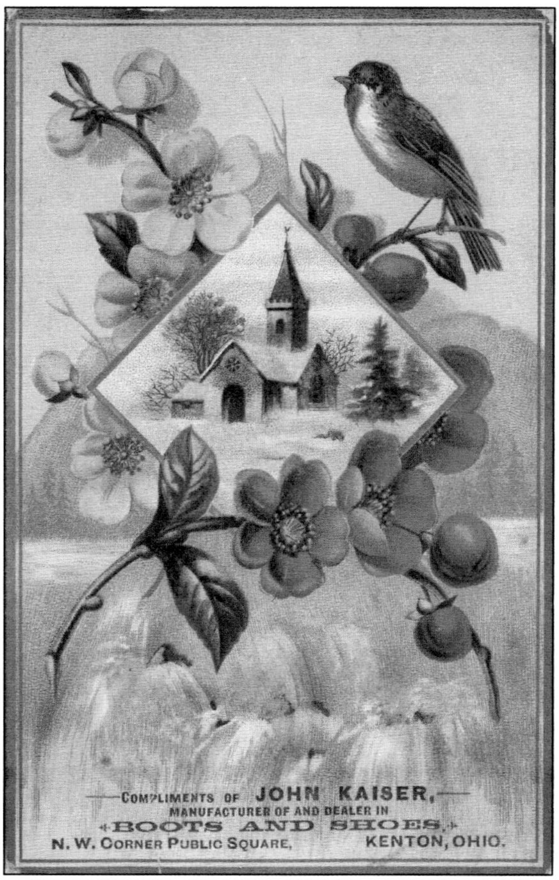

This holiday card was distributed by John Kaiser, a boot and shoe merchant on the northwest corner of the public square in Kenton, about 1900. During the late 1800s to early 1900s, numerous footwear dealers operated in downtown Kenton. John C. Miller founded the first boot and shoe store in Kenton in 1858.

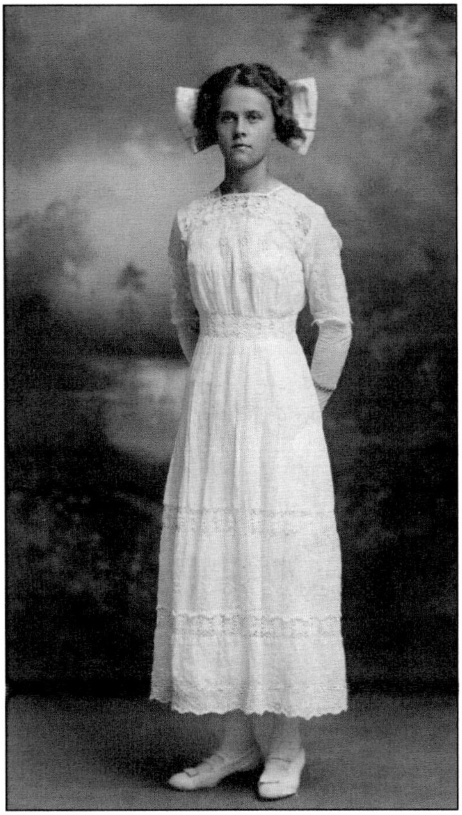

Several photography studios and galleries operated around Kenton's public square from the late 1800s to the early 1900s. Samuel M. John operated a studio in Lima from 1888 to 1895 before opening the S.M. John Photography Studio on North Detroit Street about 1896. Real Photo postcards were one of his specialties. Irene Snyder presented this postcard to her uncle Omar Snyder around 1910.

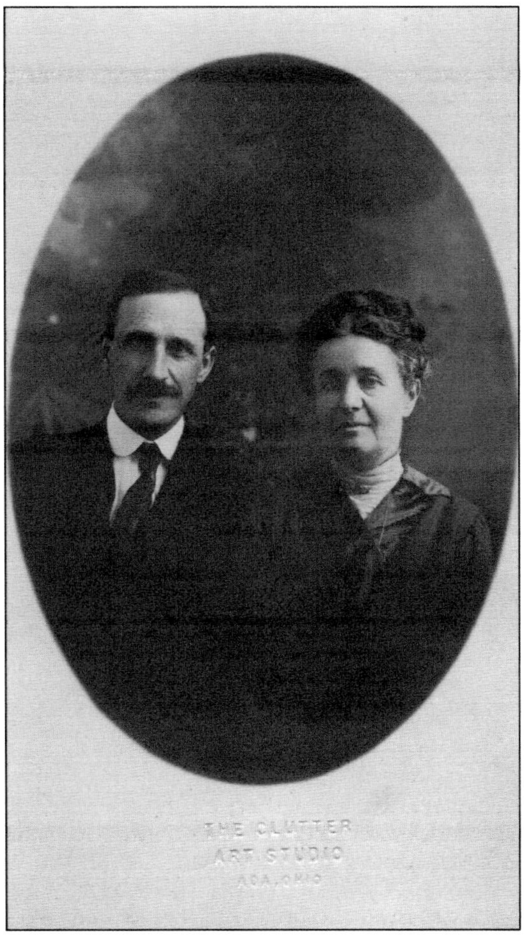

This unidentified couple posed for the Clutter Art Studio, located at 111 ½ South Main Street, sometime around 1915. Albert W. Clutter moved to Ada in 1883 and set up a small photography studio that he maintained through the 1920s. In 1885, he married Lenna E. Gilbert, the daughter of Ada photographer Martin V. Gilbert. Clutter also operated a small studio in Dunkirk in the 1910s.

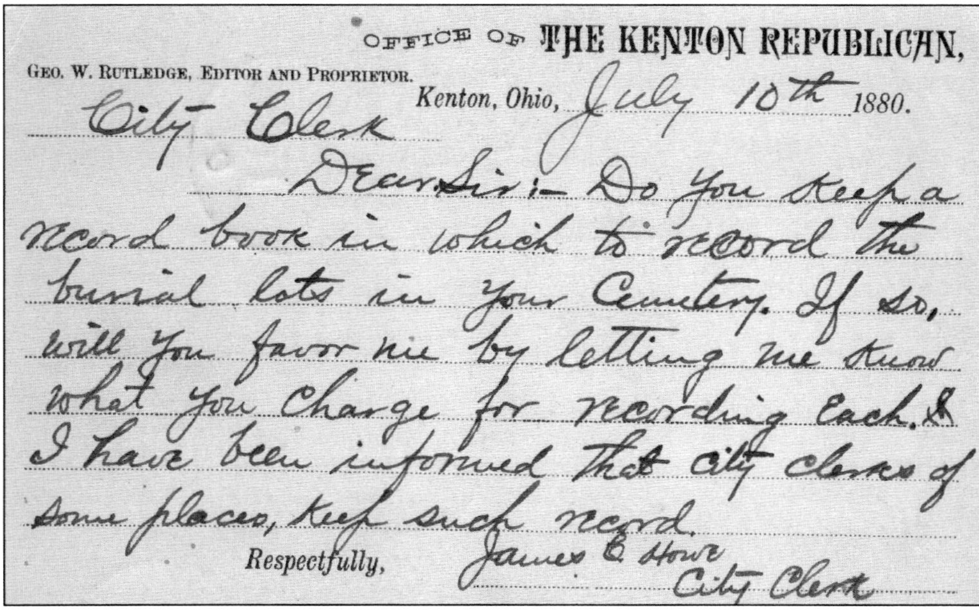

OFFICE OF THE KENTON REPUBLICAN,

GEO. W. RUTLEDGE, EDITOR AND PROPRIETOR.

Kenton, Ohio, July 10th 1880.

City Clerk

Dear Sir:– Do you keep a record book in which to record the burial lots in your Cemetery. If so, will you favor me by letting me know what you charge for recording each. I have been informed that city clerks of some places, keep such record.

Respectfully, James C. Howe
City Clerk

Kenton city clerk James C. Howe mailed this card from the office of the *Kenton Republican* in July 1880 requesting information from the city clerk of Tiffin. George W. Rutledge was editor and publisher of the *Kenton Republican* from April 1880 to May 1882. The newspaper was first issued by James S. Robinson in January 1847. Howe would own the paper from July 1895 to February 1896.

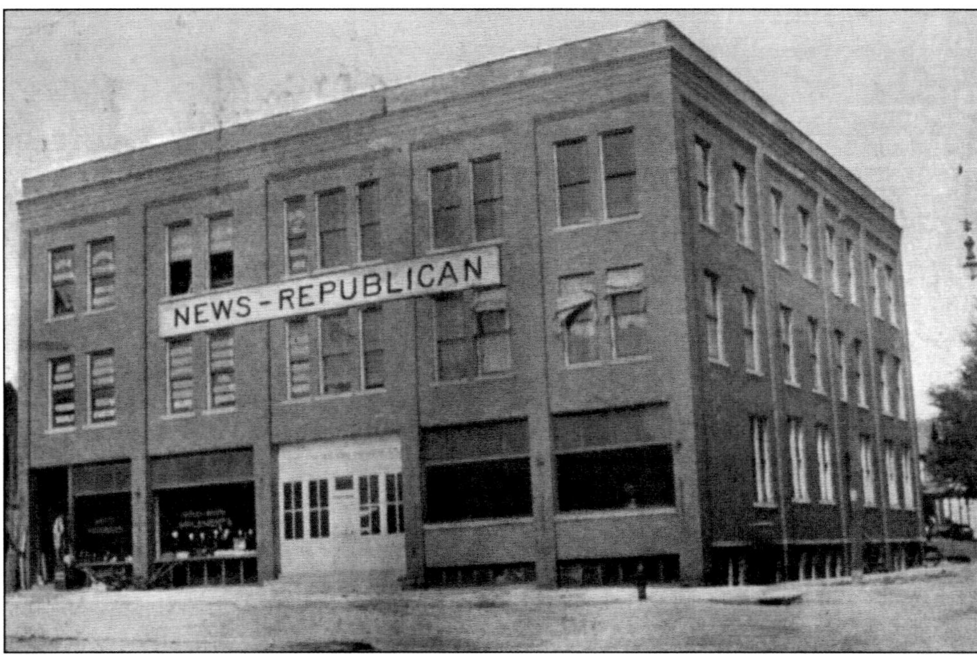

The *Kenton News-Republican* outgrew its quarters in the Palucci Block on West Columbus Street and constructed this large brick building at the intersection of South Main and East Ohio Streets in 1903. Wagner's Hardware Store, also seen in this 1909 postcard, occupied the north half (left) of the building. The newspaper was published under various names from 1847 to 1953.

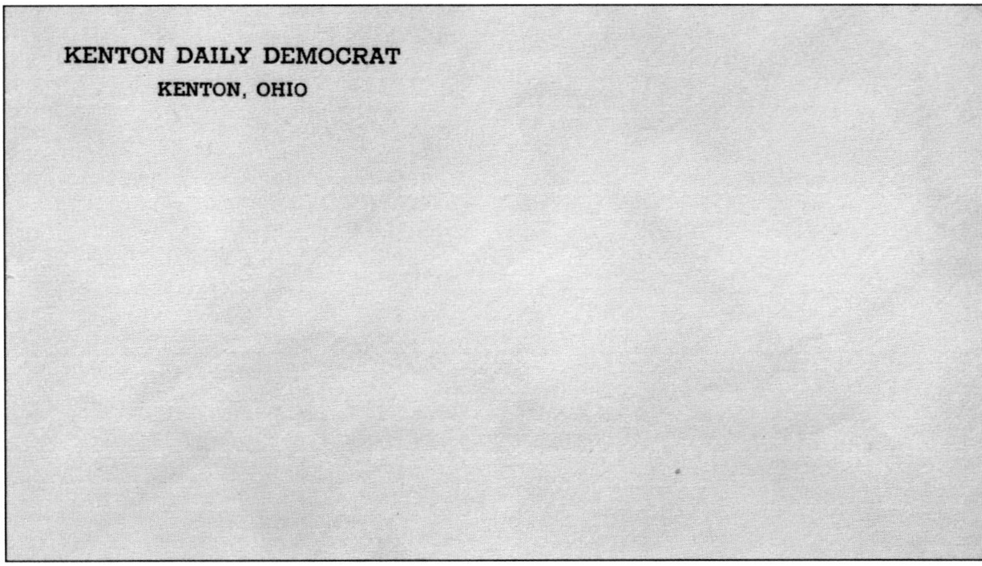

This is an envelope used by the *Kenton Daily Democrat* during the 1930 or 1940s. The first democratic newspaper in Kenton was published in 1844. The *Hardin County Democrat* appeared in 1857 and changed its name to the *Kenton Democrat* in 1866. The paper became a daily in 1892 and merged with *Kenton News-Republican* in 1953.

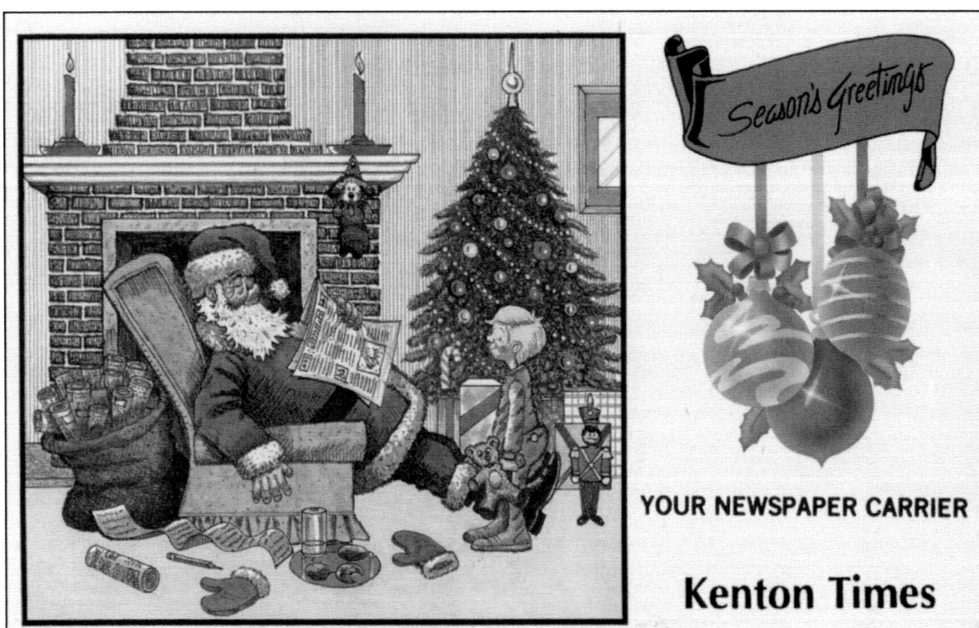

Newspaper carriers delivered this Christmas card to subscribers in the 1980s. The *Kenton Times* began publication in 1953 as a merger of the town's former newspapers and remains Kenton's only daily. Its offices are located on East Columbus Street on the site of the former Kaiser Buggy Company. Henry Kaiser began his carriage works in 1864 and moved to Columbus Street in 1873.

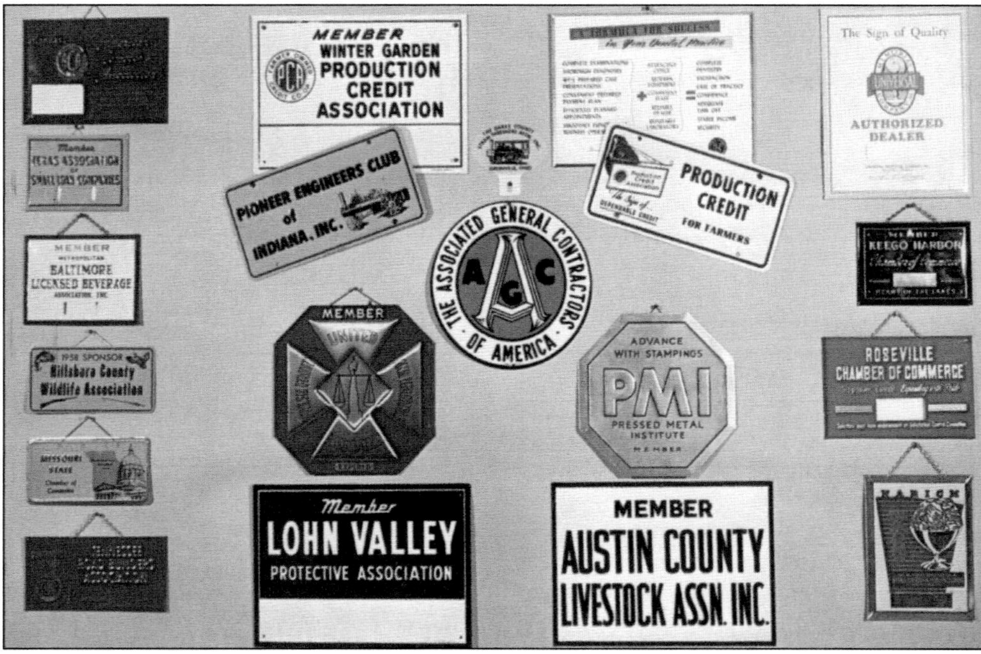

This collection of metal plaques and signs was produced by the Scioto Sign Company during the 1960s. The Scioto Sign Company was established in Kenton during 1898. It was incorporated in 1900 and, a year later, erected a three-story factory on Vine Street (Kenton Iron Products). In the 1970s, a modern facility was erected in Blanchard Township.

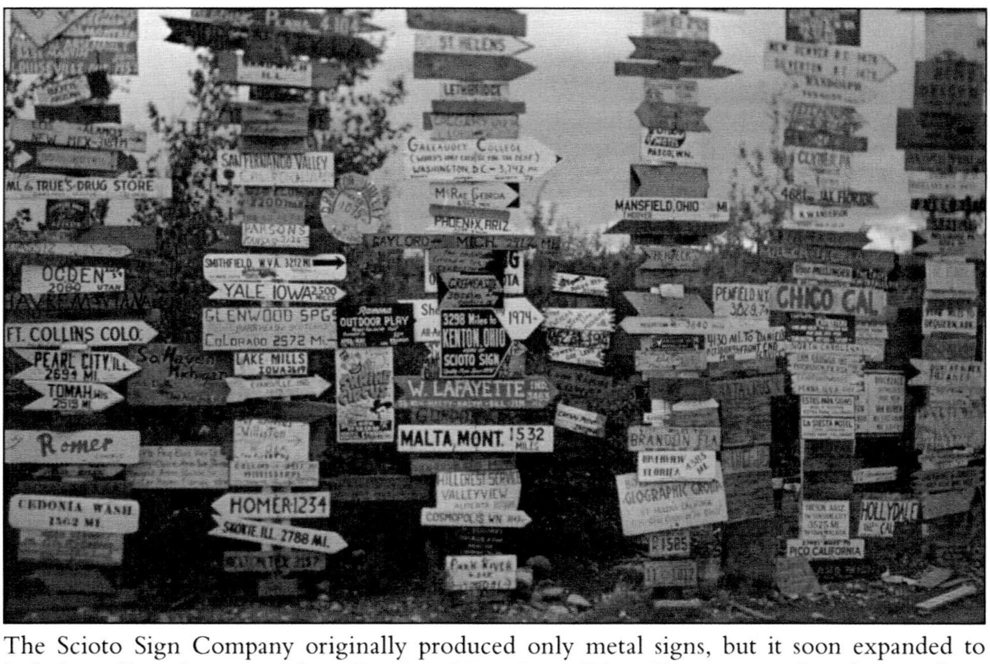

The Scioto Sign Company originally produced only metal signs, but it soon expanded to include cardboard, paper, and muslin advertising pieces. Scioto Signs are now found everywhere throughout North America, as evidenced by this postcard showing the signposts beside Watson Lake, Yukon Territory, along the Alaska Highway. This postcard was produced by the Scioto Products Company, a division of the Scioto Sign Company.

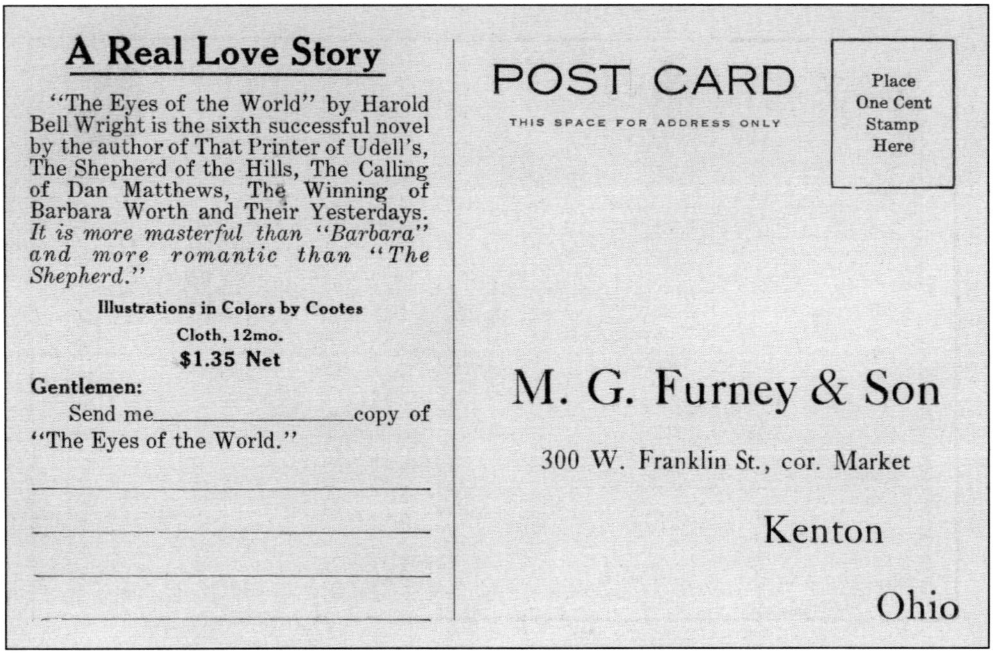

Melvus G. Furney opened a drugstore in 1886 in the Furney Block at the corner of Market and Franklin Streets. His son Claude continued the business under the name M.G. Furney & Son until it closed about 1957. William Furney, Claude's grandfather, is considered Kenton's first resident, having erected a cabin near the site of the Kenton Theatre.

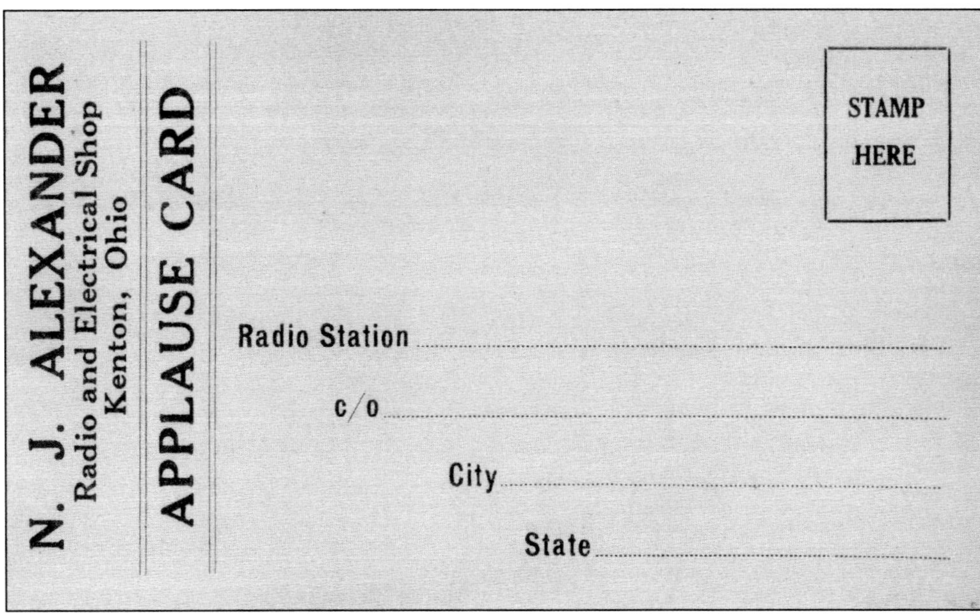

Newell J. Alexander's Radio and Electrical Shop was located on North Detroit Street in Kenton during the 1920s. The shop performed electrical and construction work in addition to household wiring. The reverse of this card allowed customers to contact local radio stations and comment on their programming.

The M. Schick Company was begun in 1884 on the north side of the public square. It dealt in clothing, boots and shoes, dry goods, rugs, millinery, and notions. This postcard promoted its 1907 spring and summer clothing lines. By 1910, it had become the largest dry goods store in Kenton, featuring over 25,000 square feet of merchandise.

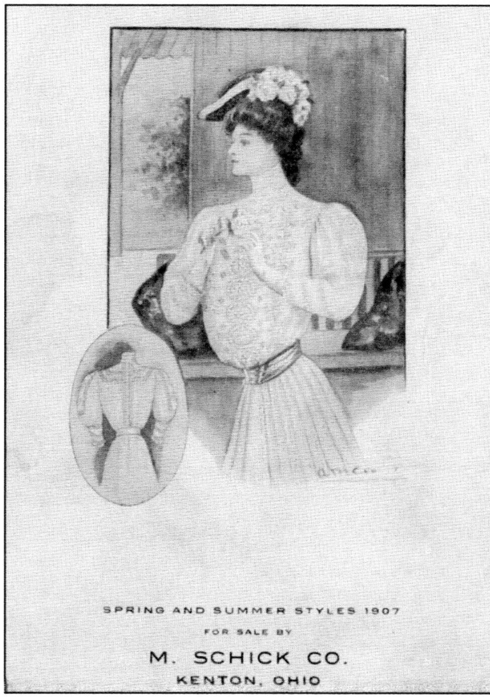

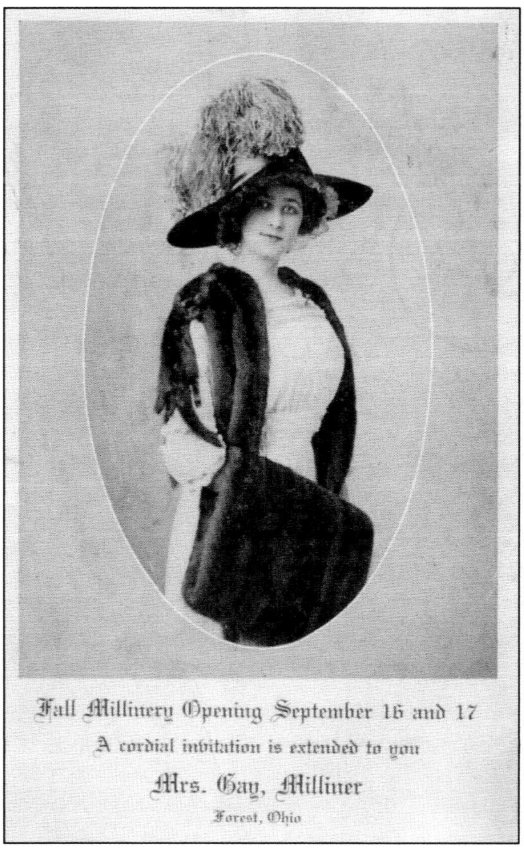

Emma S. Gay operated a millinery shop on Lima Street in Forest during the early 1900s. This postcard promoted the opening of her fall line in September 1910. Other early milliners included Mollie Elberson and Jennie Lyle in Ada, Olive Coy and Ida Pennock in Mount Victory, the Woods Sisters in Dunkirk, and Maude Price Myers and Maude Kimmell in Kenton.

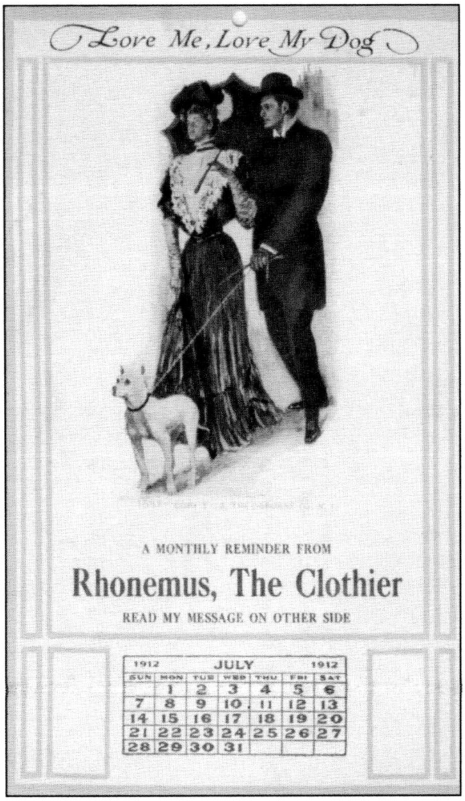

Christian E. Rhonemus operated a clothing store on North Main Street in Ada from 1901 until the early 1920s. This postcard from July 1912 is promoting the Rhonemus Clothing Store's summer line of clothing. The store specialized in clothing for men and boys. Neighboring shops included the Deming Brothers clothing store and Joseph O. Tyson's, a merchant tailor on North Main Street.

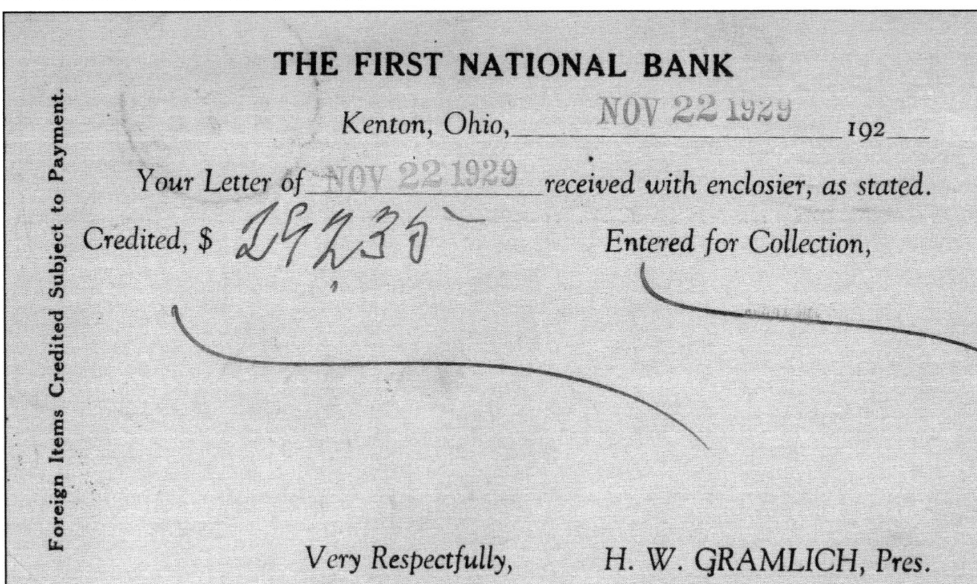

THE FIRST NATIONAL BANK

Kenton, Ohio, NOV 22 1929 192

Your Letter of NOV 22 1929 received with enclosier, as stated.

Credited, $ 24235 Entered for Collection,

Very Respectfully, H. W. GRAMLICH, Pres.

Foreign Items Credited Subject to Payment.

Henry W. Gramlich mailed this receipt postcard to a Hepburn customer in November 1929. The First National Bank was founded in 1881. It was located on the southwest corner of the square until 1968 when a new building was completed at the intersection of South Main and East Franklin Streets. The building has undergone several name changes and is now a branch of Liberty Bank.

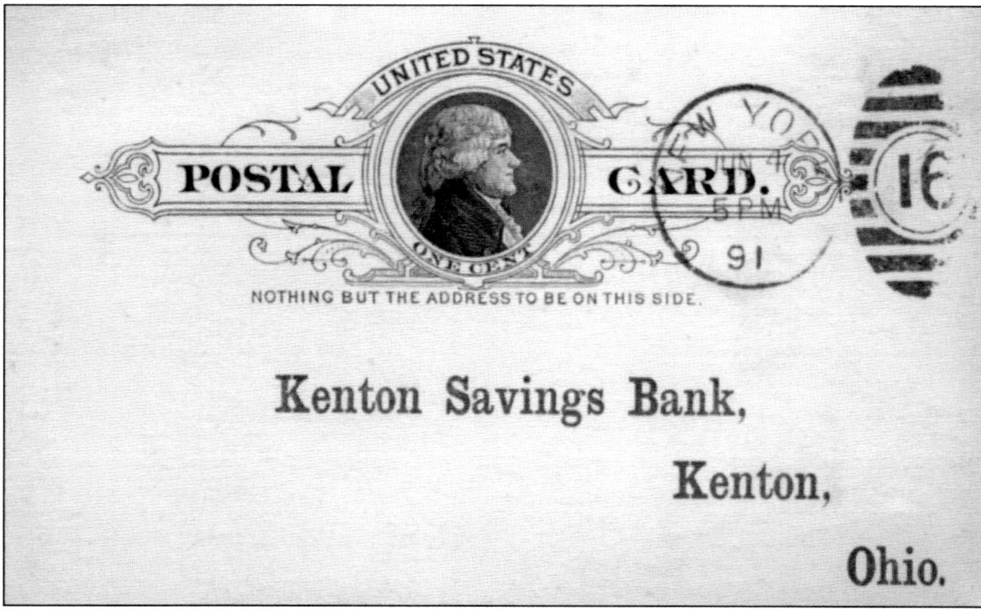

The Kenton Savings Bank was incorporated in September 1875 and opened its first office on the west side of the public square. In January 1876, the bank moved into the "bank block" at the corner of North Detroit and West Columbus Streets, where its successors remain. This preprinted postal card was mailed from the National Park Bank of New York in June 1891.

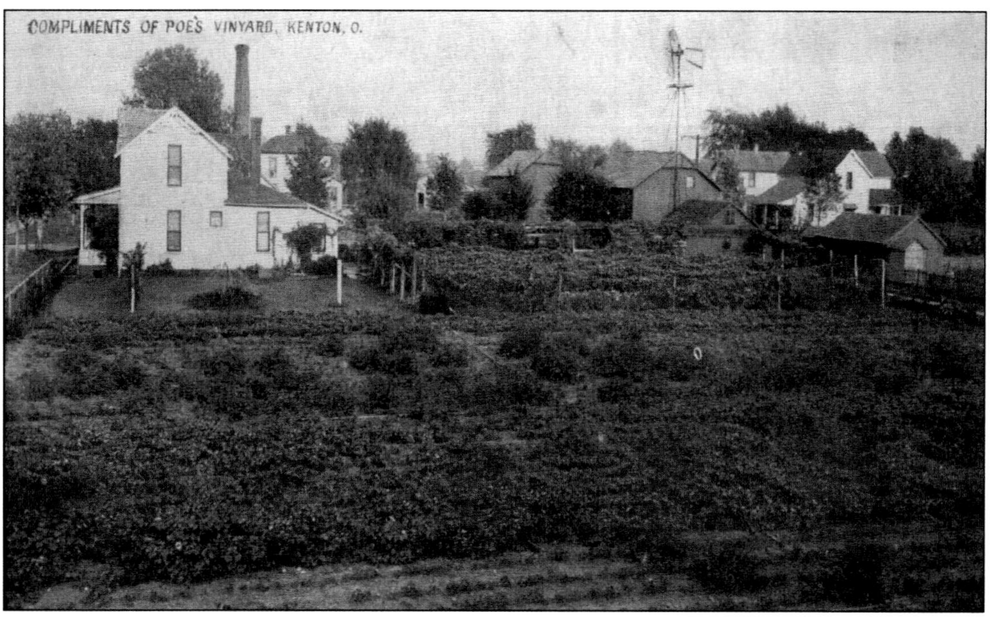

George H. Poe opened the 1.5-acre Poe's Vineyard at 330 North Avenue in south Kenton in 1900. Poe advertised and guaranteed his new line of "mammoth grapes" in 1906. By the early 1920s, the small nursery operation alongside the Scioto River featured small fruit trees in addition to the grapevines.

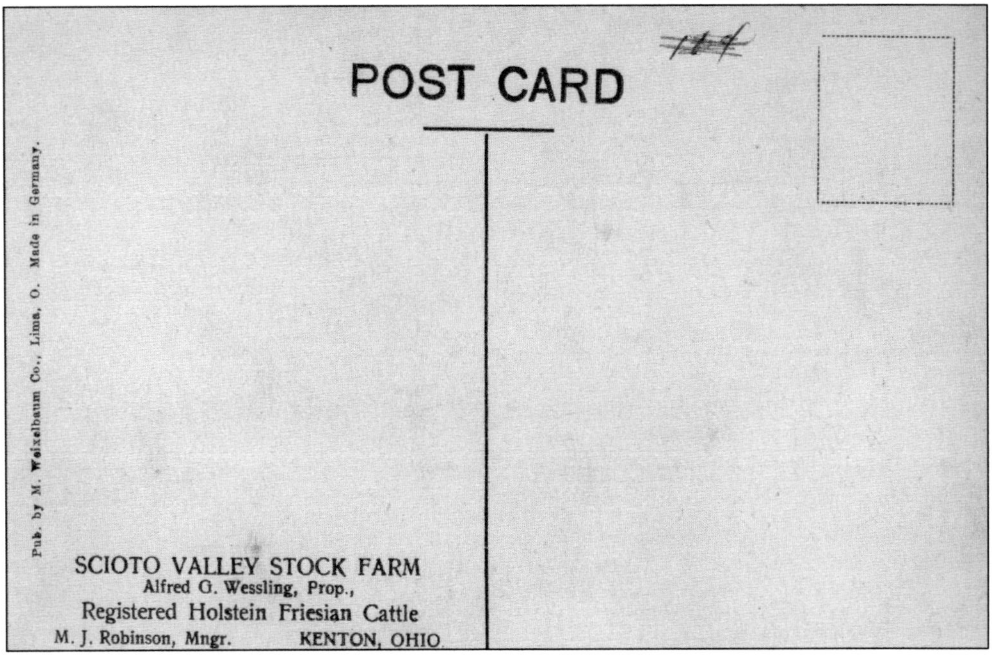

The Scioto Valley Stock Farm was owned by Alfred G. Wessling, who also operated the A.G. Wessling Cold Storage Company on South Detroit Street in Kenton. This 240-acre farm was headquartered at the historic Wheeler Tavern in Pfeiffer Station. Miniter J. Robinson was hired as the farm manager in 1905.

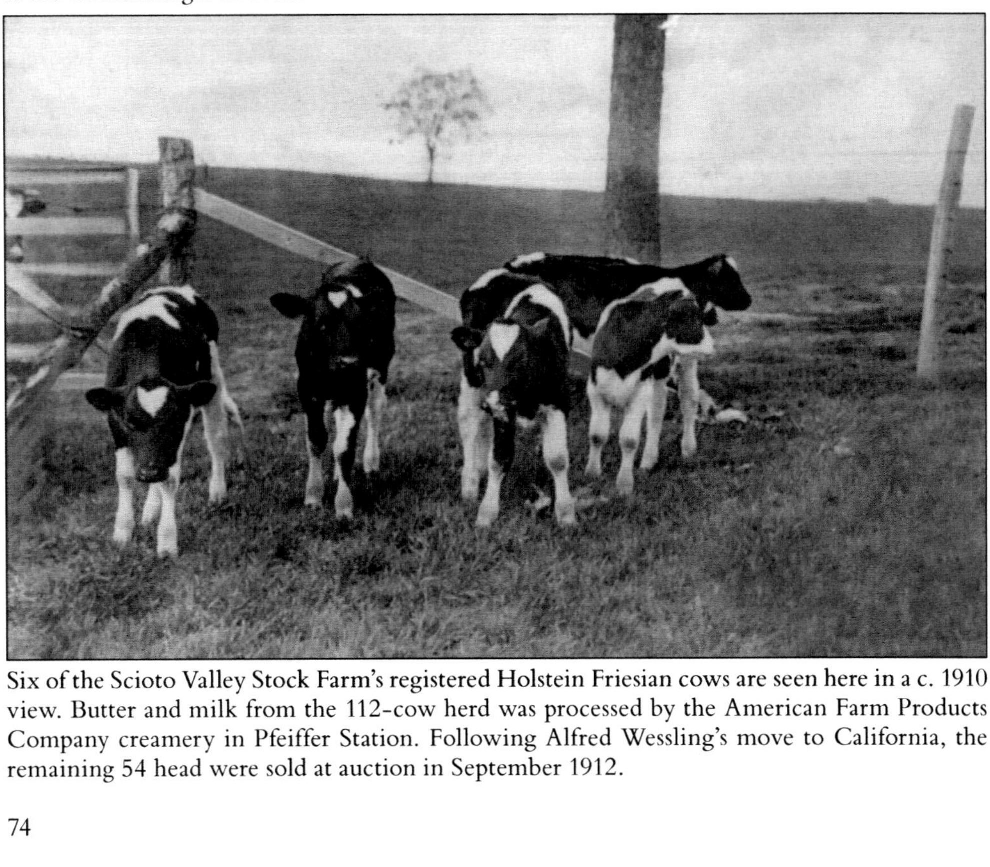

Six of the Scioto Valley Stock Farm's registered Holstein Friesian cows are seen here in a c. 1910 view. Butter and milk from the 112-cow herd was processed by the American Farm Products Company creamery in Pfeiffer Station. Following Alfred Wessling's move to California, the remaining 54 head were sold at auction in September 1912.

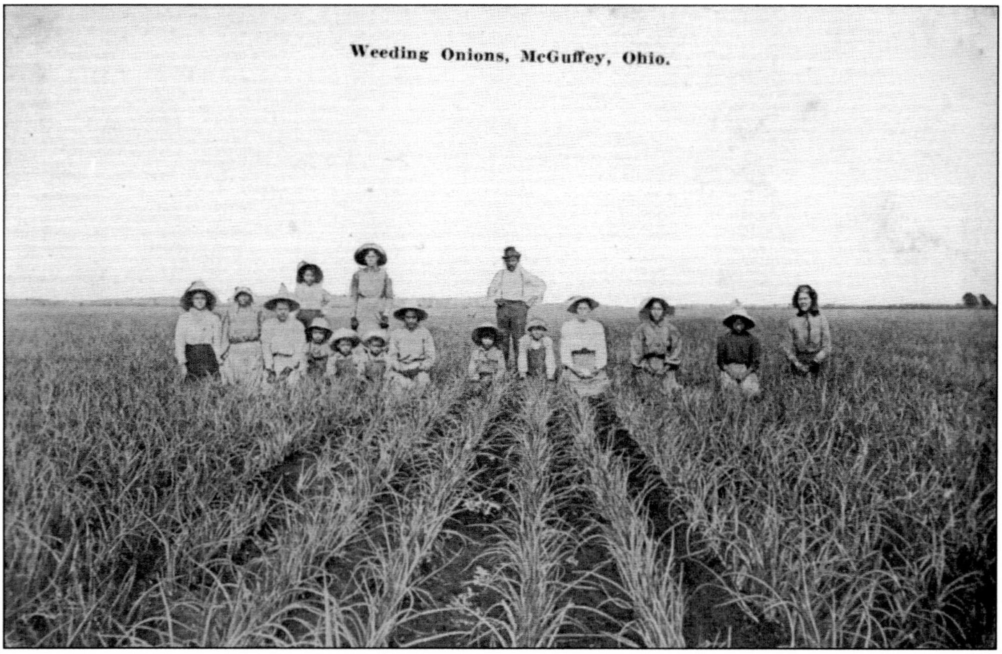

James Bowen produced this c. 1914 postcard of migrant workers who flooded the area around McGuffey and Alger looking for agricultural work. In the 1860s, efforts were undertaken to drain the Scioto and Hog Creek Marshes. Finally drained in the early 1900s, the marshlands proved to be some of the most fertile soil in the country.

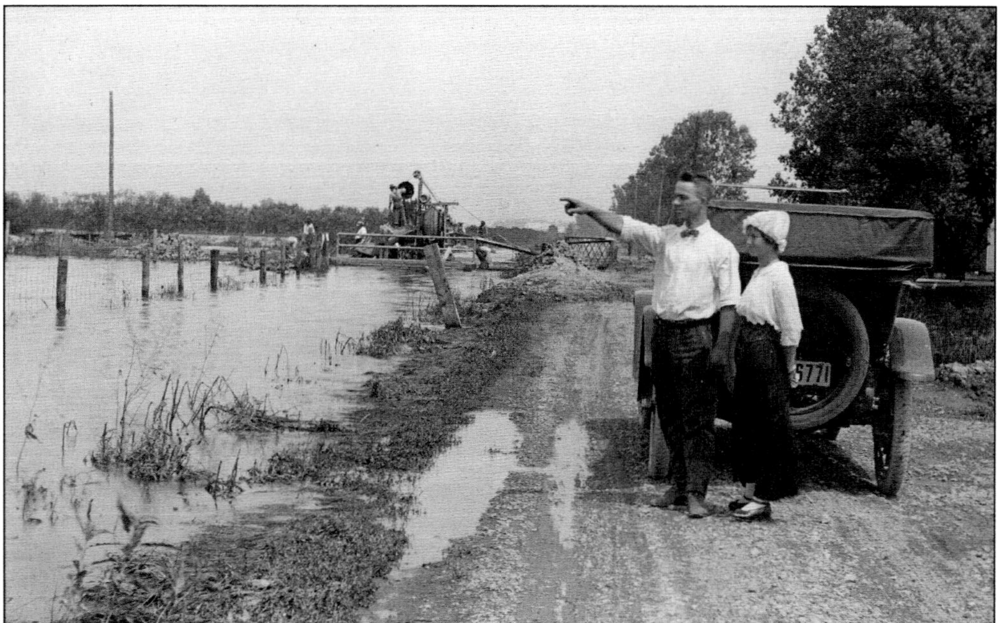

Residents examine the onion fields near McGuffey following the flood of 1913 while workers try to dredge out the ditch in the background. The Scioto Marsh, once considered the "onion capital of the world," produced thousands of crates of onions, potatoes, and beets each season. The crates were stored in large warehouses that still dot the landscape of central Hardin County.

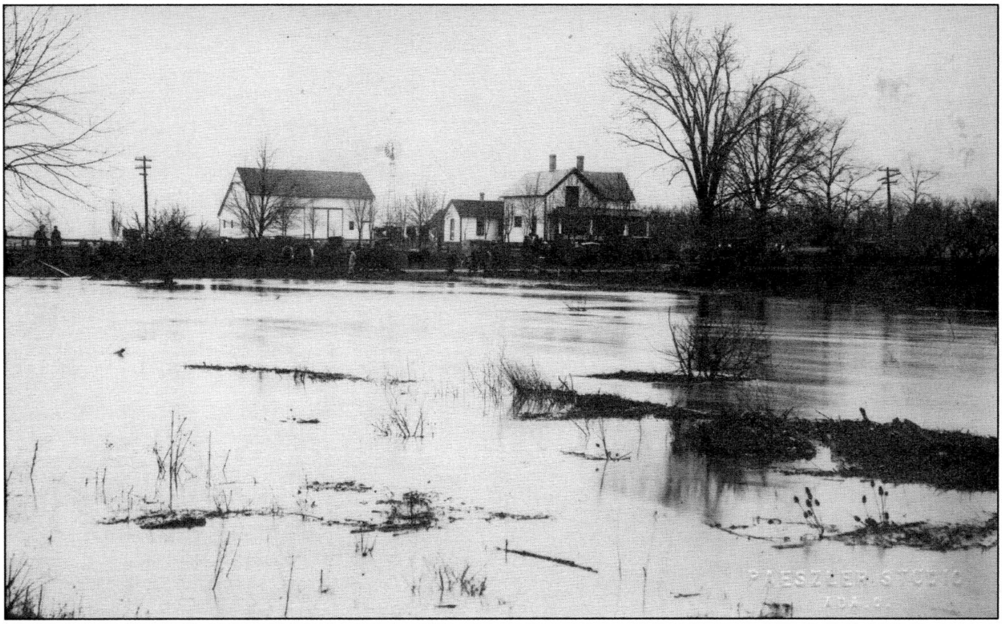

The Paeszler Photography Studio captured this image of the flooded fields beside a small farm outside of Ada following the flood of 1913. A large group of buggies and men can be seen gathered along the edge of the water. Clara Paeszler operated her studio in Ada from about 1897 until her death in 1921, when Brian Frederick, her assistant for 17 years, acquired ownership of the studio.

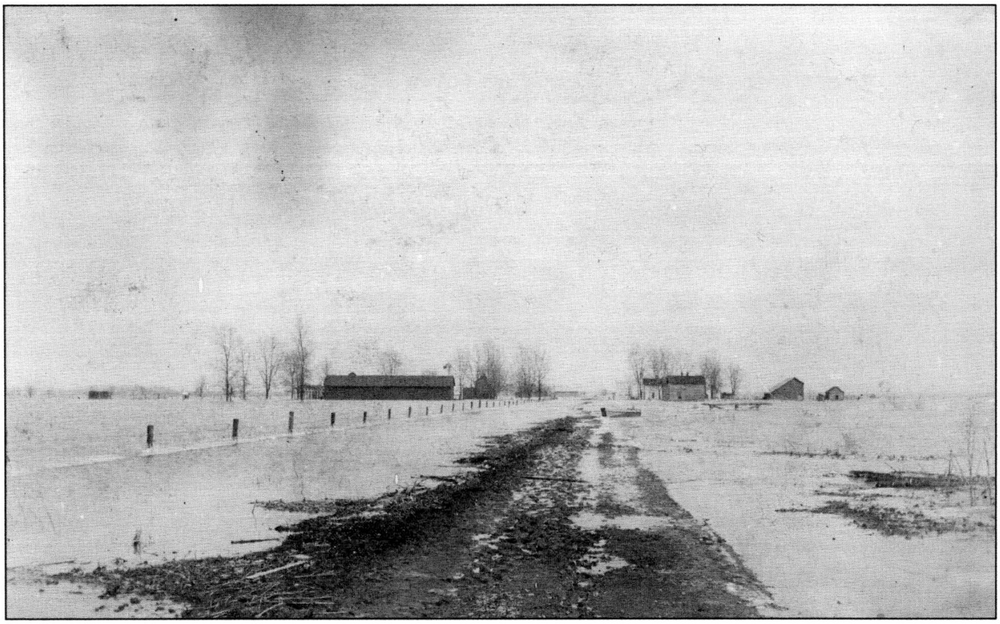

This postcard was mailed from Alger in April 1913, shortly after the flood in March. The author wrote that the "picture was taken just below the Lone Oak Bridge. Right hand is Jay's farm." Most of the former lands of the Scioto and Hog Creek Marshes were inundated, resembling the original lakes that covered the county. It would take two to three weeks for the waters to recede.

Five

Transportation

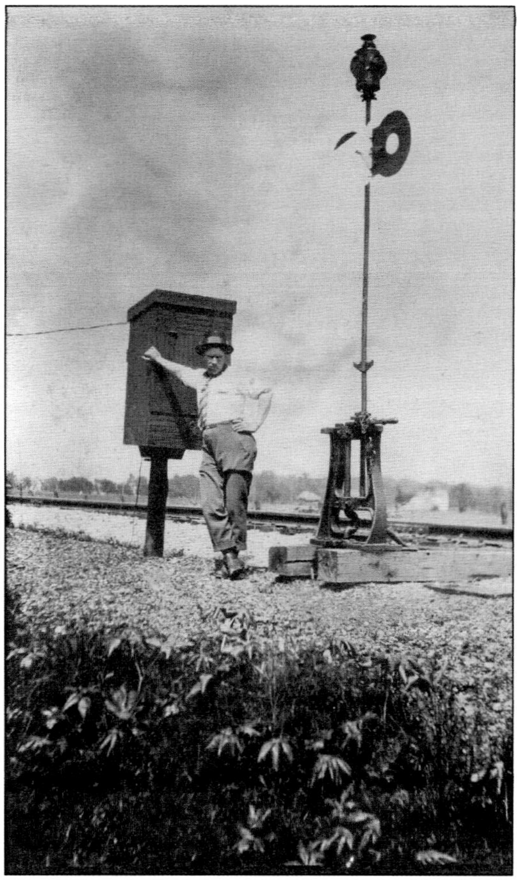

This photograph of railway worker Clyde Barst was taken beside the railroad signal near Grant. The small railroad town received its name when it was established in the 1870s during Pres. Ulysses Simpson Grant's term. Grant's Station, located in Jackson Township, began as a cooling stop along the Mad River & Lake Erie Railroad about 1852. A few homes were eventually built around the station.

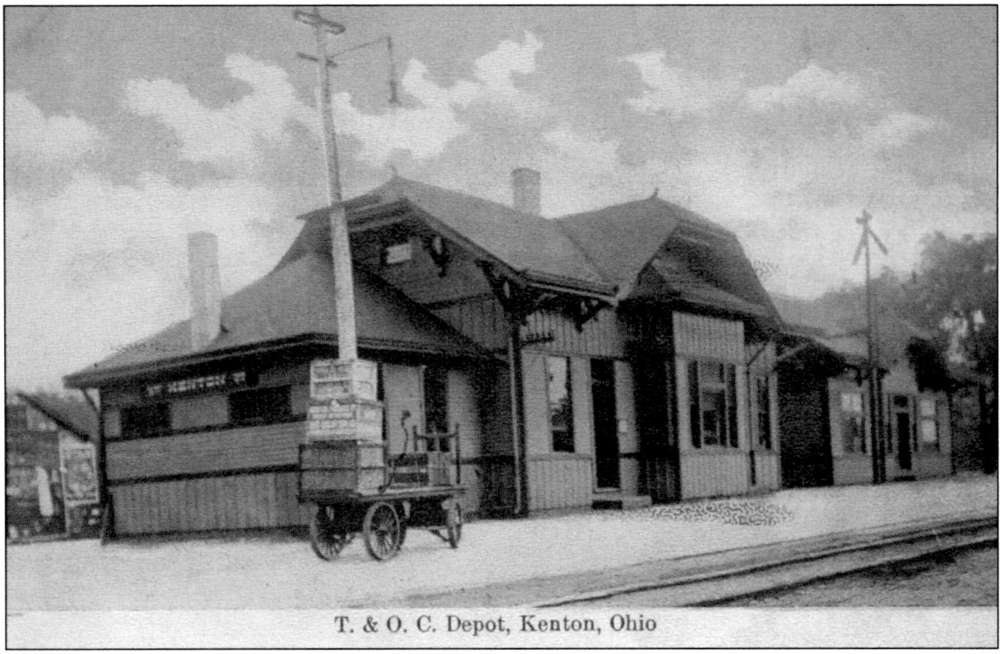

The Toledo & Ohio Central Railroad erected its freight house/depot on the south side of the railroad tracks at the intersection of West Decatur and South Main Streets about 1890. By 1911, the railroad was operating as a division of the New York Central, and shortly afterwards a new passenger depot was erected on the north side of the tracks.

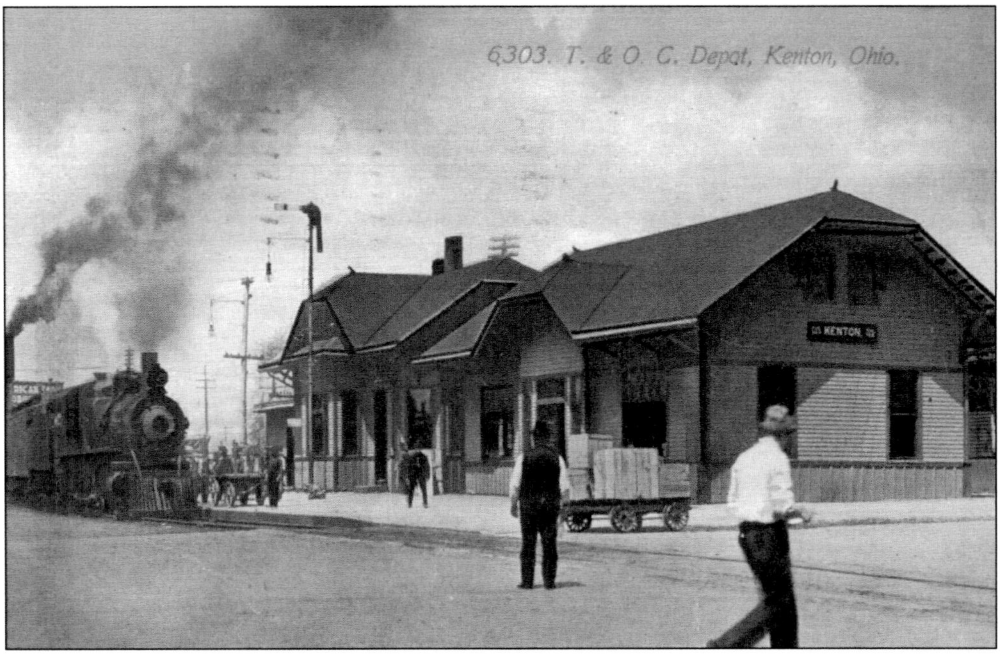

The Toledo, Columbus & Cincinnati Railroad reached Kenton by February 1890. The railway constructed a roundhouse and several maintenance shops alongside the Scioto River at the end of Dixon Street at that time. The roundhouse was closed by the 1930s, and many of the smaller shops were shuttered and eventually torn down.

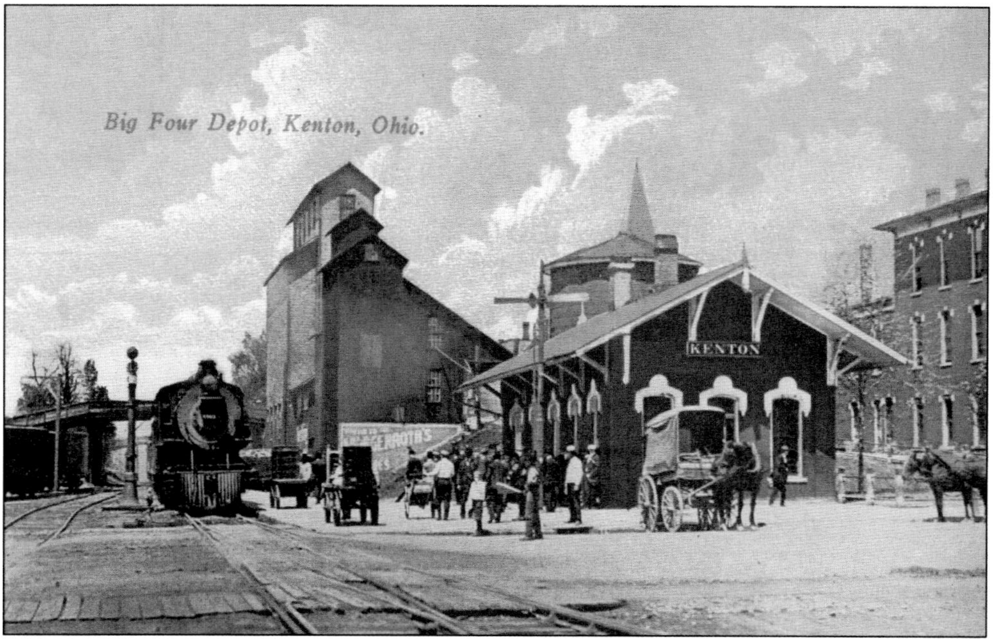

Kenton's first train arrived July 4, 1846, on the Mad River & Lake Erie Railroad. In 1855, a stock pen was placed next to the original depot to allow for easier shipment of livestock. This brick passenger depot was built around 1882 by the Cleveland, Cincinnati, Chicago & St. Louis Railroad (Big Four) to replace an earlier wooden one.

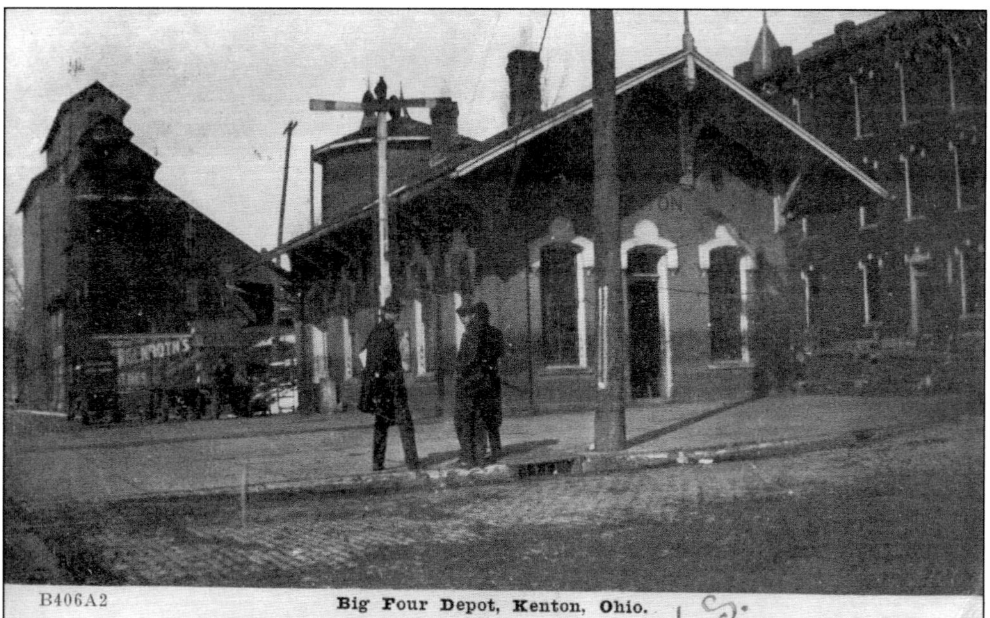

Here is a view of the Big Four Depot and water tower looking north from West Franklin Street with the Seymour & Ochs Grain Elevator to the rear. The three-story brick structure to the right was the Saint Nicholas Hotel, which closed by the 1940s. The depot was restored and has been used as the Rodgers Insurance Agency office for many years.

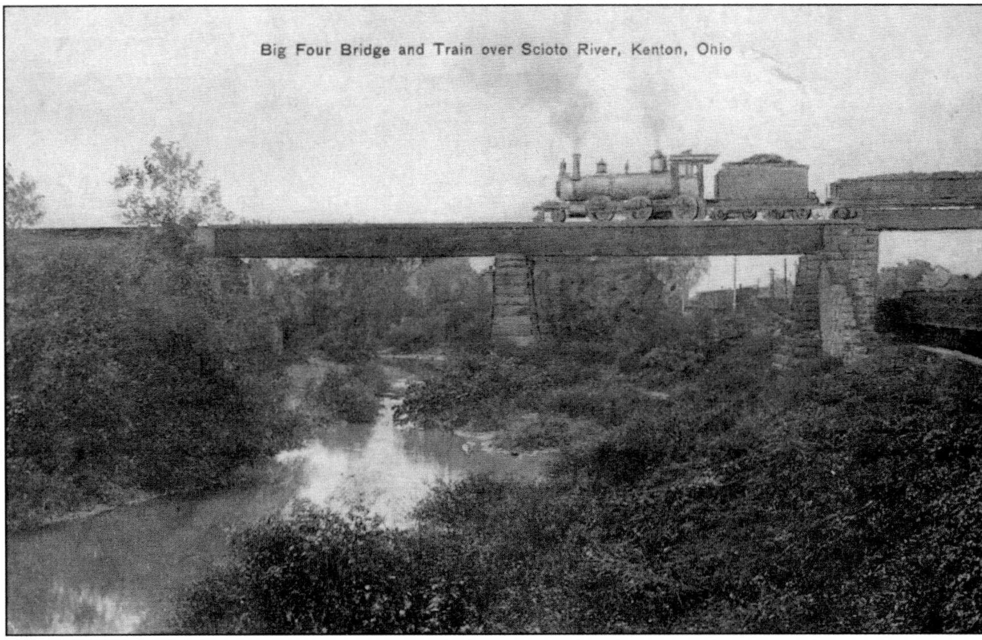

William W. Snodgrass established the Snodgrass Drug Store, Kenton's third drugstore, with his uncle in 1867. He published this early image of a Cleveland, Cincinnati, Chicago & St. Louis Railroad train crossing the Toledo & Ohio Central Railroad before continuing south over the Scioto River on the Big Four Railroad Bridge in south Kenton.

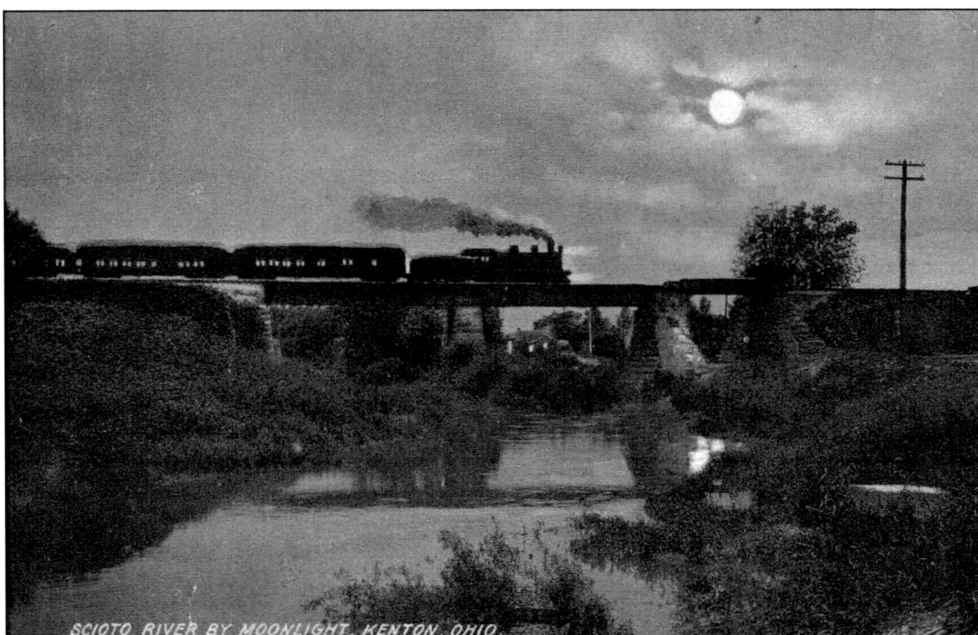

Moonlight shines down on a passenger train crossing the Scioto River over the Big Four Railroad Bridge in this 1910 postcard. In May 1866, night express trains began operating on the Sandusky & Cincinnati Railroad, the successor to the Mad River & Lake Erie Railroad. These trains were scheduled to pass through Kenton at midnight.

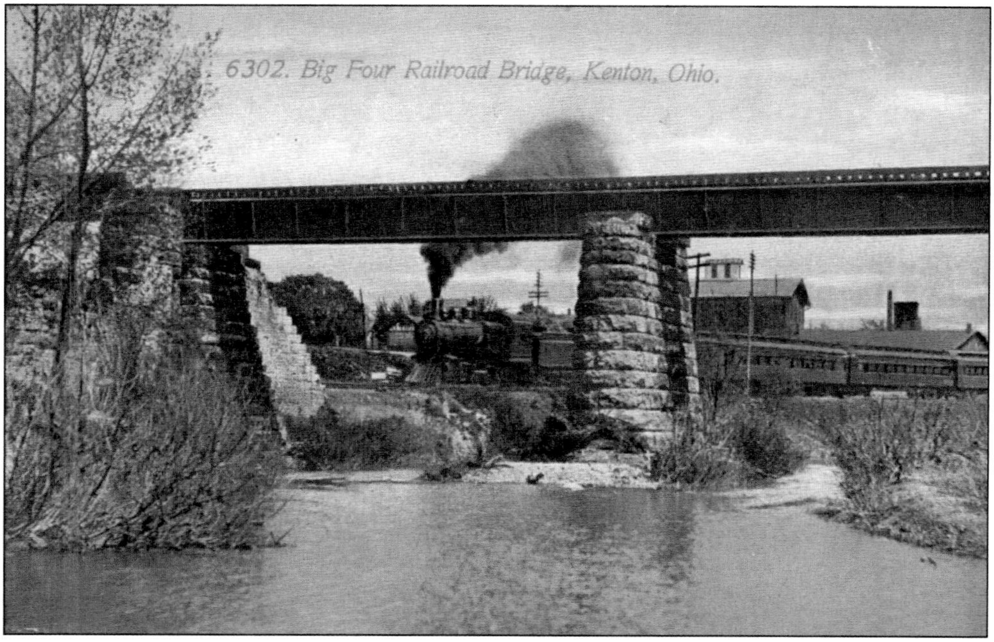

Passenger trains, such as this one heading west alongside the Scioto River, were a common site in Kenton during the late 19th and early 20th centuries. The Big Four Railroad Bridge carried these trains over the Scioto River south of town. Abandoned years ago, remnants of the bridge's stone support columns are still visible.

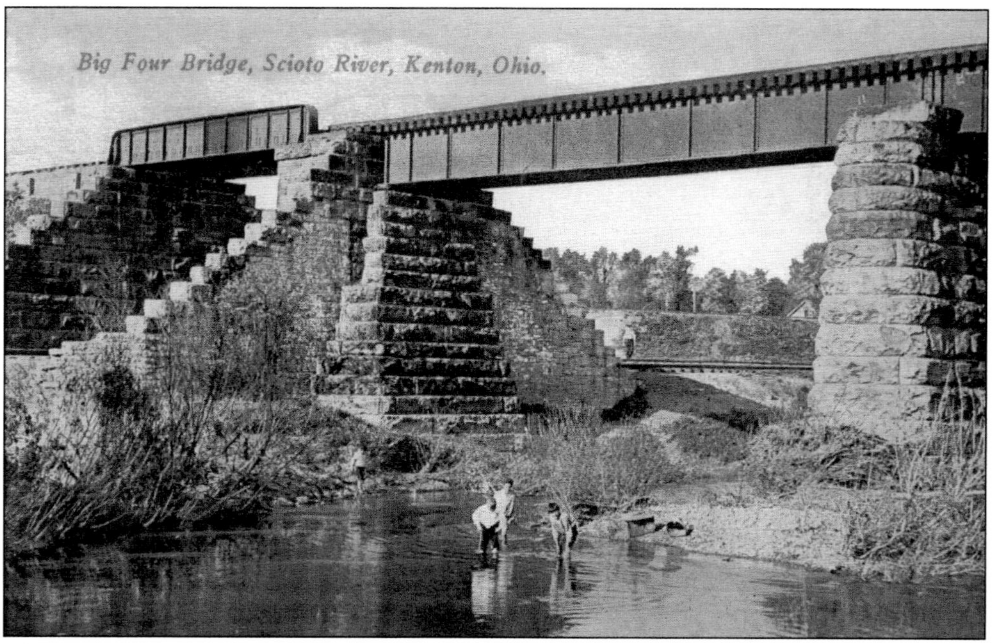

The Scioto River has always been an attraction to local children. The Big Four Railroad Bridge near the Water Works Park baseball diamond was an easily recognizable landmark and could serve as a rallying point for adventurous boys. A child can be seen walking in the background along the Toledo & Ohio Central Railroad tracks.

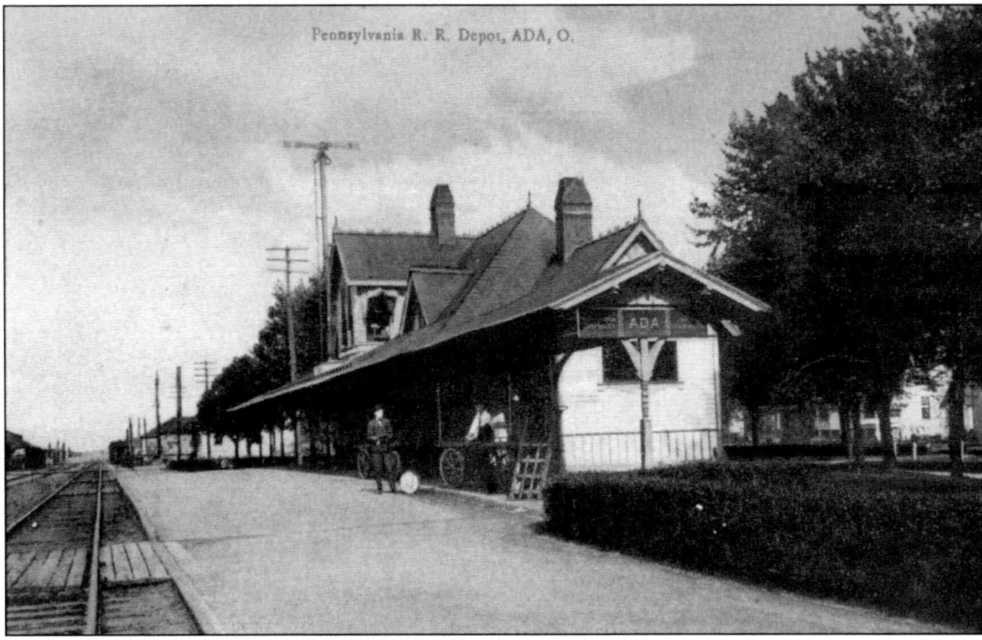

The first train passed through Ada on April 11, 1853, and the original depot was built east of Johnson Street shortly afterwards. This two-story depot was constructed in the Stick-Eastlake style by Pennsylvania Railroad workers in 1887. Located in the center of town, the restored depot was listed in the National Register of Historic Places in 1998.

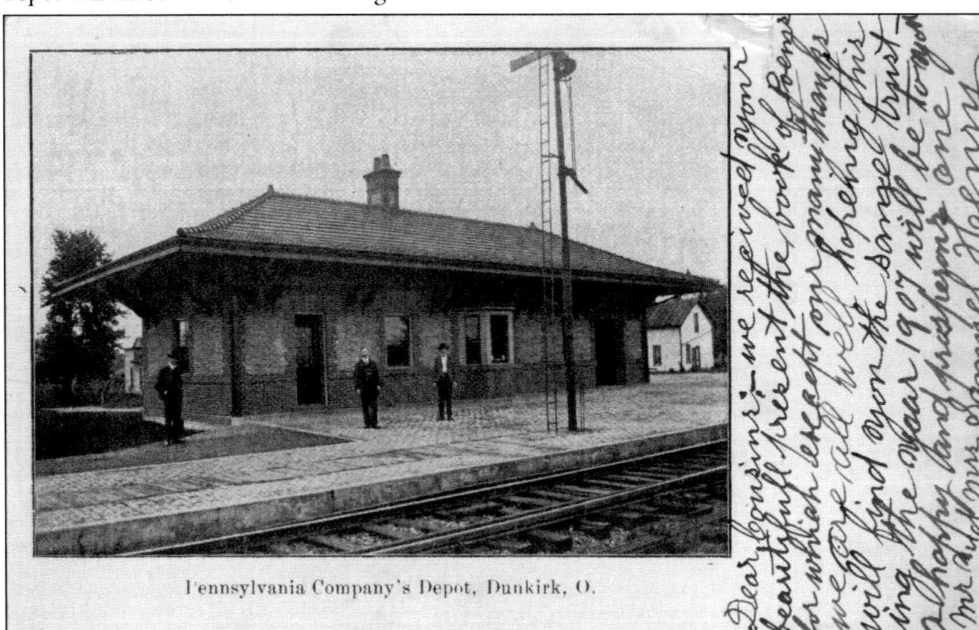

Dunkirk's original depot is believed to have been built around the time the first passenger trains reached town during 1864. The wooden structure was removed and converted to a private home about 1900. Seen here in about 1906, this brick, three-room Pennsylvania Railroad Company passenger depot was utilized until the 1950s, when passenger service began to decline in the area.

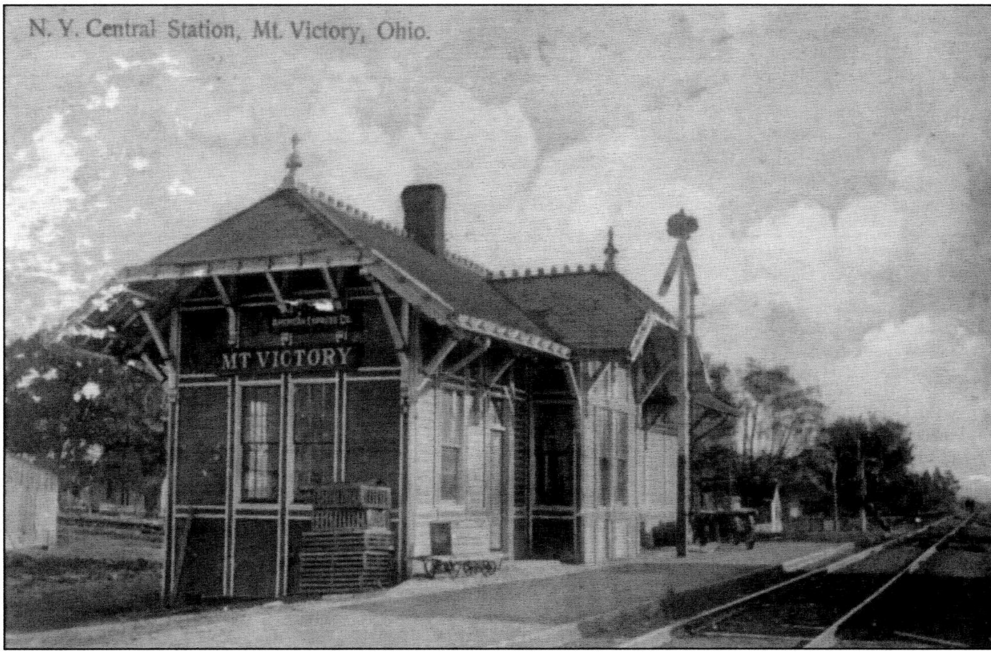

The Bellefontaine & Indiana Railroad Company completed the first line through Mount Victory in 1852. To accommodate freight and passenger service, this depot was constructed about 1900. Mount Victory sat on a trunk line of the New York Central Railroad, which was later acquired by Conrail. The last passenger train traveled through the town in 1955.

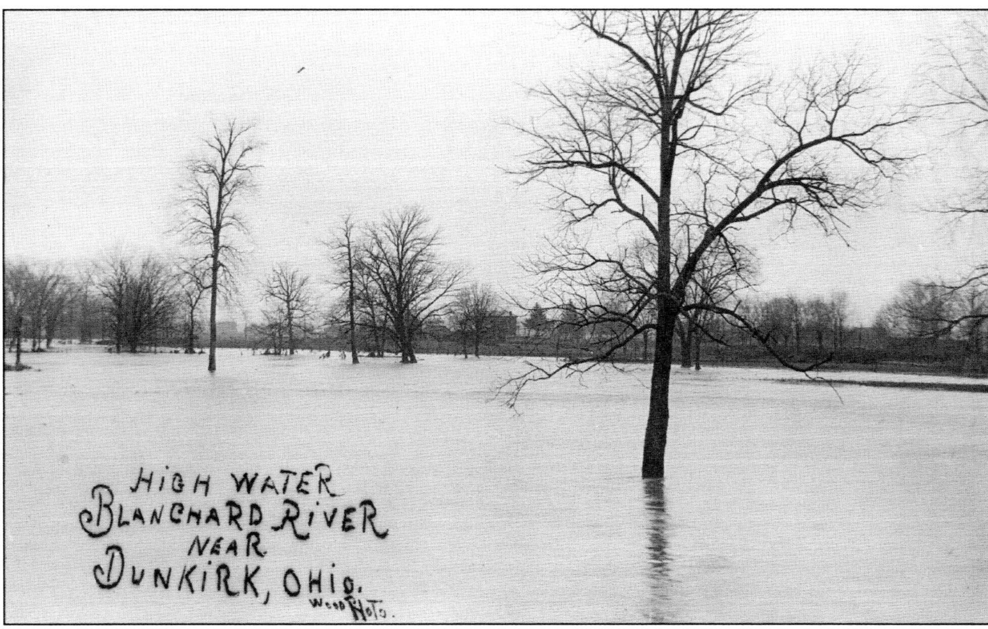

Originally known as Blanchard's Fork, the Blanchard River in Hardin County was named for Frenchman Jean Jacques Blanchard, a tailor who lived among the Shawnees during the late 1700s. The river winds its way from its headwaters in Pleasant Township northward toward Findlay. During heavy rains, it is prone to flooding, as evidenced by this c. 1910 image by the Wood Photography Studio.

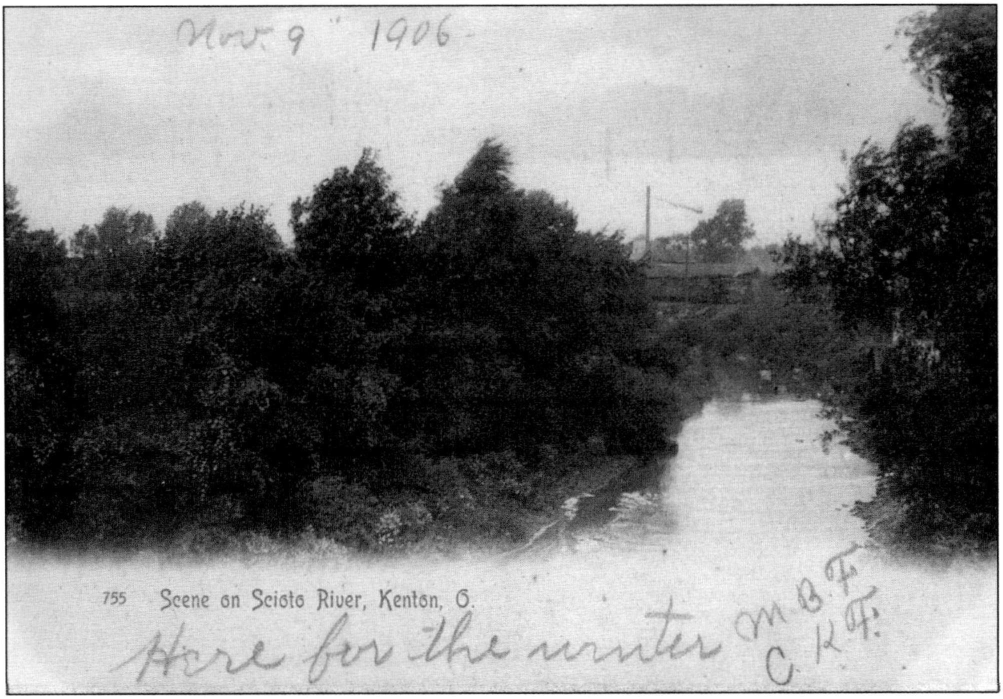

The Scioto River is seen meandering lazily through south Kenton in 1906. During 1869, Hardin County commissioner Benjamin R. Brunson advocated cutting a straight channel for the Scioto River and erecting two 100-foot iron bridges. City leaders finally eliminated the river's curve along Riverside Drive in the mid-1920s following the serious floods of the 1910s.

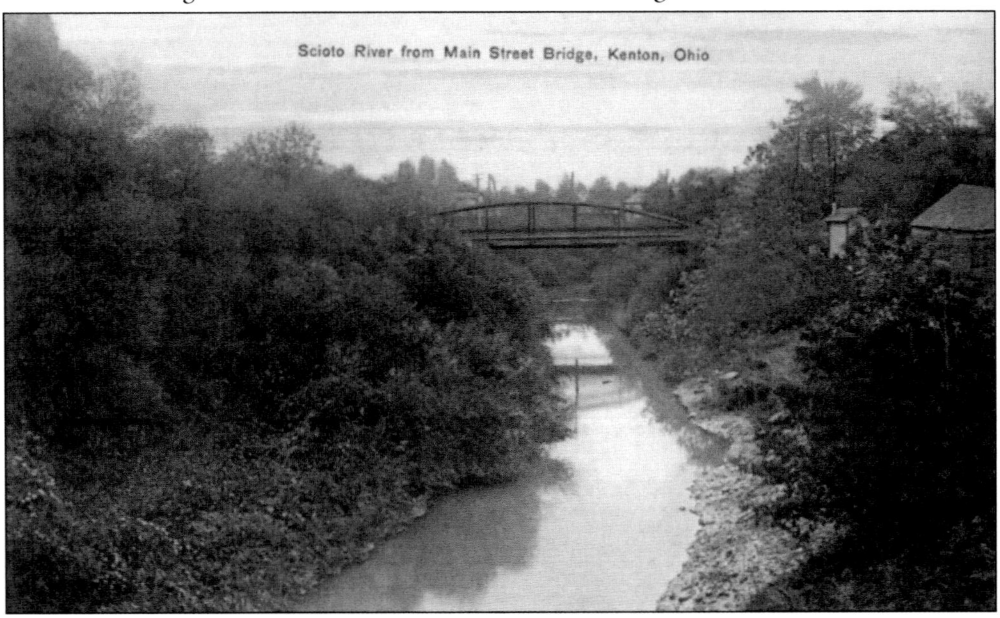

William W. Snodgrass published this image of the South Wayne Street Bridge about 1905. The Champion Iron Company fabricated and installed three 100-foot cast-iron bridges across the Scioto River during the 1890s. The floods of March 1913 and July 1915 severely damaged these bridges and several others throughout the county, forcing their replacement.

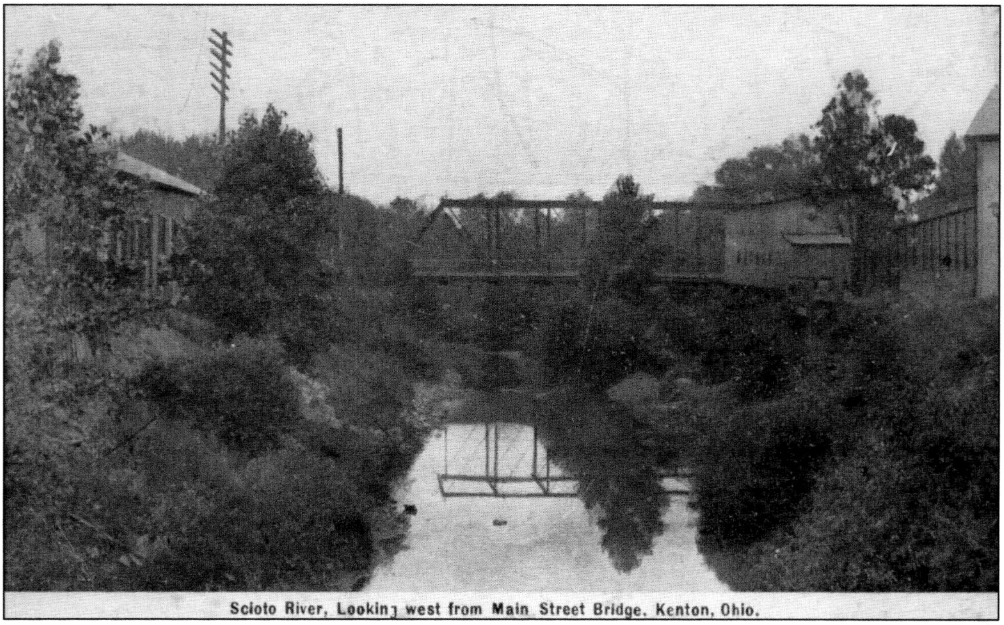

Portions of the Robinson Gage Lumber Company are visible alongside the South Detroit Street Bridge in this 1908 image. The lumber mill was established in 1897 east of the Toledo & Ohio Central Railroad passenger depot north of the bridge. Around 1910, the lumber company purchased the former Scioto Furniture Company on the south side of the river.

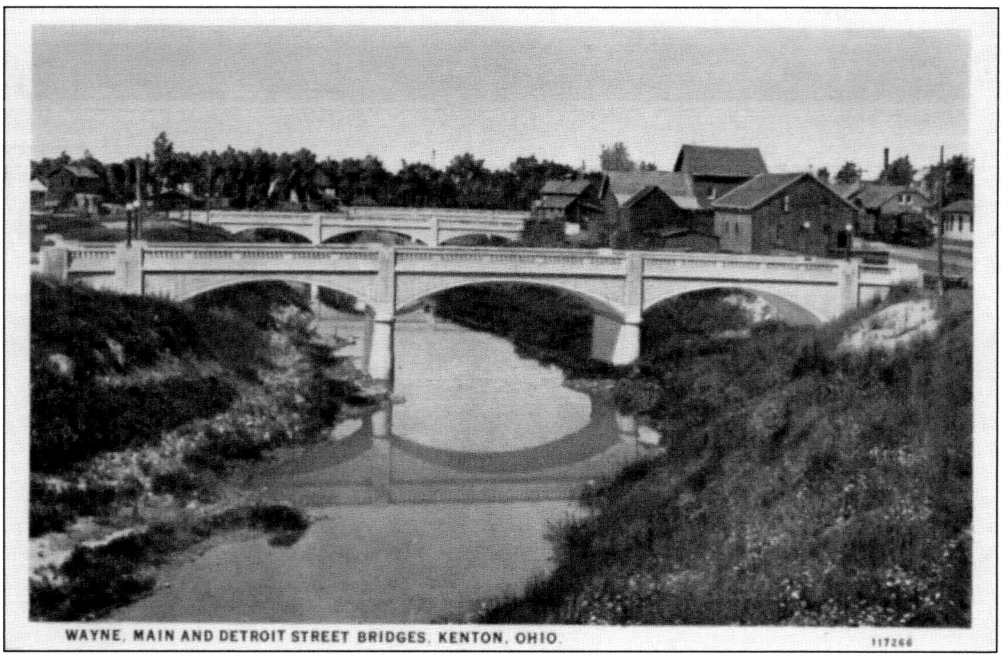

The Wayne Street, Main Street, and Detroit Street Bridges crossed the Scioto River in south Kenton. These reinforced concrete bridges were installed during the early 1920s to replace the earlier cast-iron bridges. The Robinson Gage Lumber Company and Toledo & Ohio Central Railroad freight house are visible at the north end of the bridges.

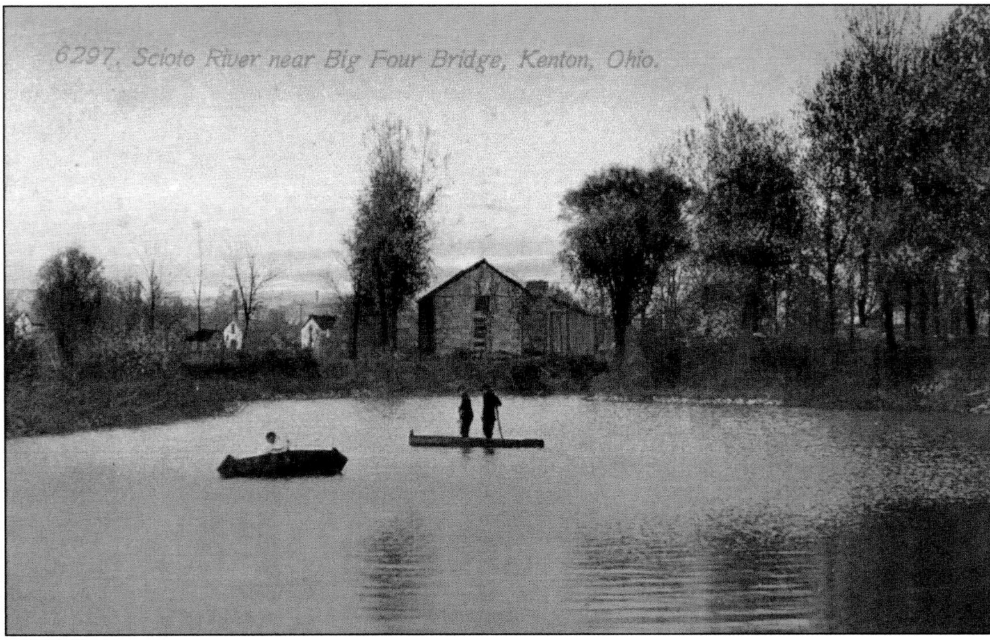

Canoeists enjoy the Scioto River south of Kenton about 1914. An early historian noted that the river was named Saint Yotok (pronounced *Sin Yoto*) by French explorer Celeron De Bienville in 1751; it was eventually Anglicized into Scioto, The name is also said to have originated within the Shawnee, Wyandot, and Iroquois languages.

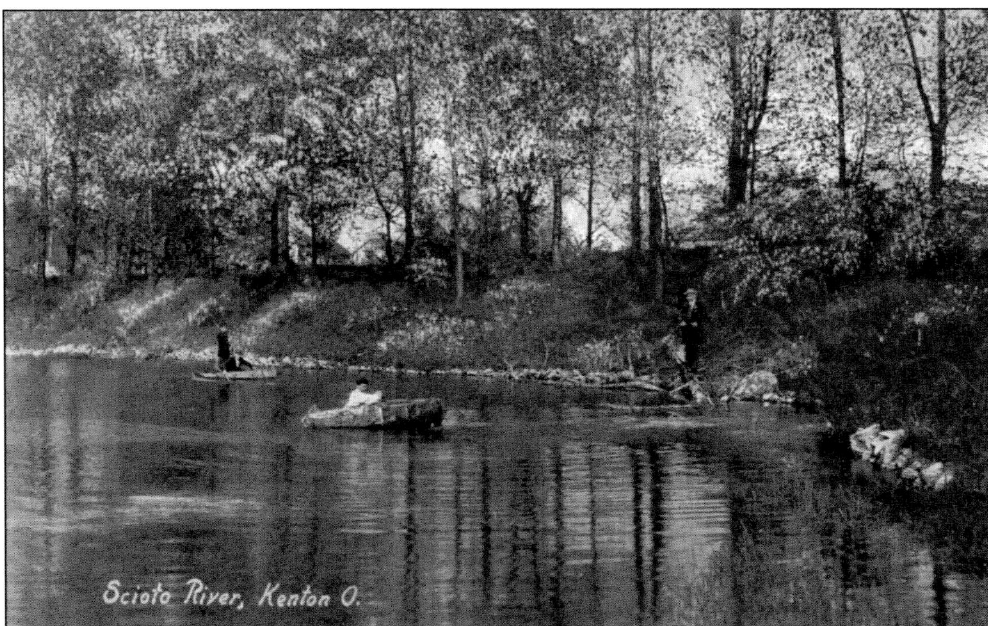

Local fishermen spend a day along the Scioto River in this idyllic view from about 1912. During the 1980s, the Scioto Canoe Livery operated along the north bank of the river near the Main Street Bridge. Recreational boaters could rent a canoe for a leisurely day trip on the river. The Scioto River Watch was established in 1990 to promote and protect the scenic river.

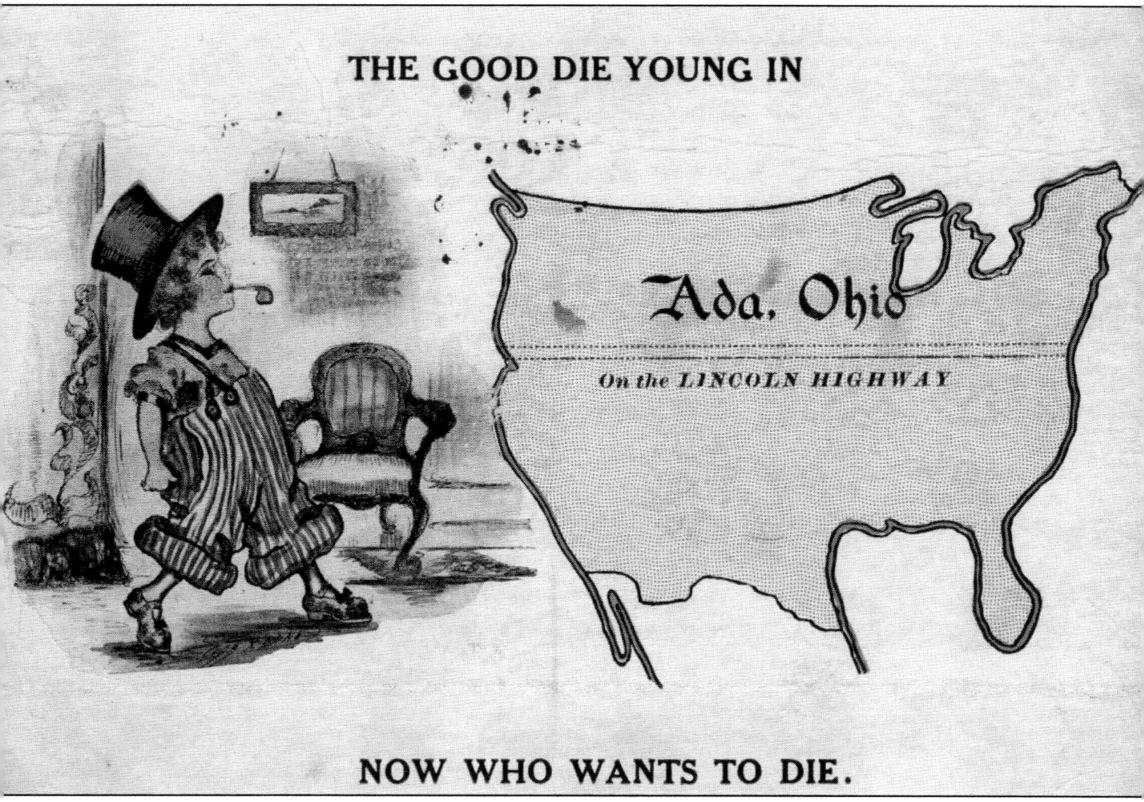

On September 14, 1913, the Lincoln Highway, America's first coast-to-coast automobile route, was announced. Between 1913 and 1919, the northern Hardin County towns of Forest, Patterson, Dunkirk, Dola, and Ada were part of the Lincoln Highway's so-called "zigzag route" through Ohio from Galion west to Lima. This path, chosen by Henry Joy over the straighter Marion to Kenton route, included at least 32 right-angle turns along current county and township roads. In addition, the route traversed 12 sets of railroad tracks, including crossing the Pennsylvania Railroad at or near each of the county towns. In 1926, the original Marion to Kenton route was reestablished as the Harding Highway and designated US Route 30-S in May 1931. The highway was renamed State Route 309 in 1975. Today, a series of signs and brick markers delineate the path of the Lincoln Highway's zigzag route through Hardin County.

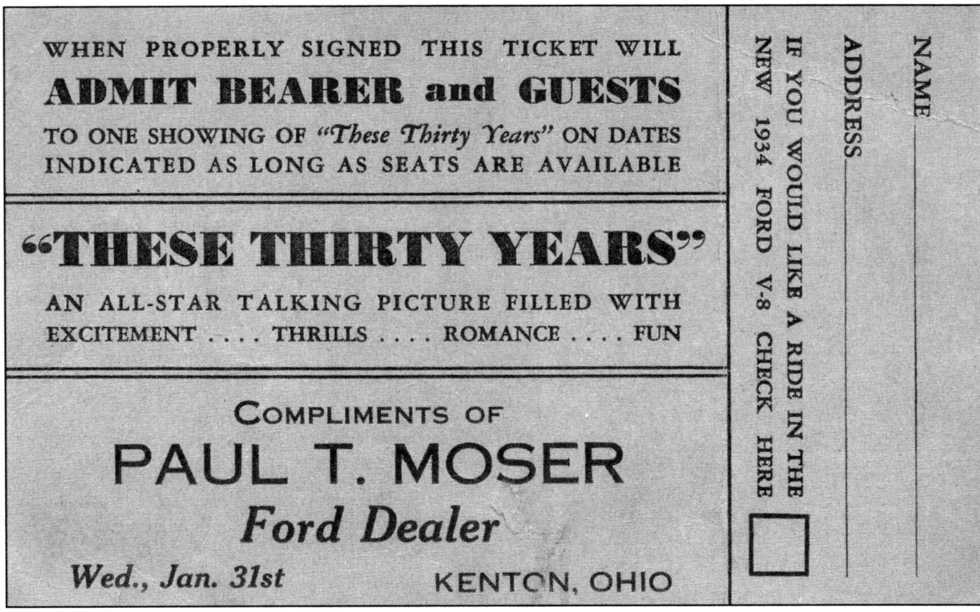

Paul T. Moser and Harold G. Short opened the Moser & Short Ford and Lincoln dealership on South Detroit Street in 1923. Following the firm's split about 1930, Moser opened his own Ford dealership on Detroit Street, which moved to South Main Street by 1940. He passed out this promotional card/movie pass in 1934 as a way to get automobile shoppers into his dealership during the Great Depression.

This early airmail envelope promoted the dedication of Hardin County's first airfield. Cedar Lawn Airport, located south of Kenton along State Route 292, opened in September 1929. The county's second airport, the Ada Air Service, opened outside Ada on July 4, 1947. The current Hardin County Airport, built south of Kenton, was dedicated by Gov. James A. Rhodes on October 1, 1967.

Six

SCHOOLHOUSES

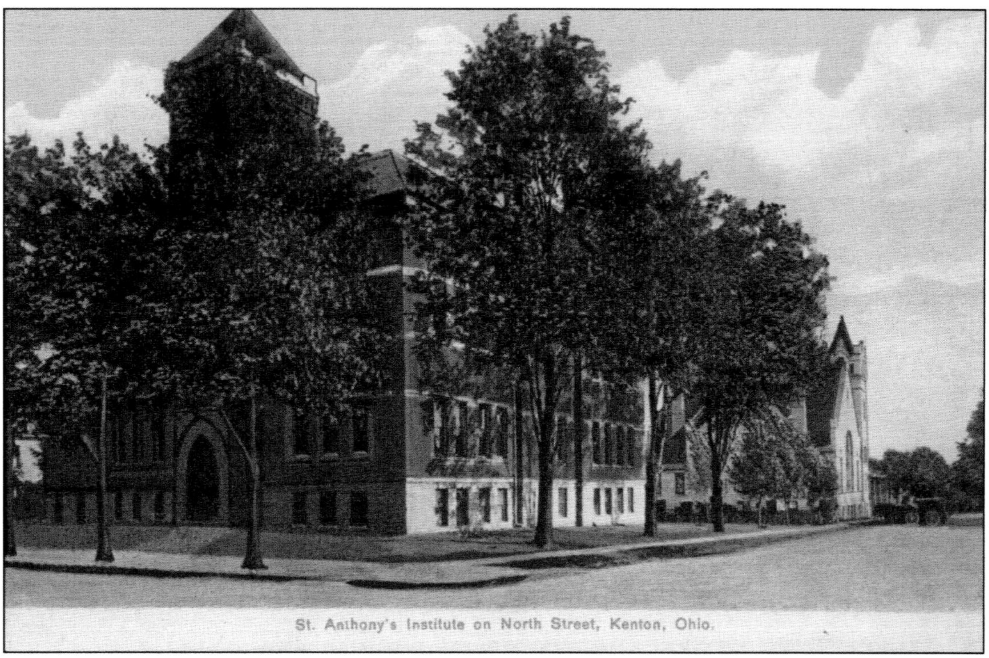

Kenton's first Catholic school was held in the church loft in 1872. A wooden schoolhouse, operated by the Sisters of Charity, was built in 1873. Saint Anthony's Institute, seen on the corner of Wayne and North Streets about 1910, was built during 1893 and 1894. It graduated its last high school students in 1934 and closed about 1973. Today, the building is operated by the church as the Saint Anthony Center.

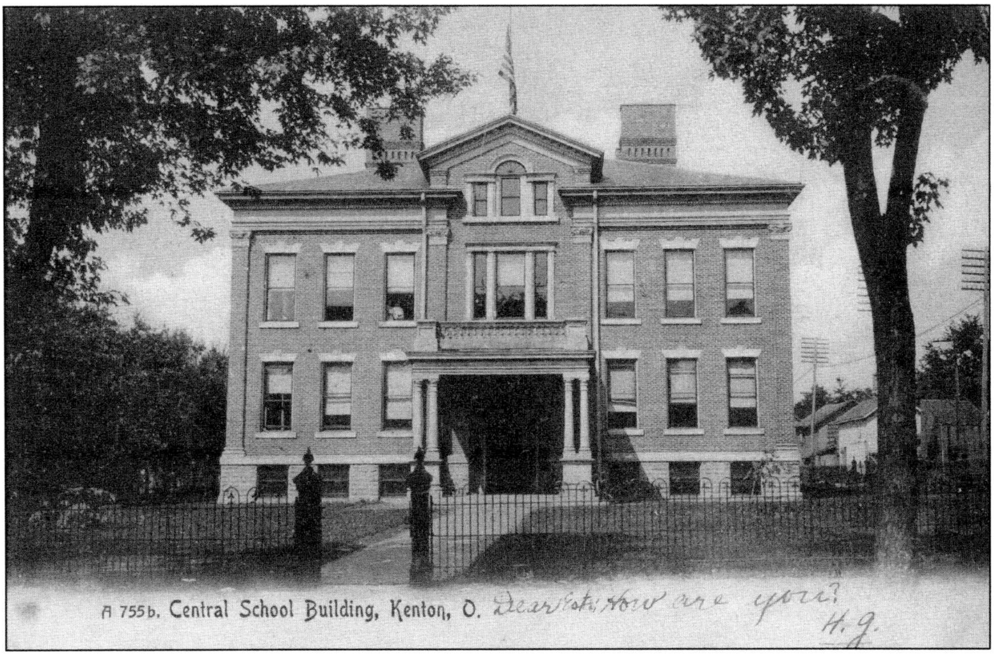

Kenton's first school was a small log house erected in 1834 on Wayne Street. The Kenton Union School District was organized about 1858. The first Central School Building was erected at the intersection of Carroll and Market Streets in 1857 and burned down in January 1899. The second Central School Building, seen here about 1906, was erected for $22,000.

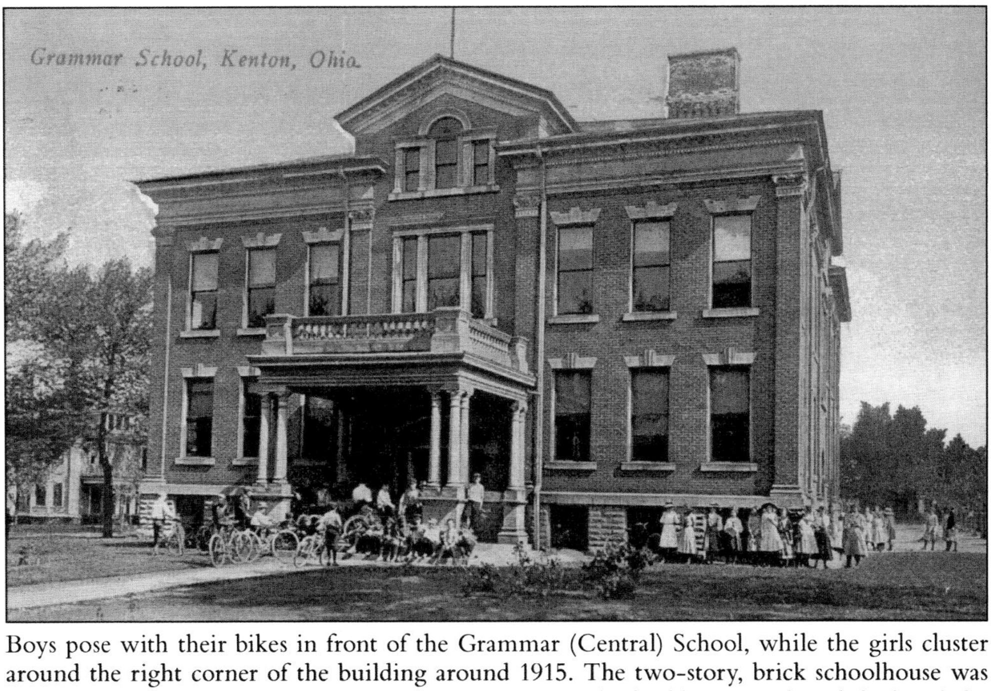

Boys pose with their bikes in front of the Grammar (Central) School, while the girls cluster around the right corner of the building around 1915. The two-story, brick schoolhouse was completed in 1901 and operated until 1965. In 1968, the building was demolished and the Oaklief Building erected. The Kenton City School District administrative offices currently occupy the building.

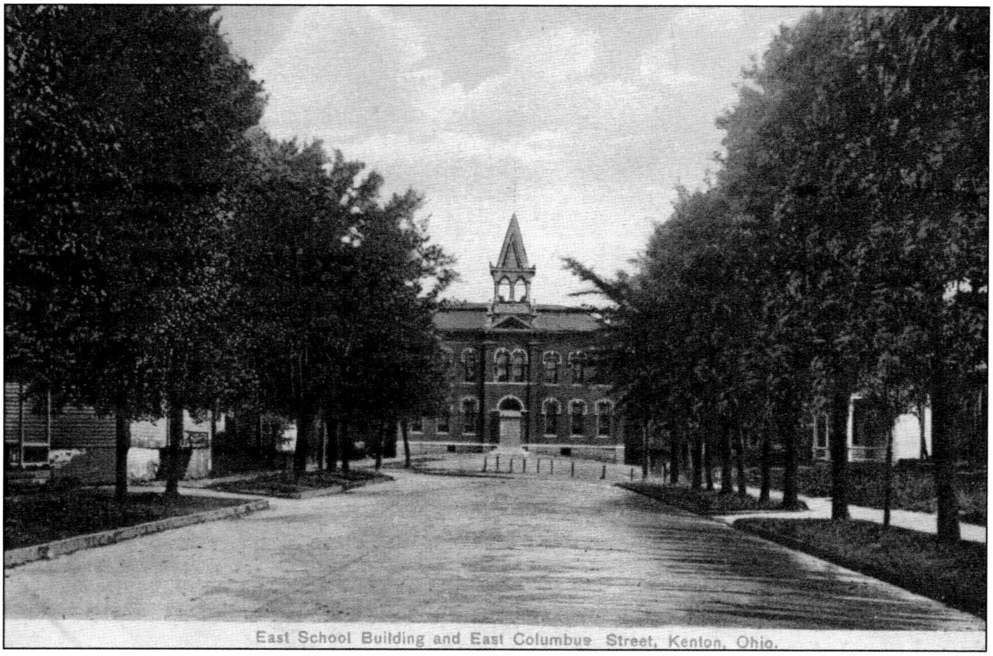

This is a distant view of Kenton's East School Building, which was situated on a triangular lot along East Columbus Street facing Barron Street. A car wash, parking lot, and abandoned service station now occupy the location. Other schools built during this period were the South School (1880) on Espy Street and the West School (1887) on Glendale Street.

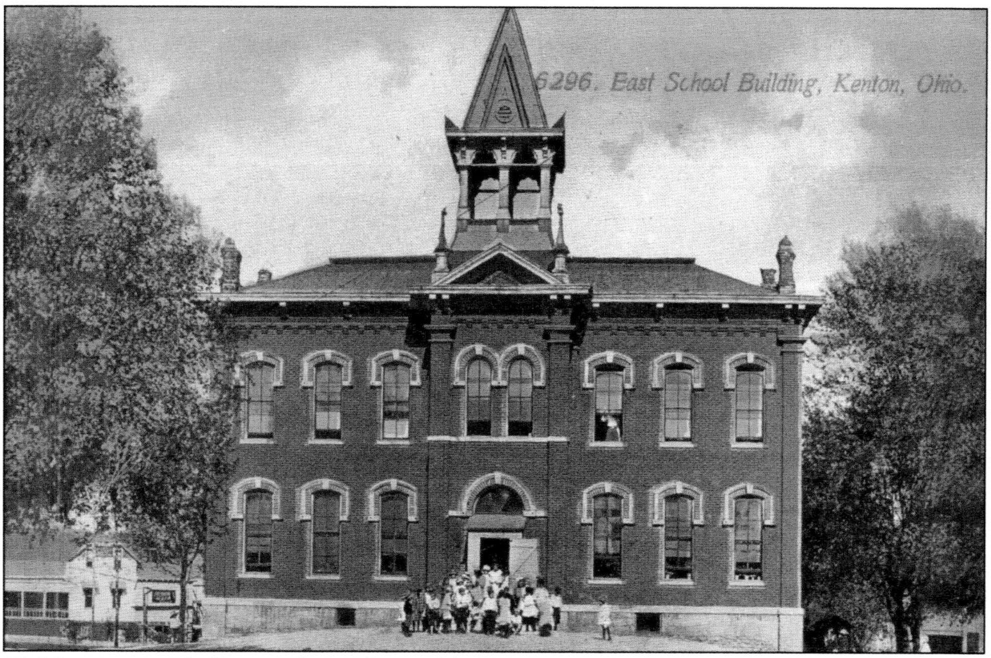

Children pose with their teacher in front of the East School Building sometime around 1910. The building was constructed in 1877 and housed students until 1940. When it closed, elementary students were taught at the former high school building on East Columbus Street. The building was eventually replaced by the Eastcrest School, which was in use from 1956 until 2010.

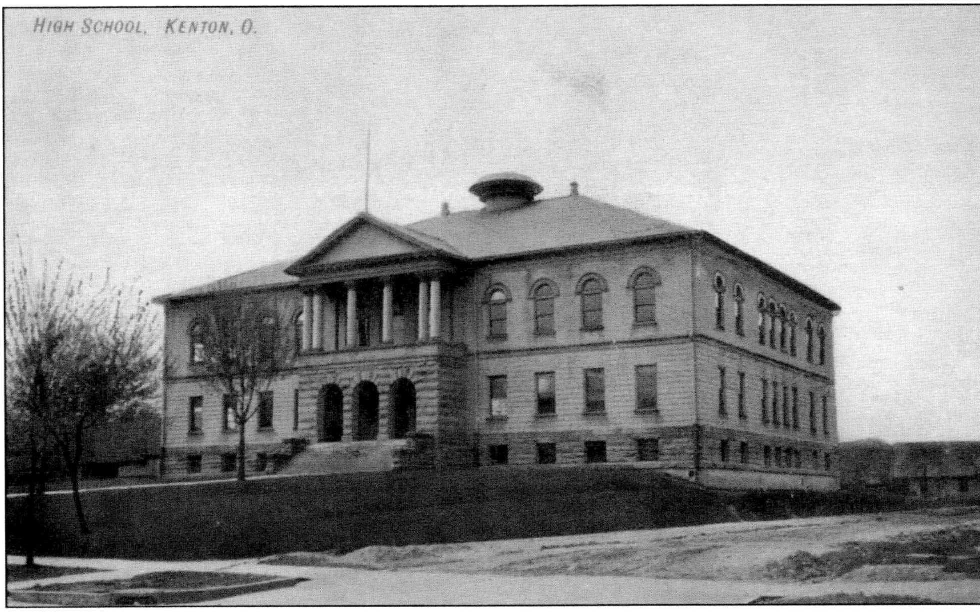

Powell & Gasson's Big Drug Store published this 1906 view of Kenton High School on East Columbus Street. The building was erected from 1894 to 1896. It served as the senior high until 1939, when it became an elementary school. In 1949, it became known as the Ellis Junior High School and was demolished in 1968 to make room for the new Hardin County District Library.

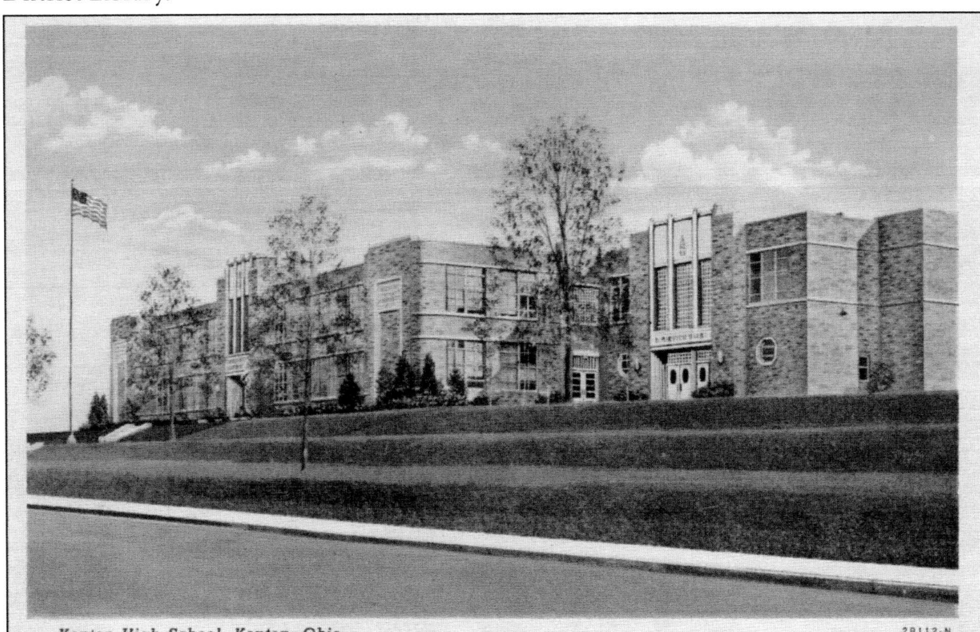

The Kenton High School building on Oriental Street was constructed during 1939 and 1940. The building was in use as a high school until the construction of the current Kenton High School on Harding Avenue in 1963. It then became known as the Kenton Junior High and, later, the Kenton Middle School in 1981. Robinson Field, the football field and track, was constructed behind the building in 1936.

Dunkirk's first schoolhouse was erected on South Main Street in 1854. Nelson F. Faze published this c. 1915 view of the Dunkirk High School on McCaskey Street. The three-story, 12-room, brick school building was erected in 1883 for $21,670. An auditorium and gymnasium were added in 1935 when the building was expanded. It was razed about 1960.

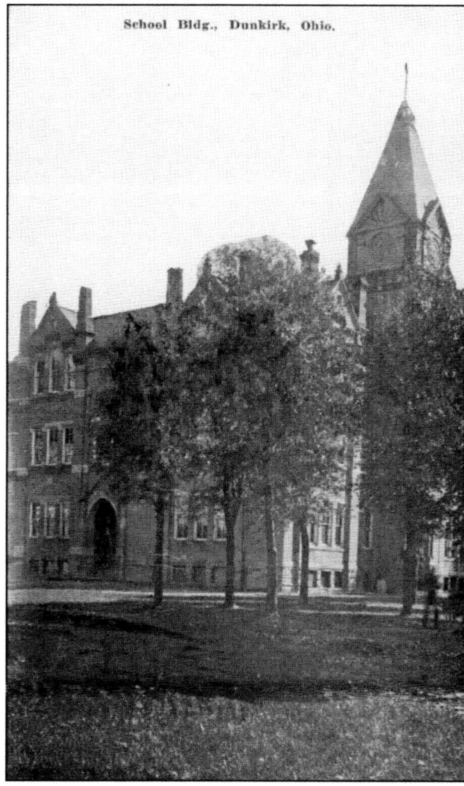

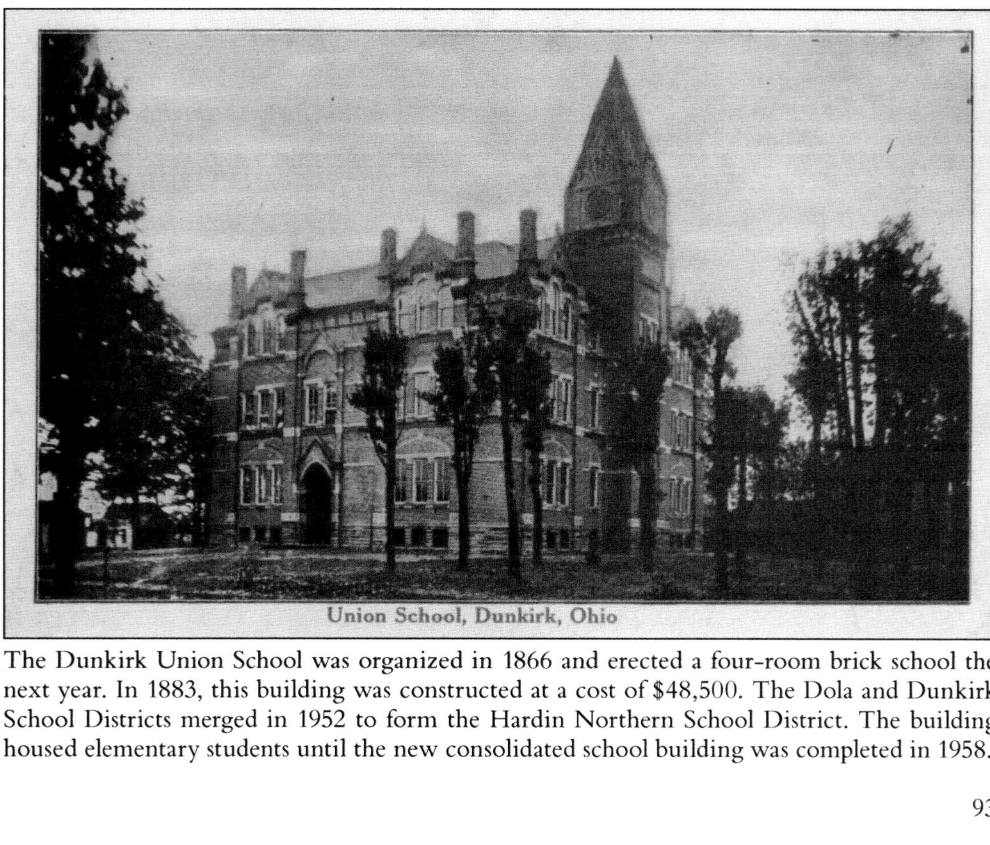

The Dunkirk Union School was organized in 1866 and erected a four-room brick school the next year. In 1883, this building was constructed at a cost of $48,500. The Dola and Dunkirk School Districts merged in 1952 to form the Hardin Northern School District. The building housed elementary students until the new consolidated school building was completed in 1958.

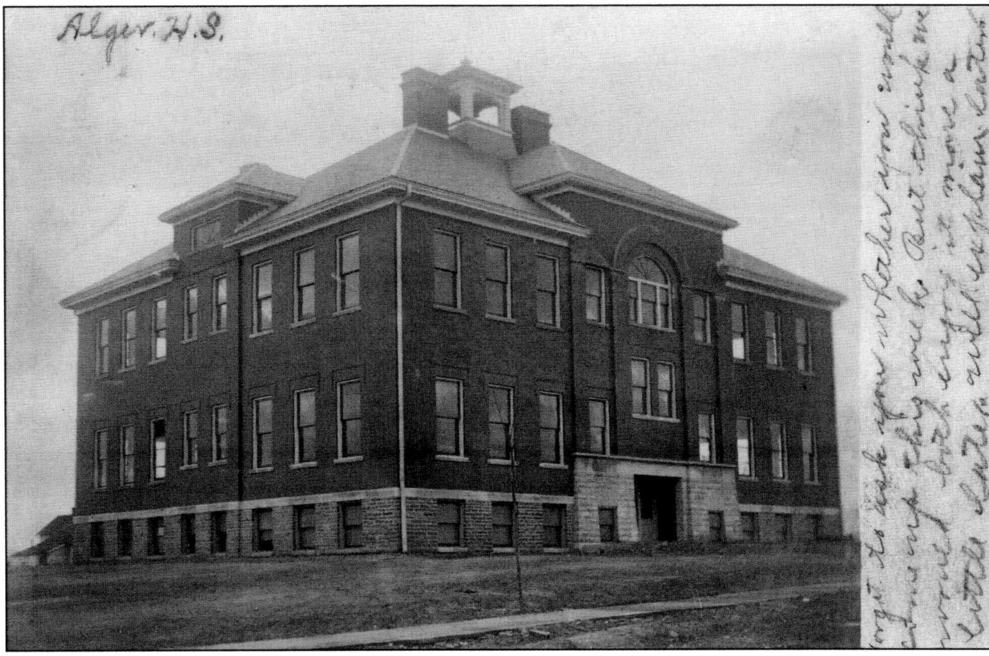

Marion Township's first school was erected in 1838. The two-story Alger High School was constructed of brick in 1906 for $18,000. In 1965, Alger consolidated with the McGuffey and Roundhead School Districts to form the Upper Scioto Valley School District. This building was utilized as a middle school until the 1970s and was razed in 1982.

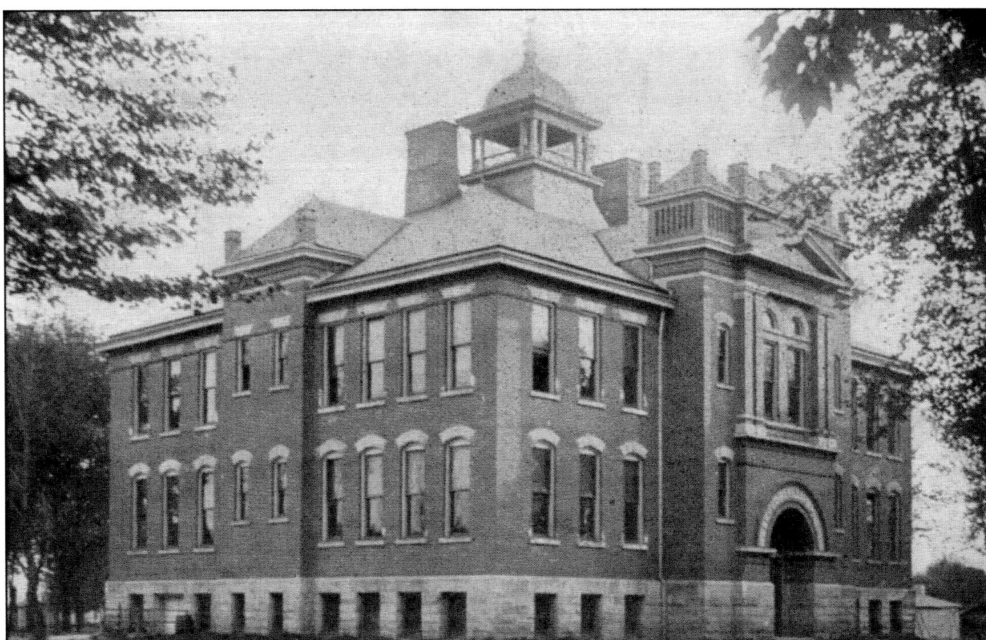

Forest's first Union School building was erected in 1872 for $7,000. The two-story, eight-room, brick Forest High School, seen here about 1910, was erected on Dixon Street for $20,000 in 1903. The Forest, Mount Blanchard, and Wharton School Districts consolidated in 1959 to form the Riverdale School District. Riverdale's new school building was completed in 1962.

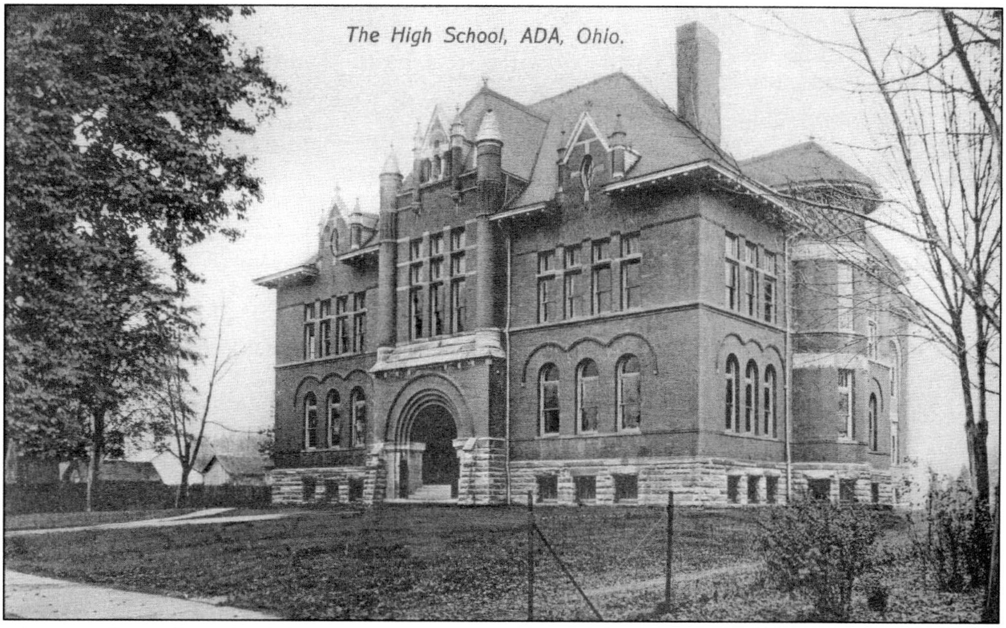

The North High School building was constructed during 1892 and 1893 on North Main Street. Ada elementary students were taught in the building from 1930 until it was sold to Ohio Northern University in 1952. The engineering department utilized the building until the Biggs Engineering Building was erected in 1971. The Liberty Township Fire Station occupies the property today.

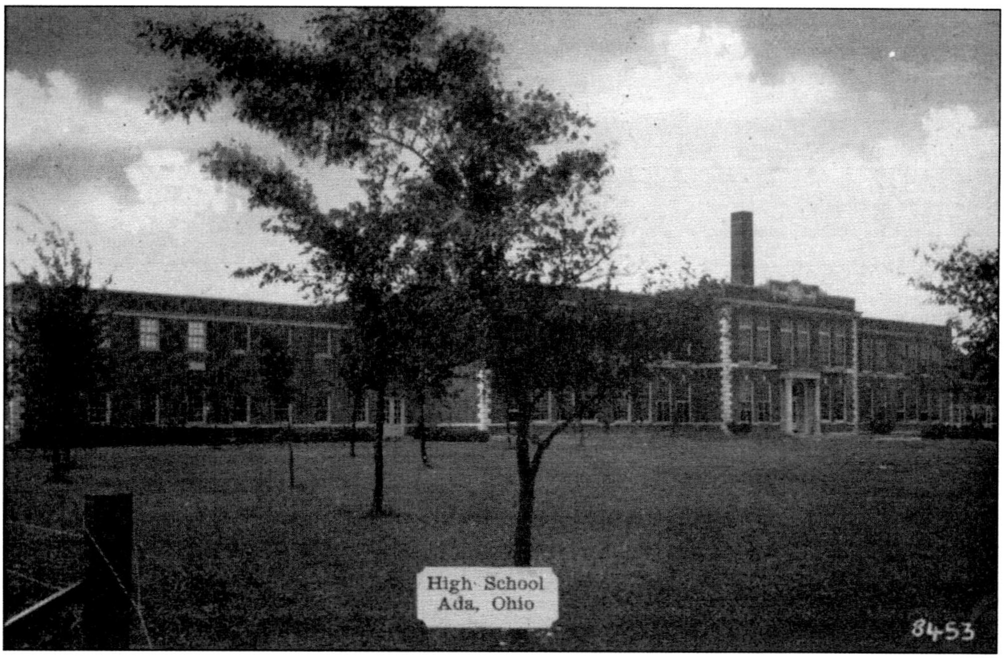

In 1929, Ada consolidated the North and South High Schools into the new Ada Exempted Village School District. The Ada High School, seen here about 1945, accommodated students from Ada and nearby Liberty Township. A grade school addition on the west side was built in 1951. The current Ada High School on Grand Avenue was constructed in 2008.

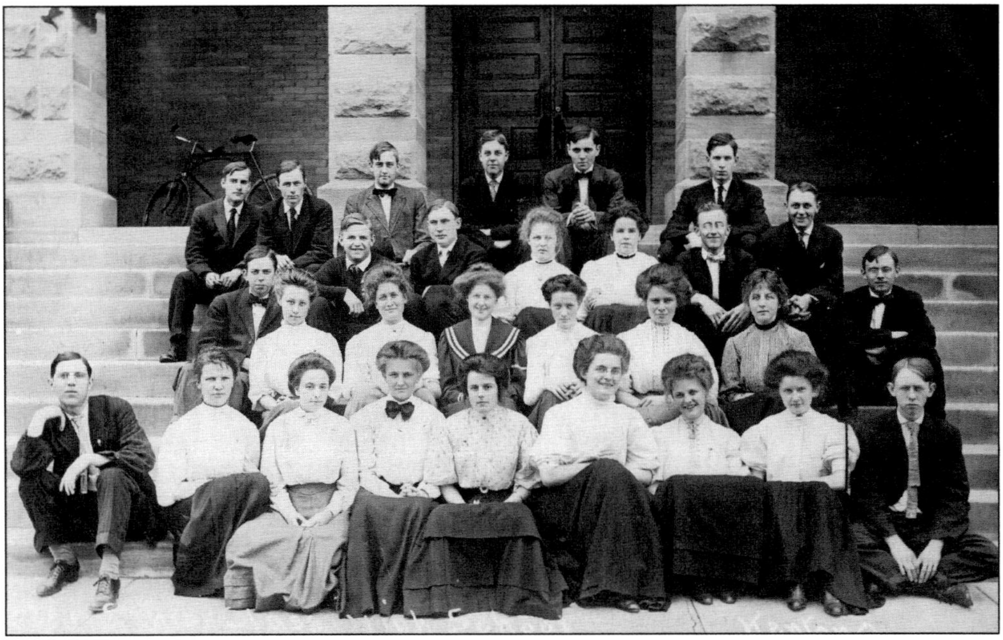

The 1908 senior class of Kenton High School poses for an image produced by the Leiter Postcard Company of Lorain. The class is seated on the steps in front of the Kenton High School on East Columbus Street. The mailer, Hazel White, is seated fourth from the right in the front row.

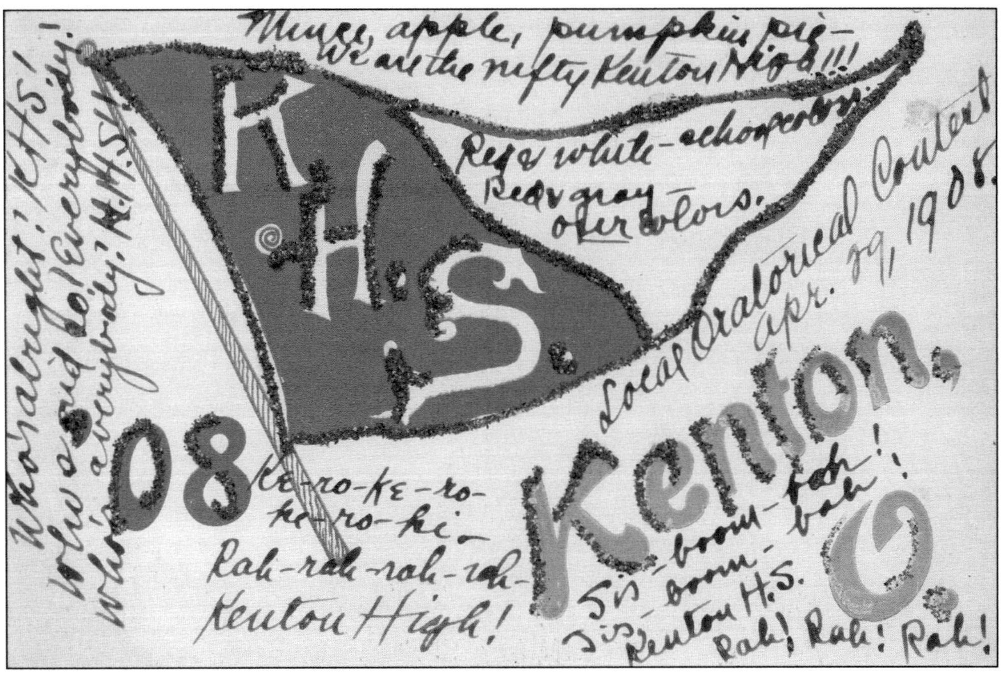

Thomas & Company of Findlay produced this souvenir Kenton High School Class of 1908 pennant postcard. The author, Hazel White, embellished it with glitter and local cheers such as "Mince, apple, pumpkin pie–We are the nifty Kenton High!" It also promoted a "Local Oratorical Contest" on April 29, 1908.

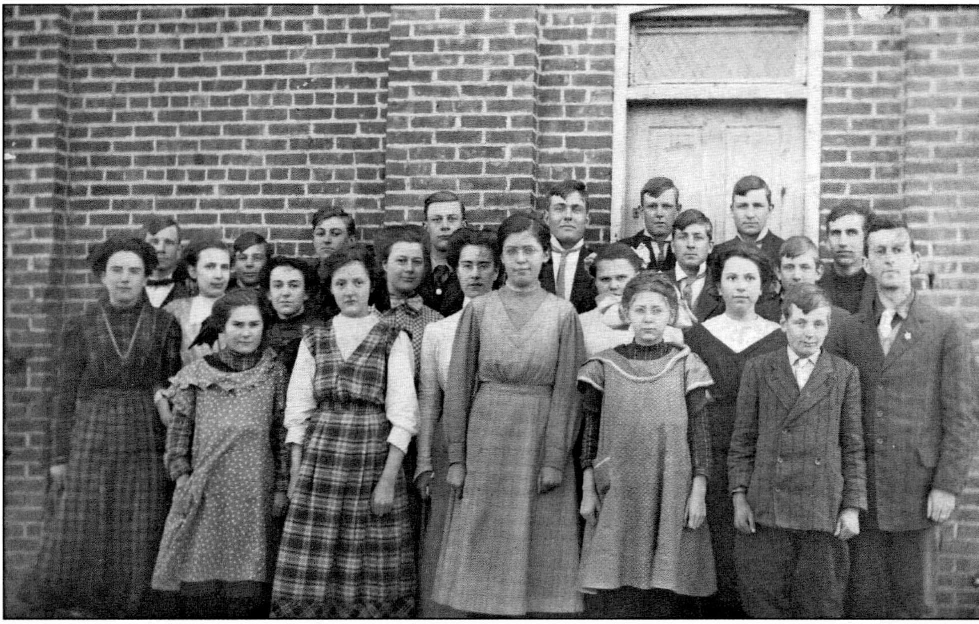

Students stand in front of the Dola School for this early class photograph. The Dola High School was built in 1912 to replace an earlier structure. Dola's last class graduated in 1952. Following the Hardin Northern consolidation, the Dola School hosted the high school students until 1954.

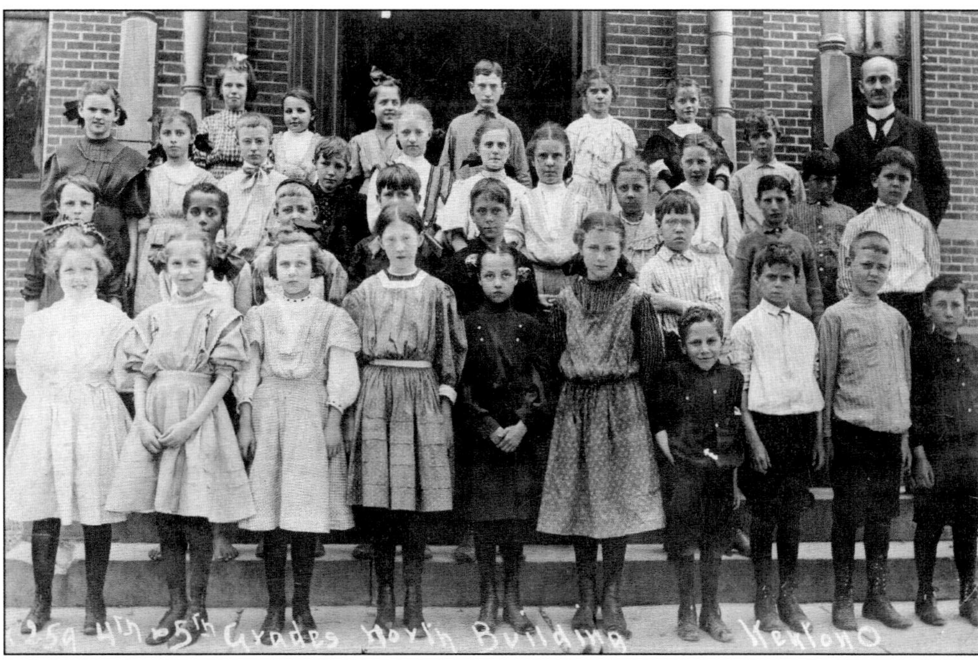

Fourth- and fifth-grade students pose on the steps in front of the North School Building in Kenton for this early photograph. The North School was constructed in 1887 on East Eliza Street and served the district until 1956 when the Westview School opened. The site is now a community park named in honor of Kenton native Brig. Gen. John Michael Murray.

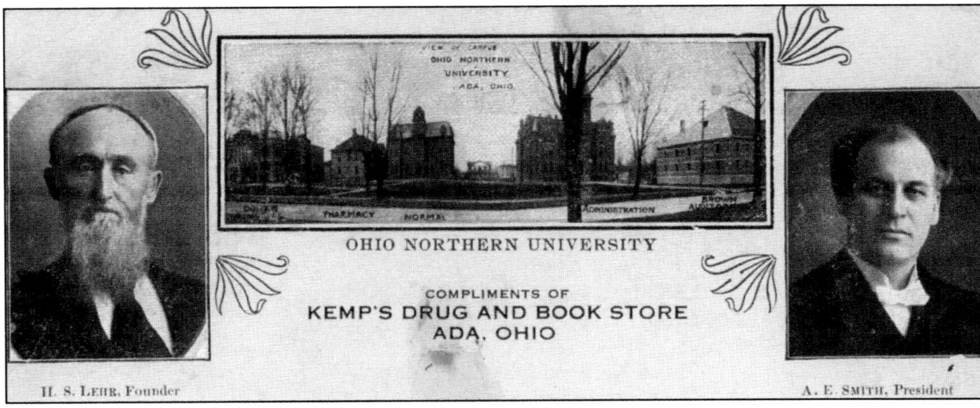

The Kemp Drug Store published this c. 1905 postcard featuring Dr. Henry Solomon Lehr and Dr. Albert Edwin Smith. Dr. Lehr founded the Ohio Normal University in 1870 and served as its president until 1900. He was succeeded by Dr. Leroy Belt, who held the position until 1905. Dr. Smith served as president from 1905 until 1929.

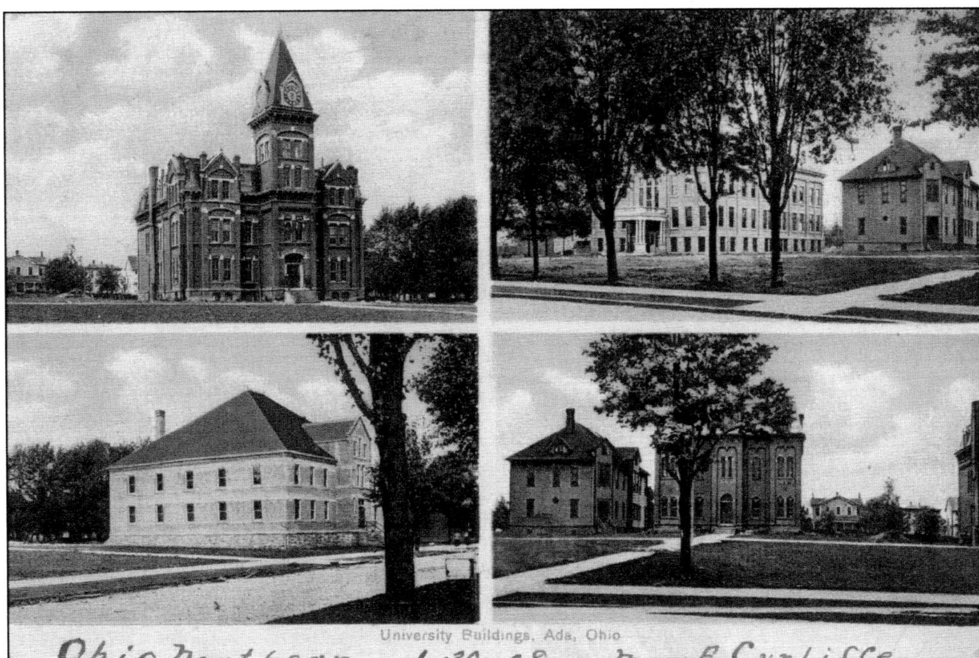

The Charles R. Wilson Company, a drug and bookstore located on Ada's Main Street, published this 1908 view of the buildings on the campus of Ohio Northern University. The buildings are, clockwise from the upper left, the Administration Building (1879), Duke's Memorial (1903), Sheep Shed (1883), Normal Building (1871), Pharmacy Hall (1894), and Brown Auditorium (1905).

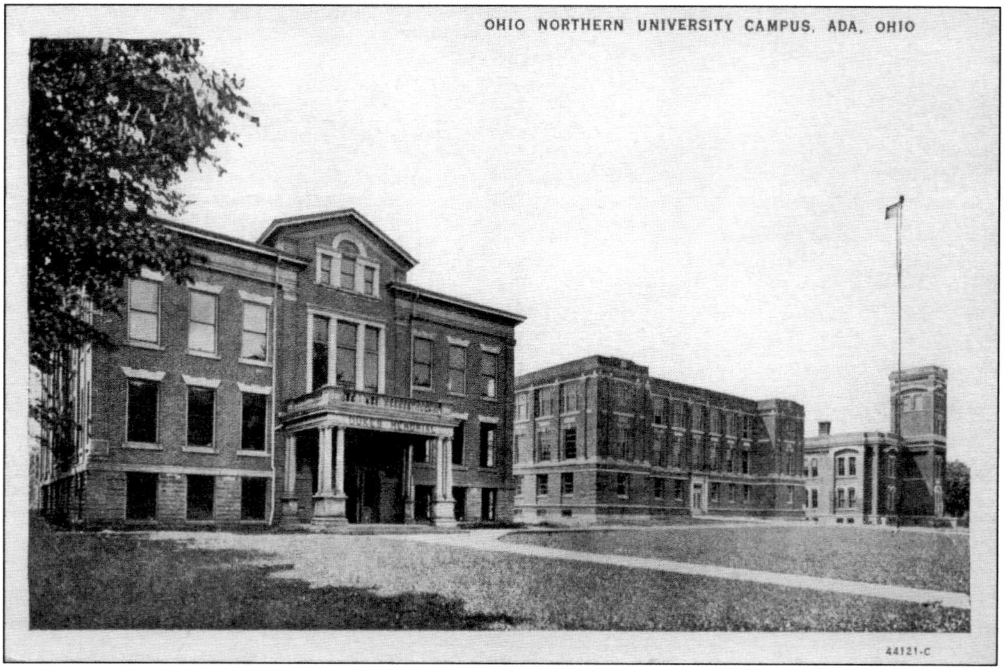

The Ohio Normal University in Ada was established in 1870 as the Northwestern Ohio Normal School. The institution was sold to the Ohio Conference of the Methodist Episcopal Church in 1899. Its name was changed to Ohio Northern University in 1903. This image shows the campus as it looked about 1920.

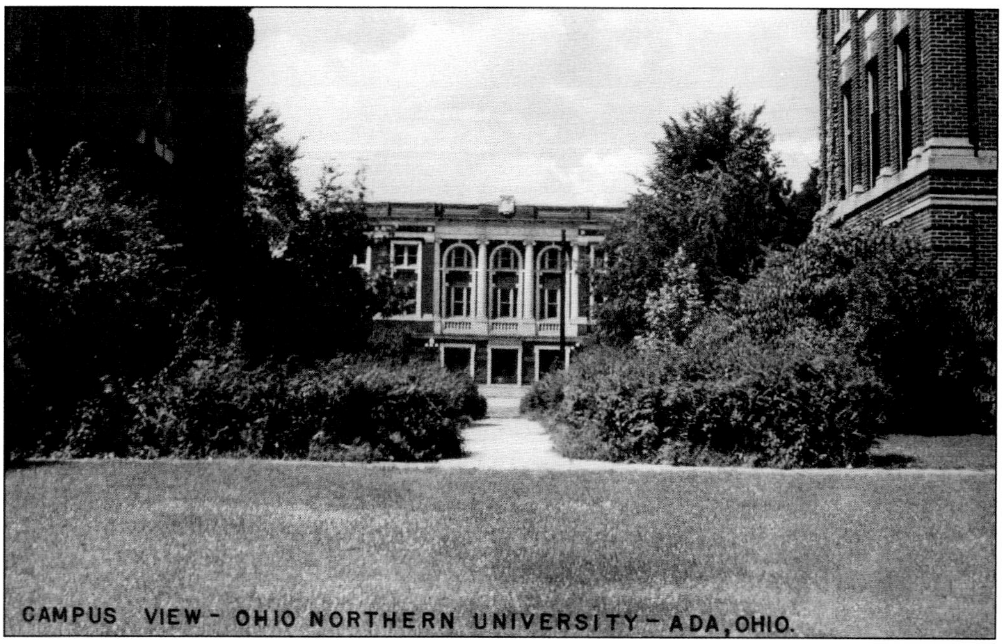

Presser Hall is visible in the background of this image by the R. Ewers Photography Studio. The building, named for Theodore Presser, Ohio Northern University's first music professor, was constructed in 1929 for the music department. The Heterick Memorial Library occupied the building from 1953 to 1968. In 1985, the music department returned to the renovated building.

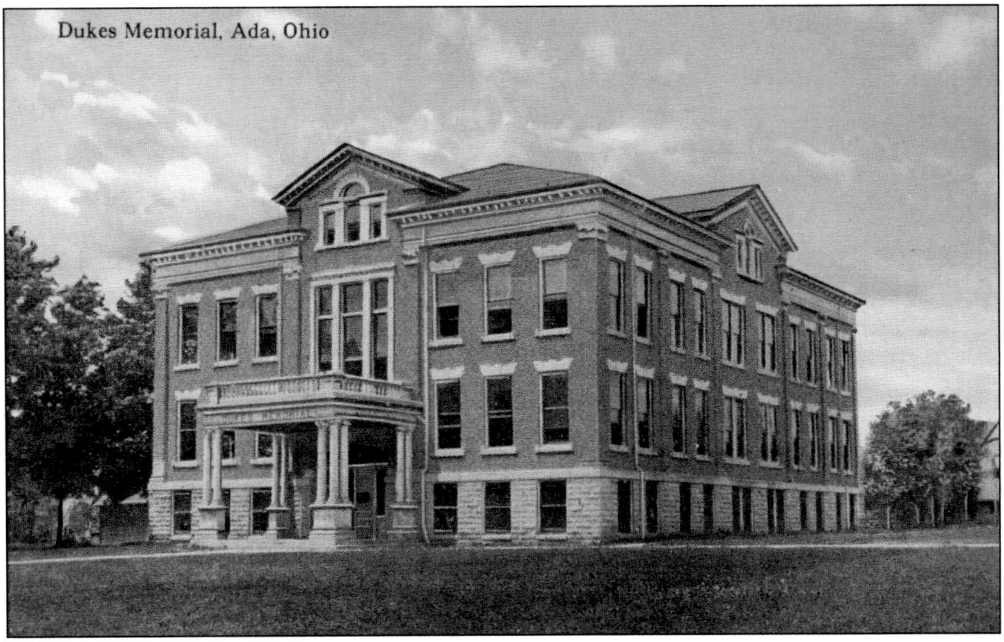

The Dukes Memorial building on South Main Street in Ada was constructed between 1902 and 1903 following the donation of $10,000 by Louis Dukes. The building underwent renovations in 1952 and 1994. From 1903 until 1966, the building housed the College of Pharmacy prior to completion of the Robertson-Evan Pharmacy Building.

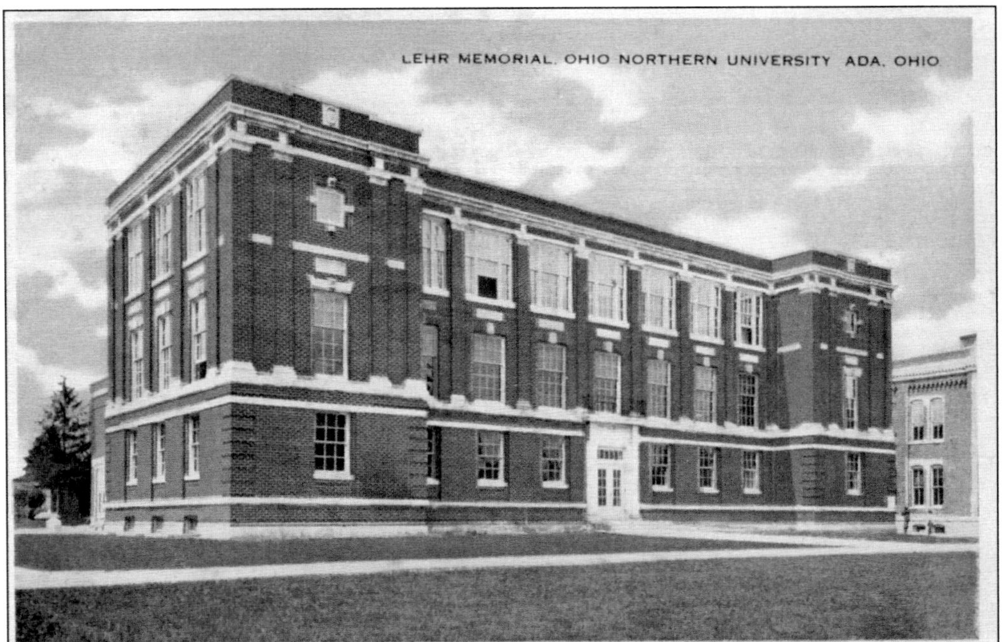

The Lehr Memorial, named for Dr. Henry Solomon Lehr, was constructed between 1913 and 1915 on the site of the original Normal School building. The structure housed administrative offices and classrooms. The building featured a 1,600-seat auditorium in the rear. Between 1915 and 1930, the building also served as the university's library.

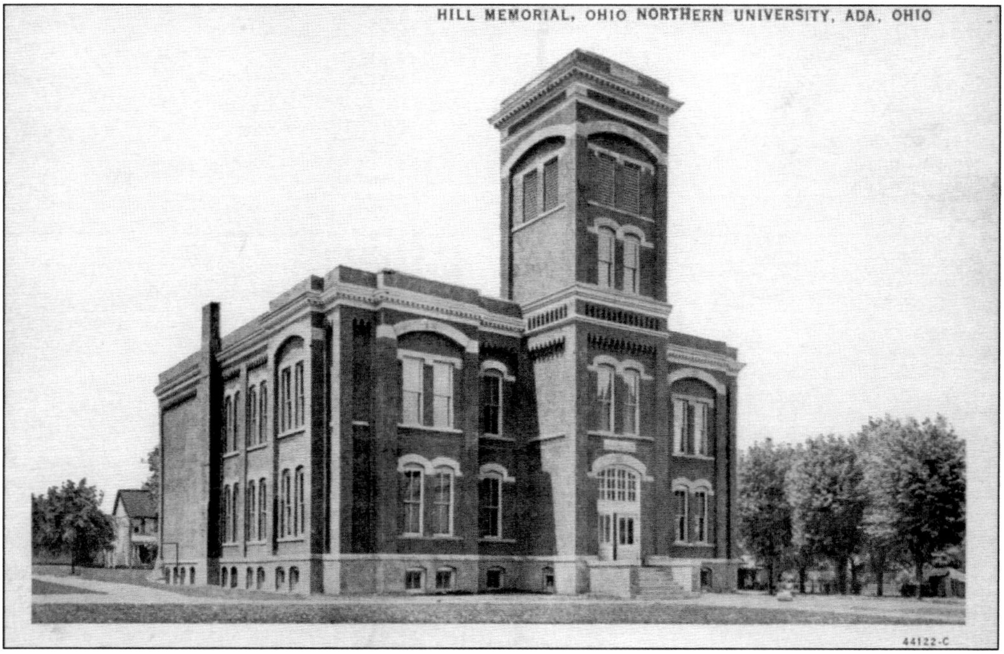

Ohio Northern University's original Administration Building was erected on South Main Street in 1879. A November 1913 fire left only the exterior walls standing. In October 1914, the reconstructed building was renamed Hill Memorial in honor of Dr. John Wesley Hill, an itinerant Methodist minister who retired to Ada in 1895.

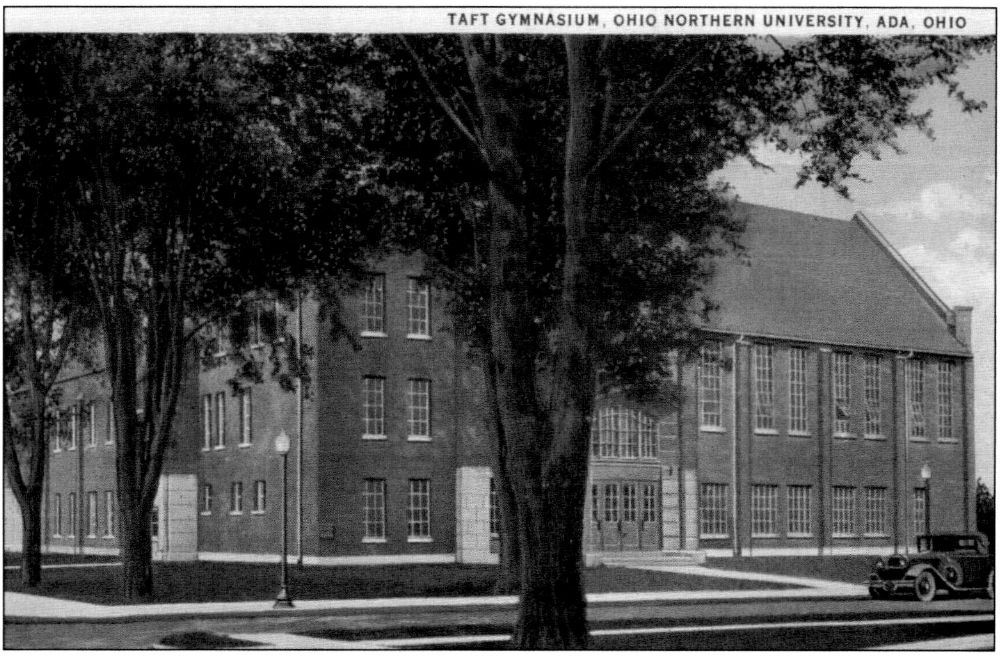

Taft Gymnasium on South Union Street, named for John H. Taft, was dedicated in 1929. It was the first athletic facility built on campus and also hosted dances and social functions. A highlight was Dr. Martin Luther King Jr.'s speech in January 1968. The last basketball game was played in 1974 before the building found new life as the Department of Technology.

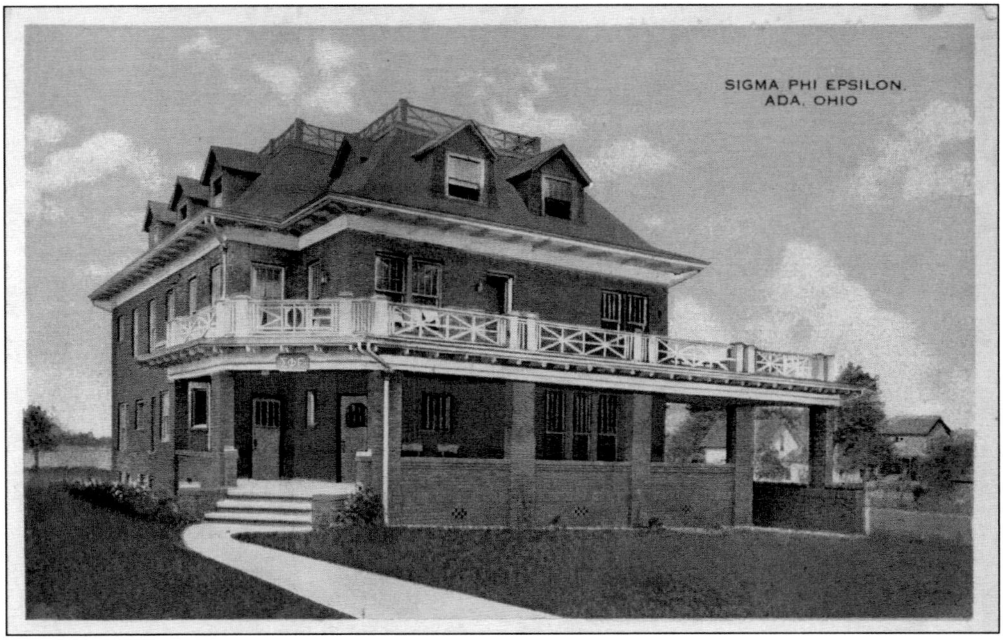

The Theta Nu Epsilon (Alpha Sigma Phi) fraternity was established in 1903, and the Tau Kappa Kappa (Alpha Xi Delta) sorority was chartered in 1904. Sigma Phi Epsilon was located on South Gilbert Street prior to building the first fraternity house on campus during 1916. As the campus expanded west in the 1960s, new fraternity and sorority houses were constructed.

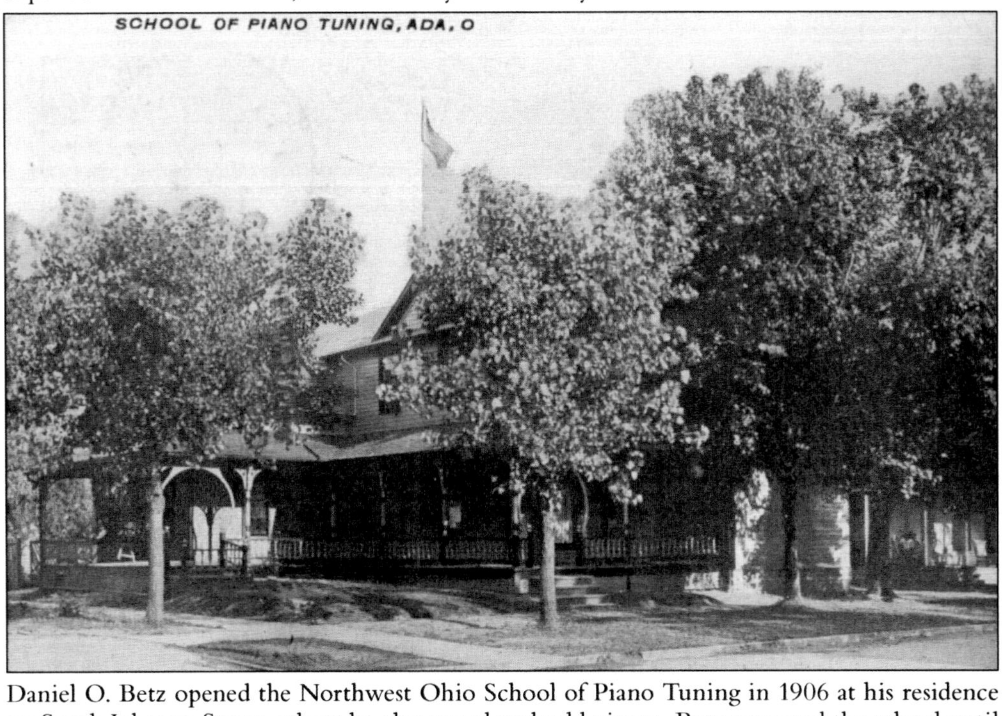

Daniel O. Betz opened the Northwest Ohio School of Piano Tuning in 1906 at his residence on South Johnson Street, where he also tuned and sold pianos. Betz managed the school until about 1927. Betz also operated the Ada Music House, later known as D.O. Betz, Pianos and Furniture, on North Main Street from about 1911 until the early 1930s.

Seven

Houses of Worship

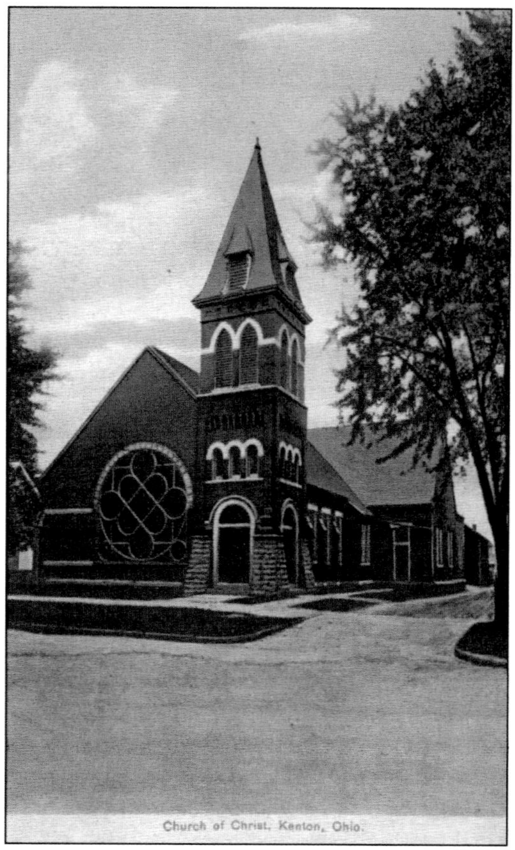

Kenton's First Christian Church (Disciples of Christ) was organized in February 1854. That same year, a small frame church was erected on North Main Street for $1,300. The congregation reorganized in April 1871 and erected the present brick church in 1887, which was renovated in 1937. The original church structure was moved to Summit Street and subsequently used by the Second Baptist Church congregation.

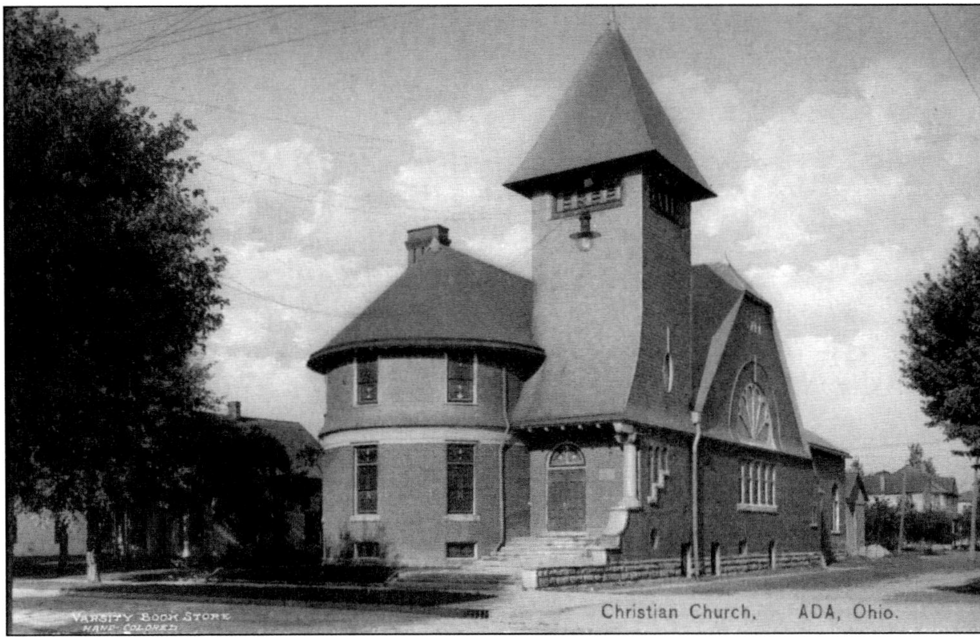

The Varsity Book Store published this 1909 view of the Christian church on South Main Street in Ada. The congregation can trace its history to about 1840, when the first religious services were held in Liberty Township. Shortly after his arrival, Dr. Henry S. Lehr was part of the group that formed the core of the Disciples of Christ in Ada.

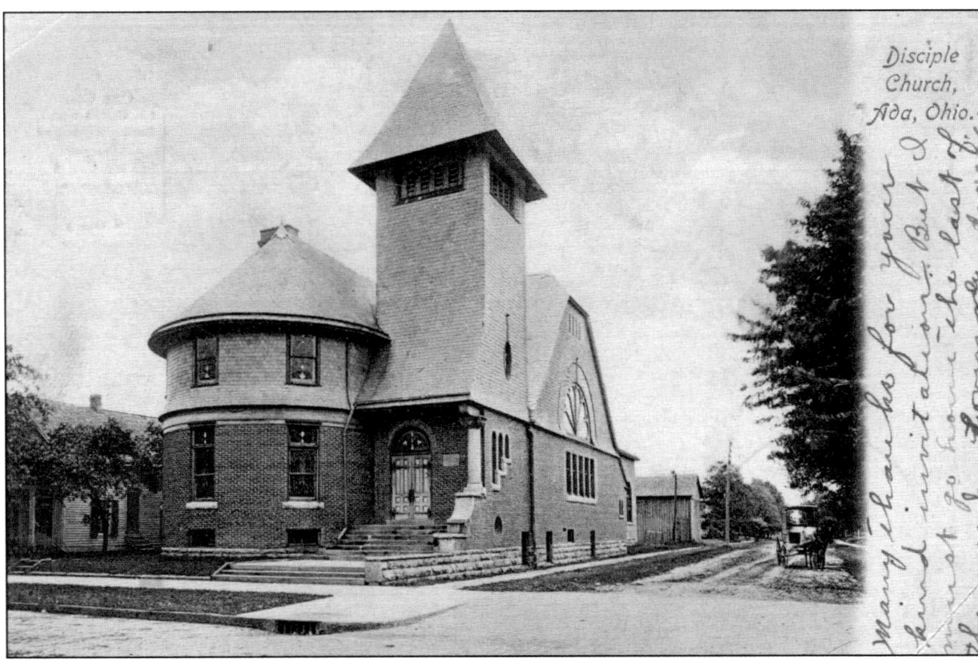

The Disciple Church of Ada was organized in 1866. The empty lot at the intersection of South Main and Long Streets was purchased in 1874 for $200 and soon a small wood-frame church was erected. The current brick church, seen here about 1907, was established in 1892 and dedicated in February 1893.

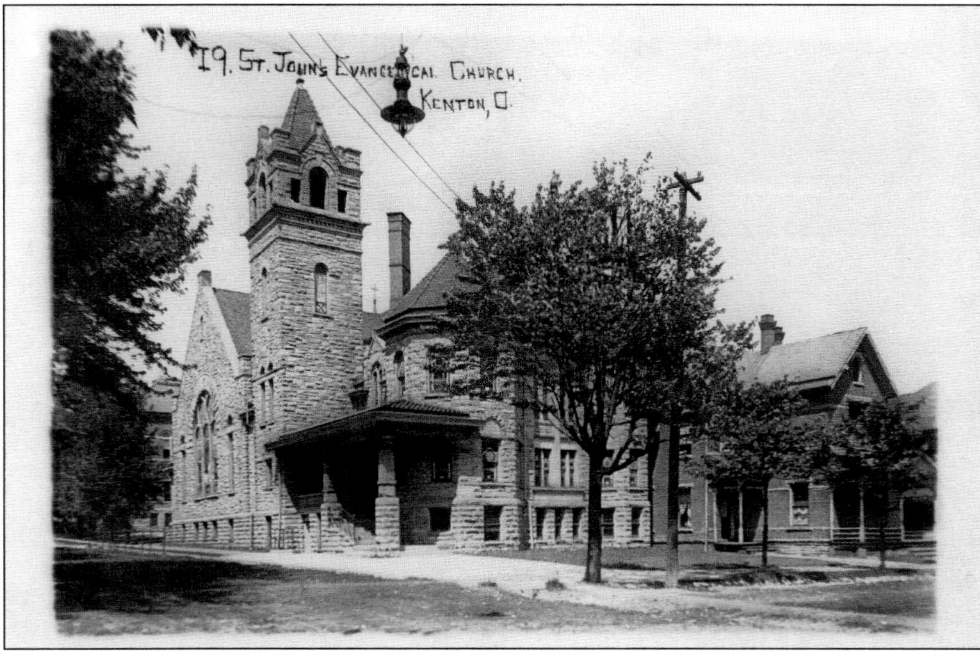

Organized five years earlier, Kenton's Lutheran congregation erected the first St. John's Evangelical Church at the corner of East Carroll and North Wayne Streets in 1844. In keeping with its German heritage, church services were held in the language until about 1920. The church parsonage can be seen to the right of the church.

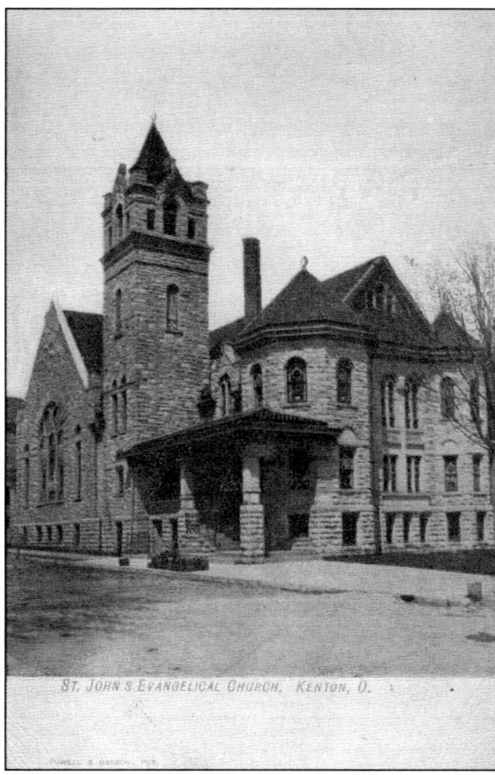

Powell & Gasson's Big Drug Store in downtown Kenton published this image of St. John's Evangelical Lutheran Church about 1906. The original church was enlarged and rededicated in January 1877. The current church was erected and dedicated in August 1903. The church expanded in 2004 and now encompasses the area of the parsonage.

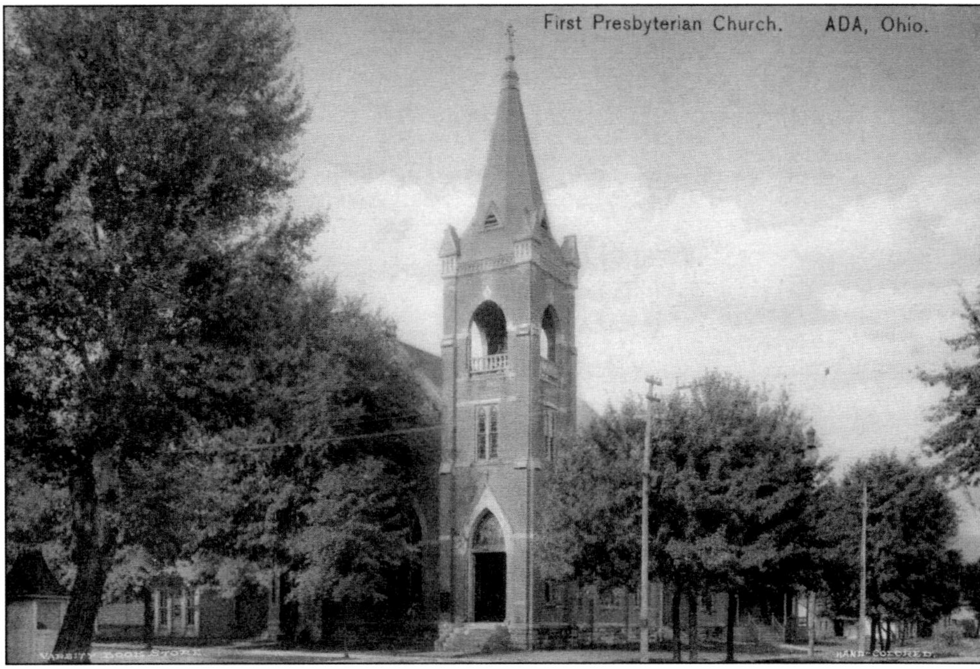

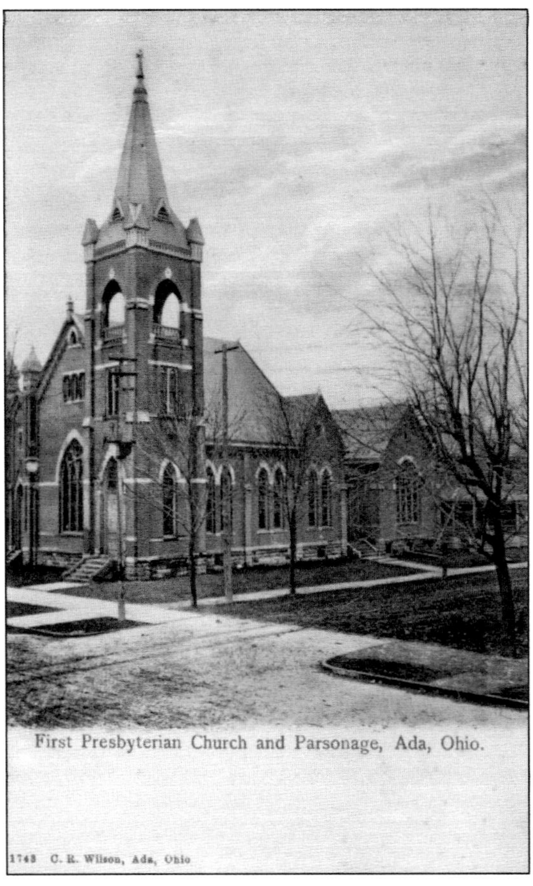

Ada's First Presbyterian Church was organized in Huntersville in August 1841 before transferring to Johnstown in 1855. The original wood-frame church began construction in 1861 and was dedicated in 1867. To make room for erecting the current church, the earlier building was sold and moved. The Varsity Book Store produced this postcard showing the church on South Main Street as it looked about 1909.

The current First Presbyterian Church was constructed at the corner of South Main and Mill (Lincoln Avenue) Streets beginning in May 1890. The church held its dedication during May 1891. Charles R. Wilson published this c. 1910 image of the church and parsonage, which was erected in 1902. The church expanded westward in 1925, connecting it to the parsonage.

The First Presbyterian Church was organized in Forest in 1849. Their first church was a wood-frame structure built in 1876 on the southwest corner of Dixon and Warner Streets. In May 1904, the current stone church was erected on the same site. The Ohio Bank Note Company of Kenton produced this postcard as part of its Forest series about 1906.

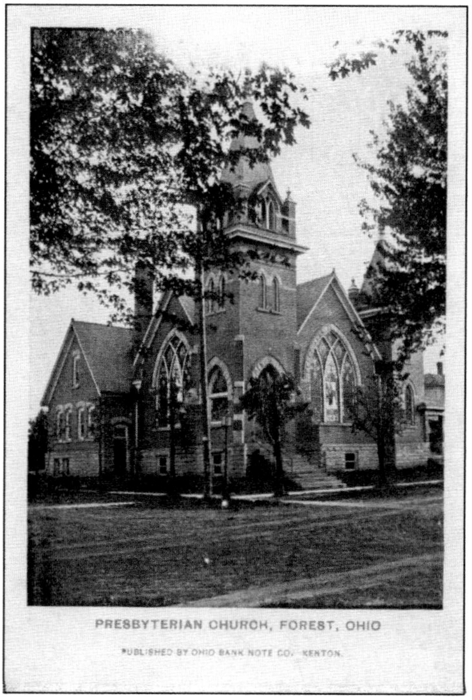

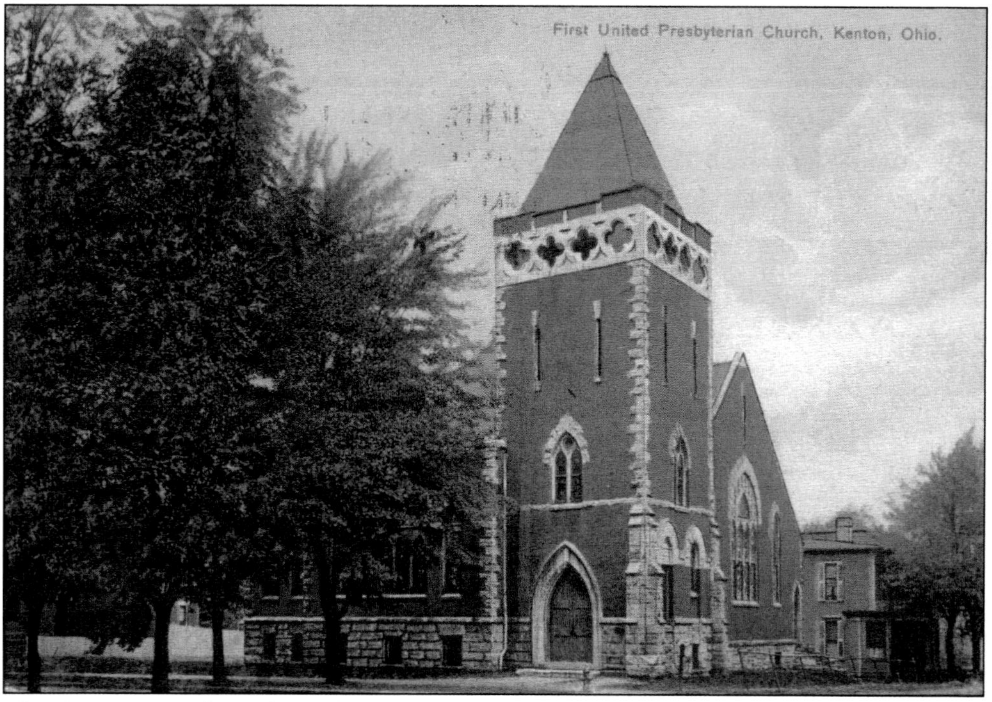

The Associate Reformed Presbyterian Church of Kenton organized in 1836, while the Associate Presbyterian Church organized in 1841. The two churches merged in 1858 to create the United Presbyterian Church. In 1890, the congregation erected this church at the corner of North Market and West Carroll Streets in Kenton. Today, it serves as the home of the TLC Ministries.

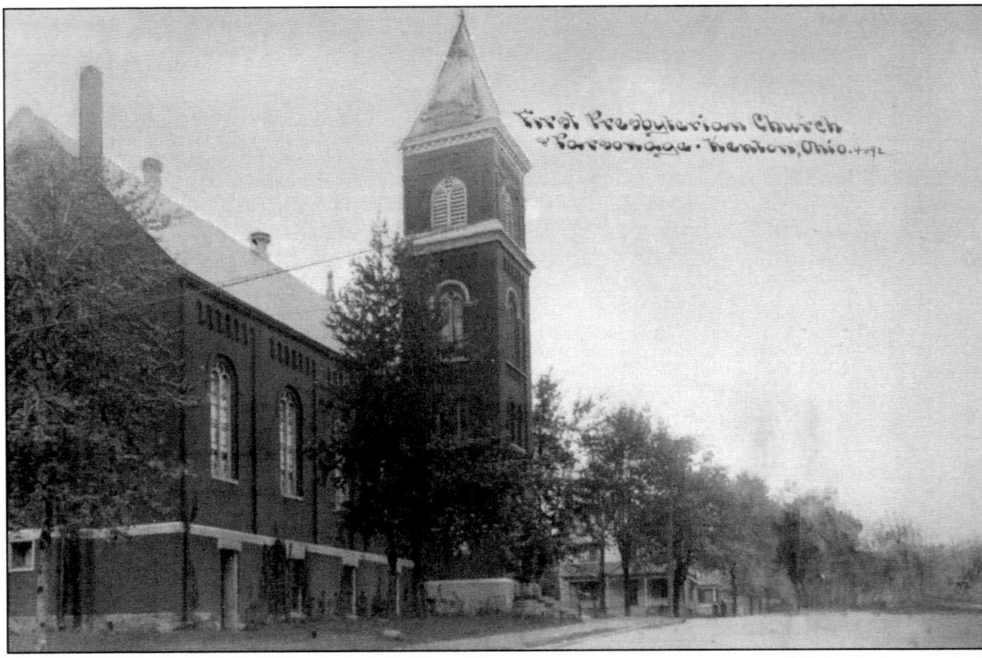

This postcard of Kenton's First Presbyterian Church and parsonage was published about 1910. The congregation was organized in 1836 and erected a frame church on the corner of West Columbus and North Market Streets during 1843. This church was sold and the congregation erected a second church in 1867, which was destroyed by the "Big Four Fire" in May 1881.

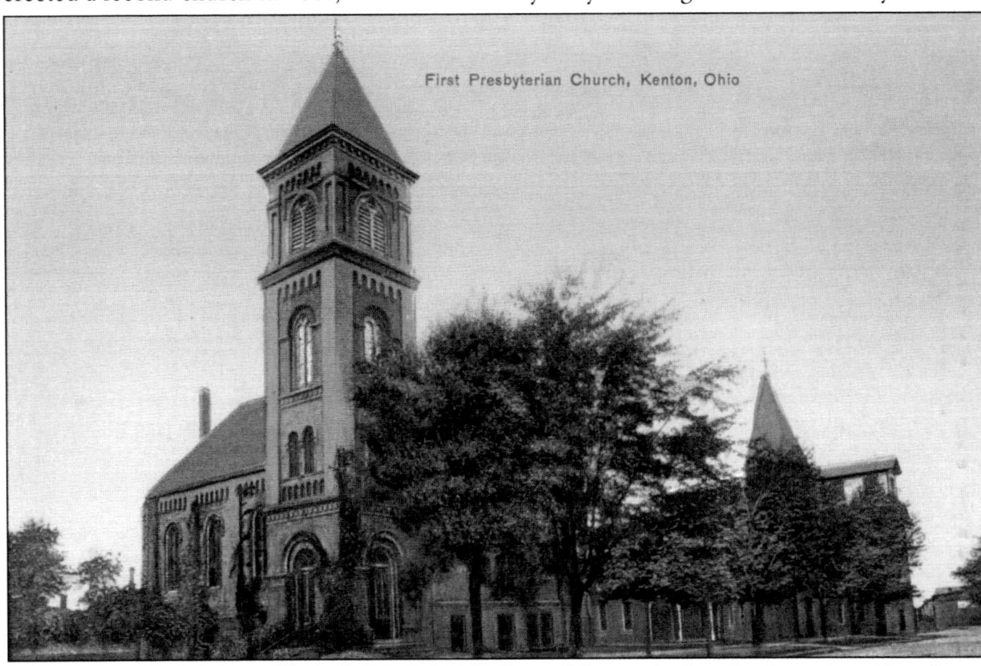

William W. Snodgrass published this c. 1905 view of Kenton's First Presbyterian Church and German Reformed Churches on West Columbus Street. The current First Presbyterian Church was erected from 1882 to 1886 and dedicated in 1887. The lot and home across the street was purchased later for use as a parsonage.

The First Reformed United Church of Christ was organized in July 1859. During its first 10 years, the congregation met on the third floor of the Goodin Block on Franklin Street. In 1867, the group purchased the former First Presbyterian Church building and moved it two doors west. The frame church was destroyed during the Big Four Fire in May 1881.

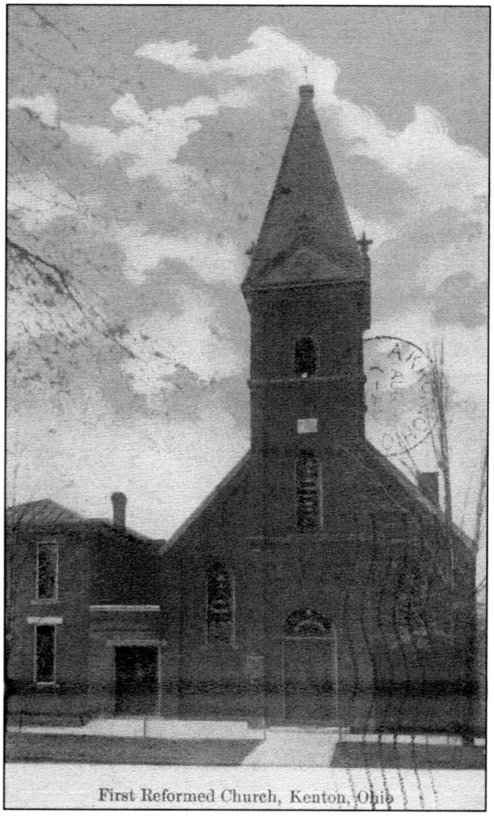

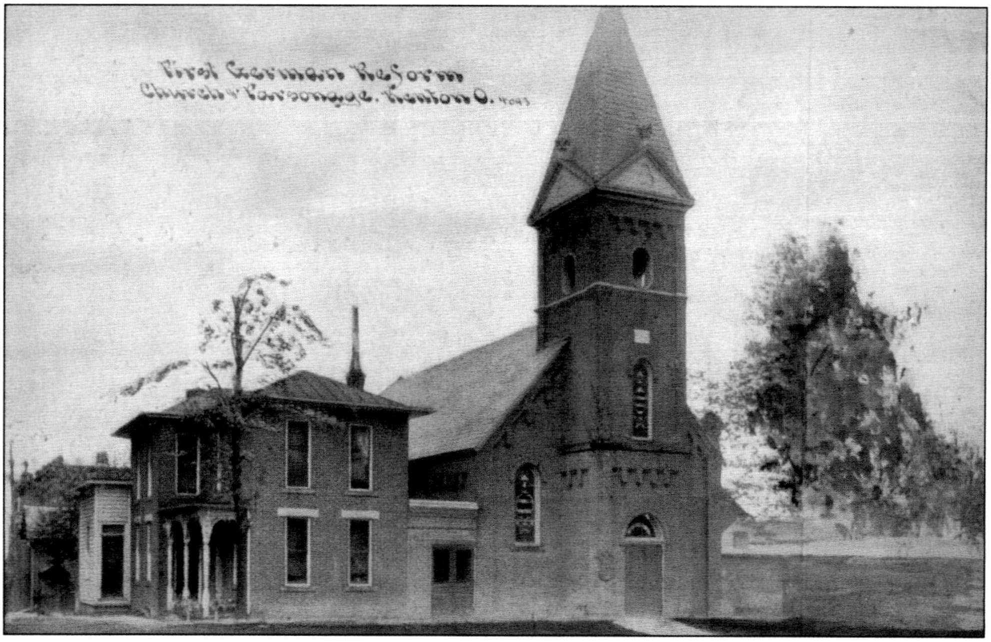

This image of the First German Reformed Church and parsonage was captured about 1905. The current brick church on West Columbus Street was erected in 1883. The parsonage was erected just to the east in 1890. The Saint Nicholas Hotel is visible to the left rear of the church.

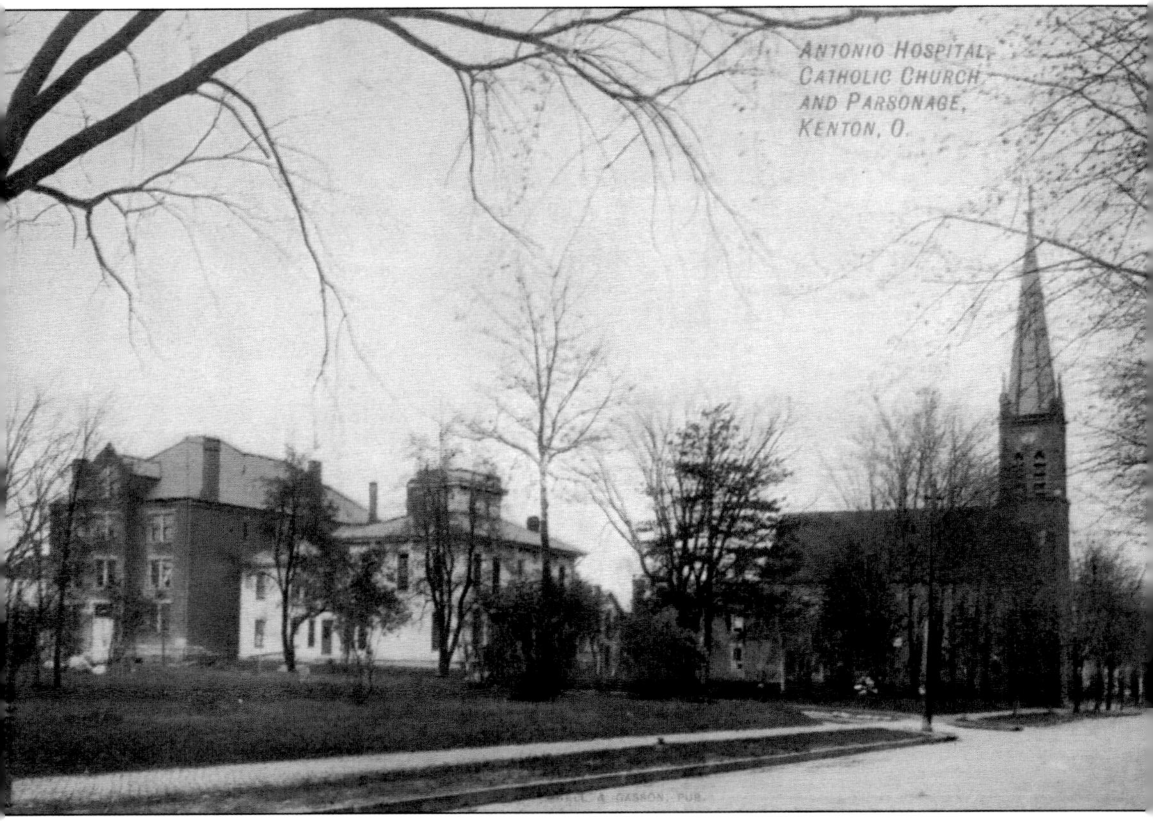

Rev. Anthony Siebenfoercher arrived in December 1871 and was instrumental in developing the Immaculate Conception Roman Catholic Church complex along North Street in Kenton before he retired in August 1905. The church had been dedicated in 1866, and he oversaw many additions to the building before it was considered complete in 1887. The original parsonage was sold, and a new one was built beside the church in 1869. Saint Anthony's Institute, the parochial school, was established in 1872. Saint Mary's Catholic Cemetery, surrounded by Grove Cemetery east of town, was purchased and consecrated in 1872. In 1880, a lot was purchased across the street to erect a brick convent for the Sisters of Charity. The nine-room Saint Mark's Hospital, to the left, opened in 1897 and was later renamed in honor of the priest. A small home was purchased near the hospital for a nurse's home. Reverend Siebenfoercher oversaw two additions to the hospital in 1900 and 1905.

The construction of Kenton's Immaculate Conception Church was started with the laying of the cornerstone by local stonemason and architect Ambrose Burkhart in July 1864. The brick church was dedicated in December 1866. Among additional improvements made were the enlarging of the sanctuary in 1883, the erecting of a steeple with bells in 1887, and the installation of a large main alter in 1893.

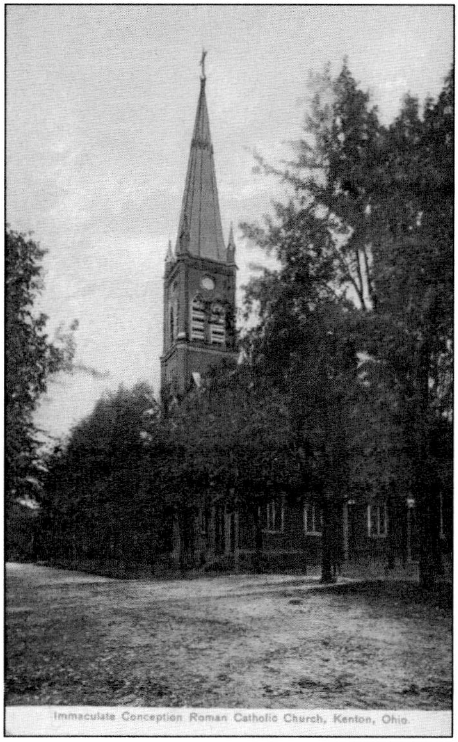

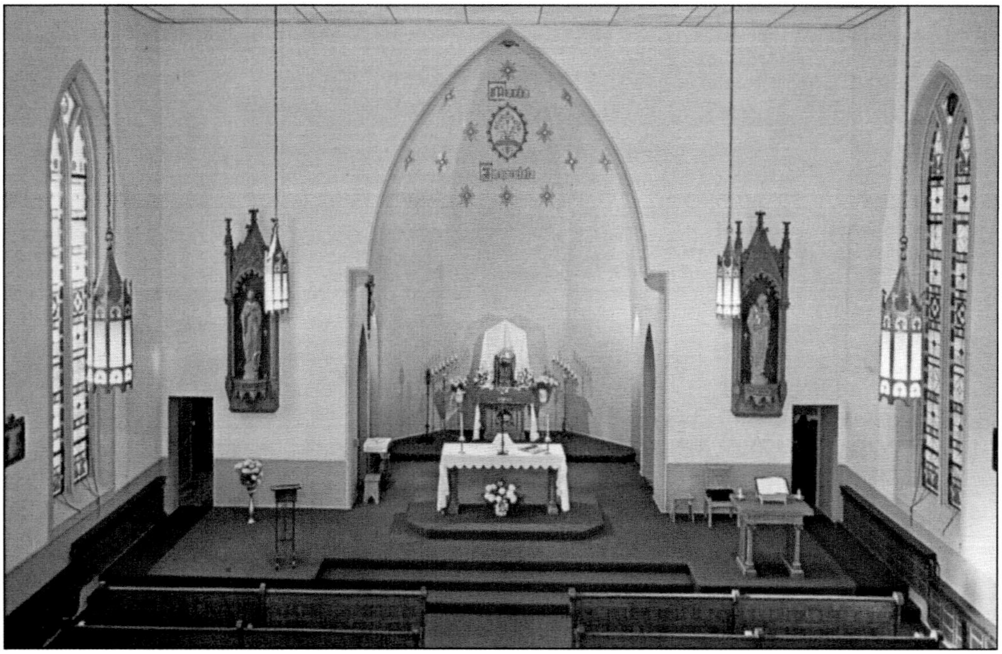

The interior of the Immaculate Conception Church at the corner of North Cherry and East North Streets is seen during 1967. The Catholic Church was organized in Kenton about 1856 and held its first meetings in members' homes. Rev. Patrick Henneberry led the movement to erect a church structure in 1864. Early maps list the church as Mary Immaculate Church and St. Mark's Roman Catholic Church.

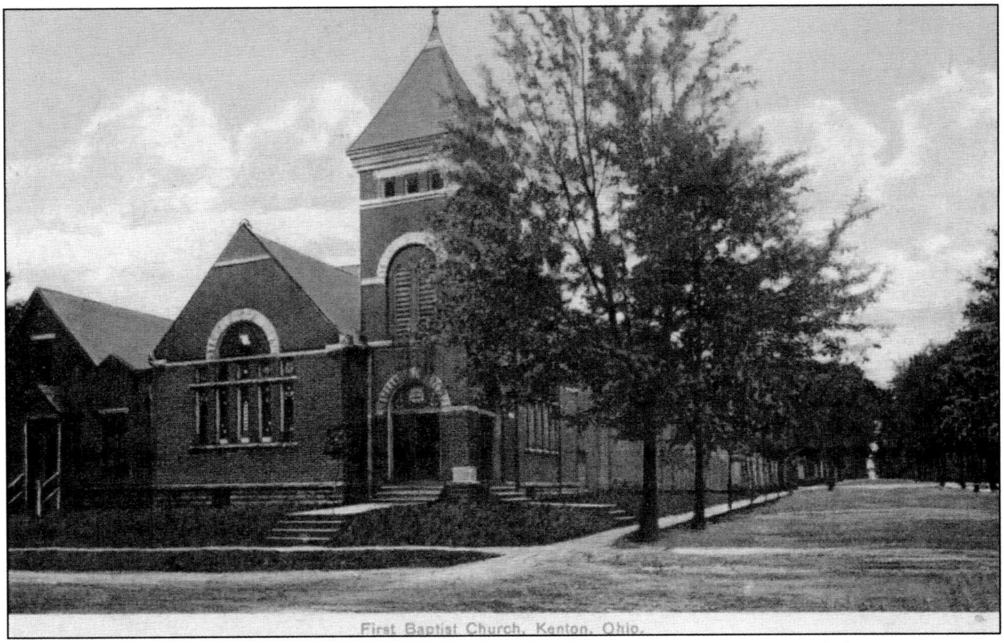

Kenton's First Baptist Church was organized in 1850 and erected a small wood-frame structure two years later. This brick church on North Wayne Street was dedicated in November 1890 and collapsed during renovations in 1926. Following a *Kenton News-Republican*–led campaign to rebuild the structure, it was completed in 1927. The congregation erected a modern church east of Kenton in 1977.

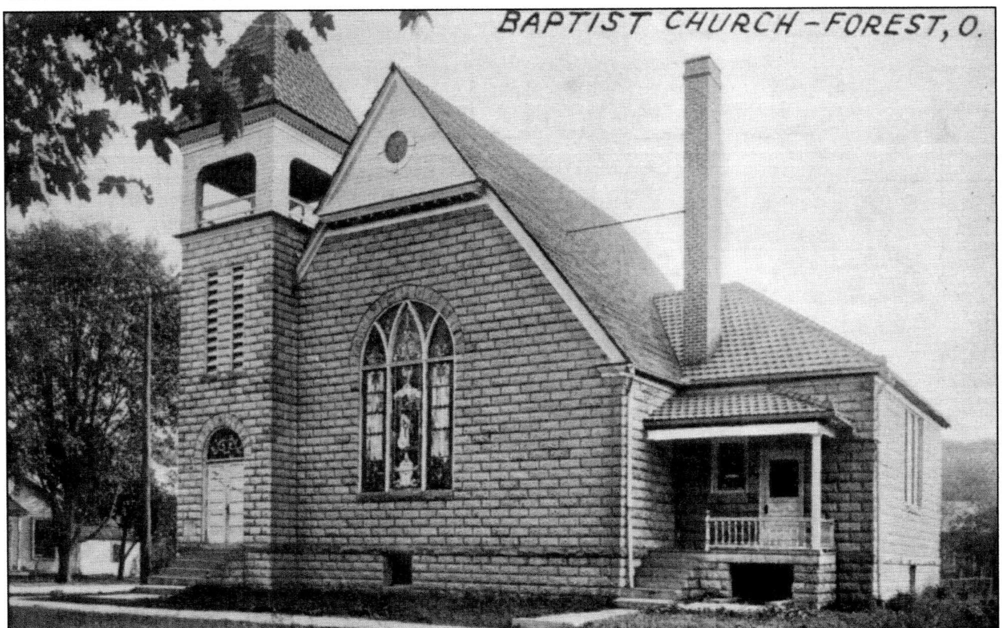

Forest's Baptist Church was informally organized around the Civil War; a new congregation was organized in 1903. The concrete-block church, photographed here about 1911, was erected in 1904 at the corner of North Martin and West Gage Streets. An educational wing was added to the east side in 1971.

The First Methodist Church, organized in Kenton about 1833, built a log church in 1839. A brick church was erected in 1851 on North Main Street. Fire destroyed this building in 1890, and the current church on the opposite side of the street replaced it in 1891. Daniel Sullivan built his home (Sullivan-Johnson Museum) on the former site in 1896.

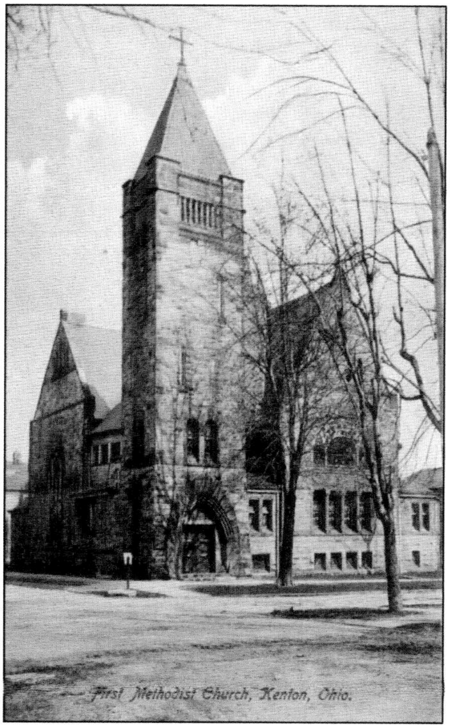

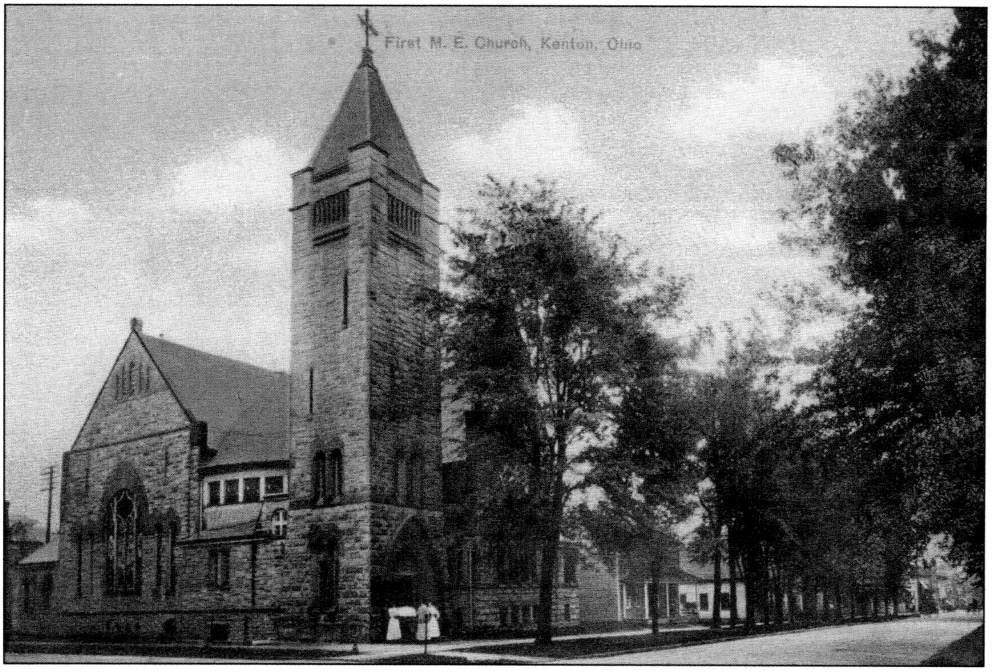

William W. Snodgrass published this 1911 view of Kenton's First Methodist Episcopal at the intersection of North Main and East North Streets. The church cornerstone was laid in May 1890, and the building was completed in 1891. The parsonage just south of the church was built in 1874. In 1972, the church merged with the Evangelical United Brethren to form the First United Methodist Church.

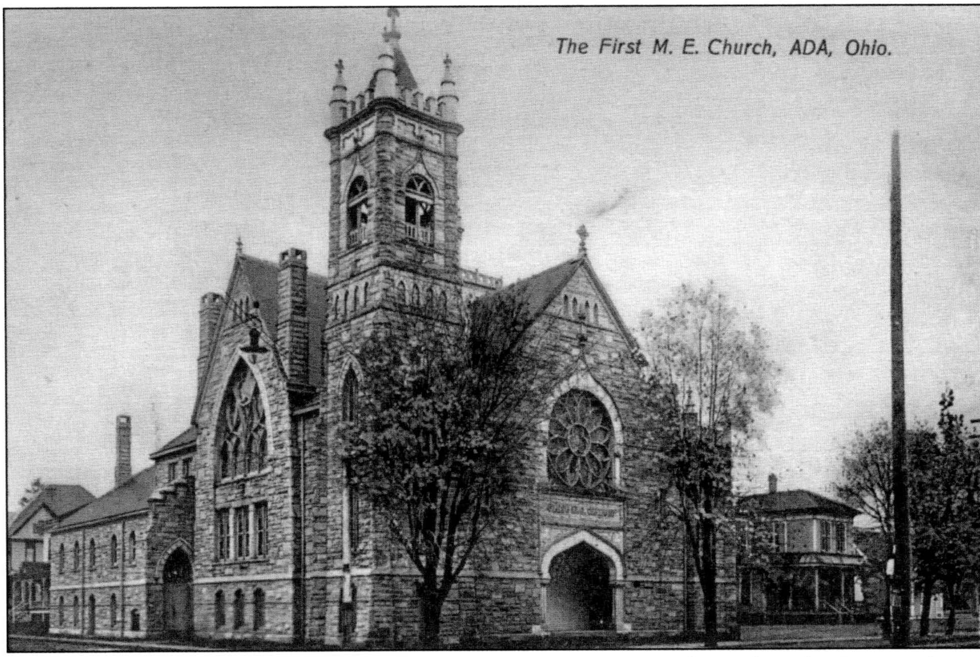

This is the First Methodist Episcopalian Church and parsonage located at the intersection of Main and Hoosier (Highland) Streets in Ada. In 1850, the Methodists held their first church services in Liberty Township. This congregation was organized in 1855 and dedicated its original wood-frame church in 1861 and again in 1871.

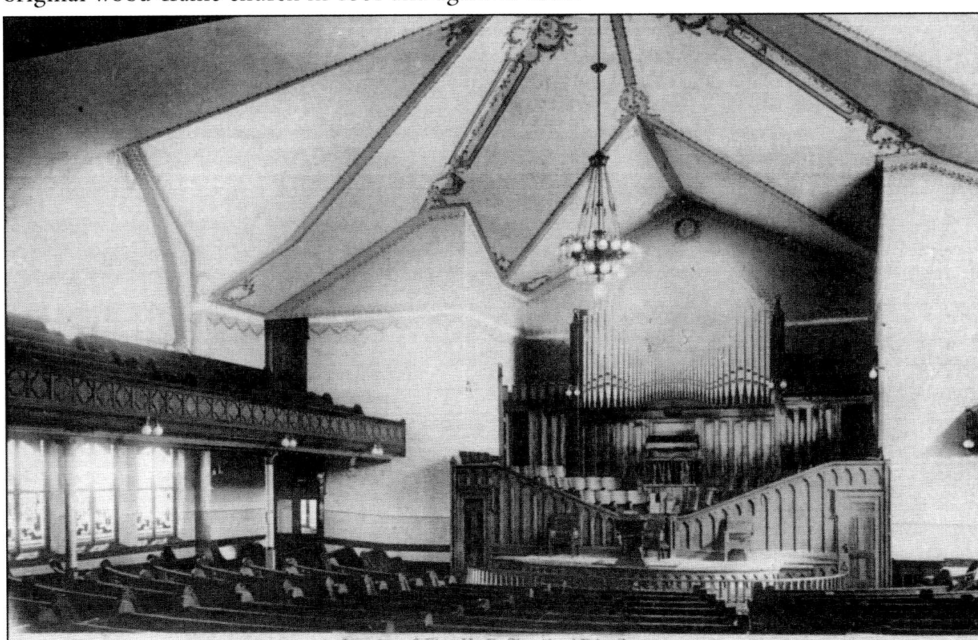

This interior view of Ada's First Methodist Episcopal Church was mailed by a student to his mother in 1911. The Central Ohio Methodist Conference held its meetings here in 1894. In 1897, two lots were purchased for the purpose of erecting a new stone church. The current church's cornerstone was placed in 1898, and the church was dedicated in 1899.

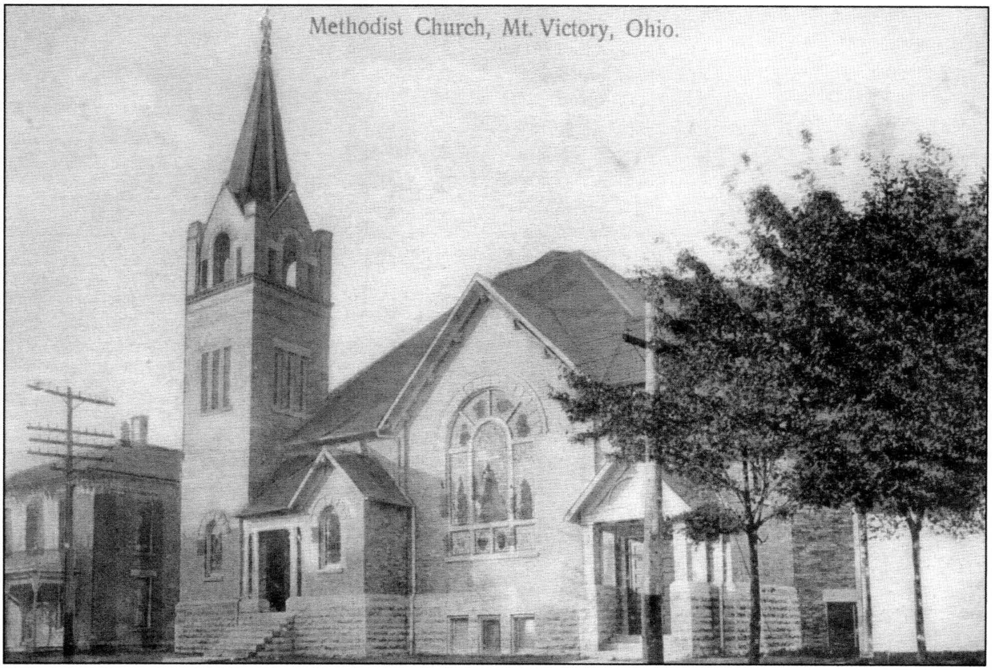

Mount Victory's congregation organized in 1853. In 1860, it purchased the former United Brethren Church. The small wood-frame church was sold in 1879 and replaced by a brick church later that year. The cornerstone of the current Methodist church on South Main Street was laid in 1903. The $15,000 building was dedicated in February 1904 and featured stained-glass windows by Tiffany.

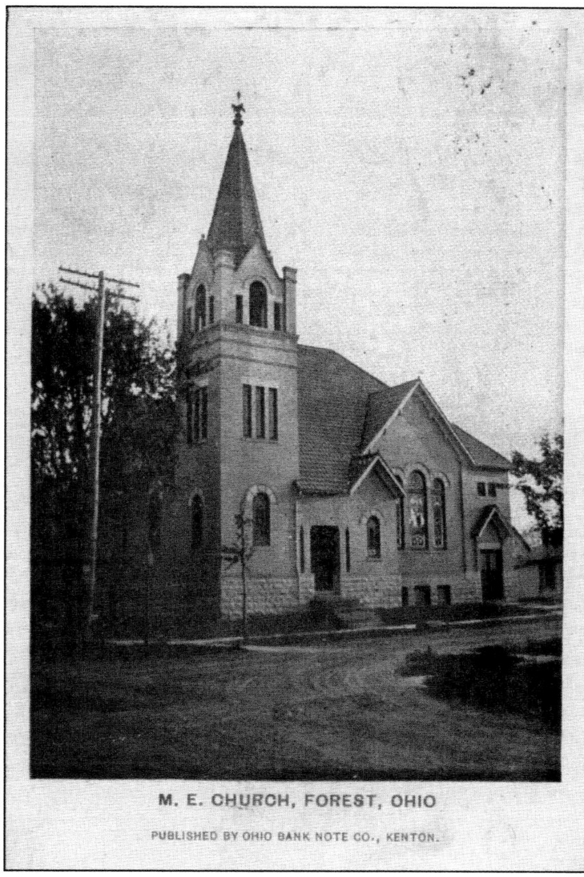

Forest's Methodist Episcopal Church was organized in 1860. The congregation constructed its first church in 1865. A second church was built in 1900 but soon burned. The current church at the intersection of Gormley and Dixon Streets was dedicated in May 1903. The Forest Methodist Protestant Church was organized in 1869 and dedicated its church in January 1871. The two Methodist congregations merged in 1939.

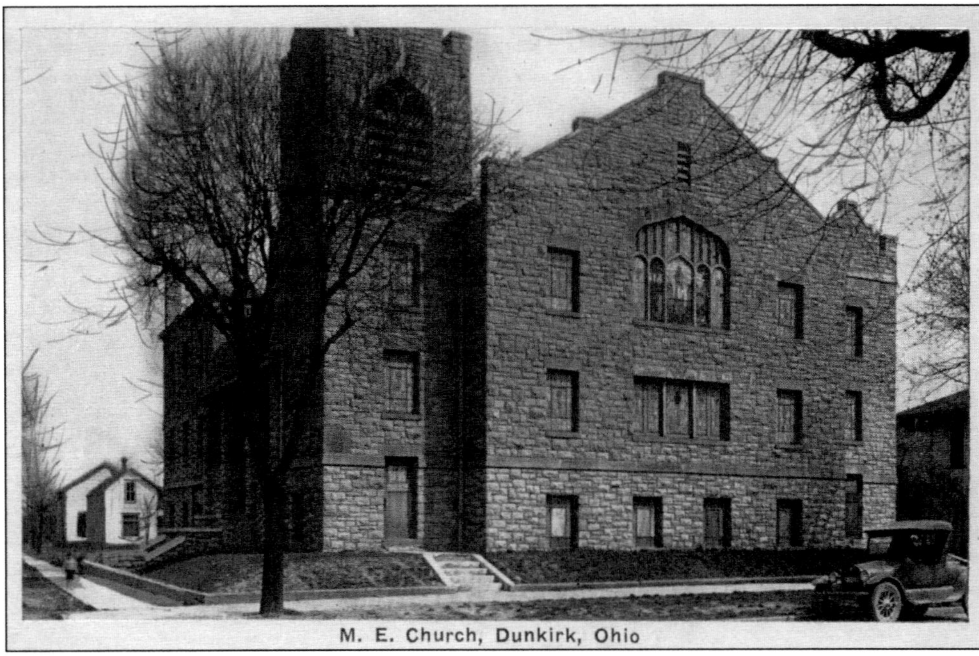

Dunkirk's Methodist Episcopal Church was organized in June 1835 in the Miller Schoolhouse on this lot along South Lincoln Way (Main Street). The first church building was erected in 1871 for $1,500 and remodeled in 1901. The stone building, seen here in about 1920, cost $45,000 and was dedicated in October 1916. It was renamed the Trinity Methodist Church in 1968.

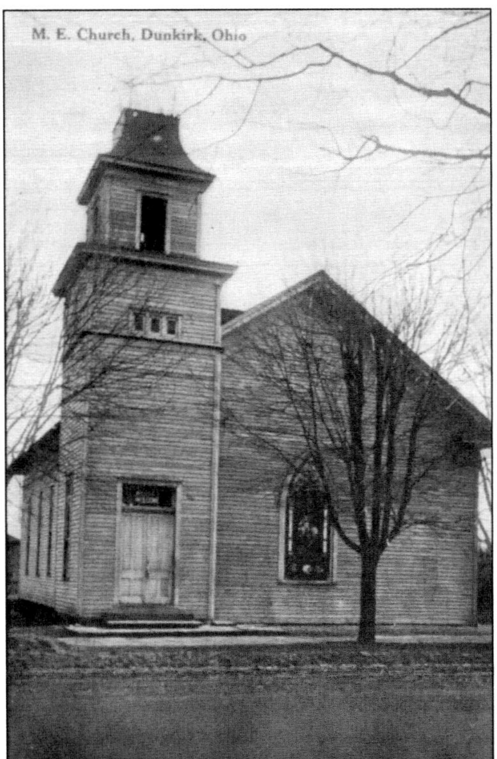

The Wesleyan Methodist Church was organized in December 1877. In the fall of 1878, the congregation erected a small wood-frame church on South West (Buckeye) Street for $1,000. Thomas & Company of Findlay published this view of the church in 1910.

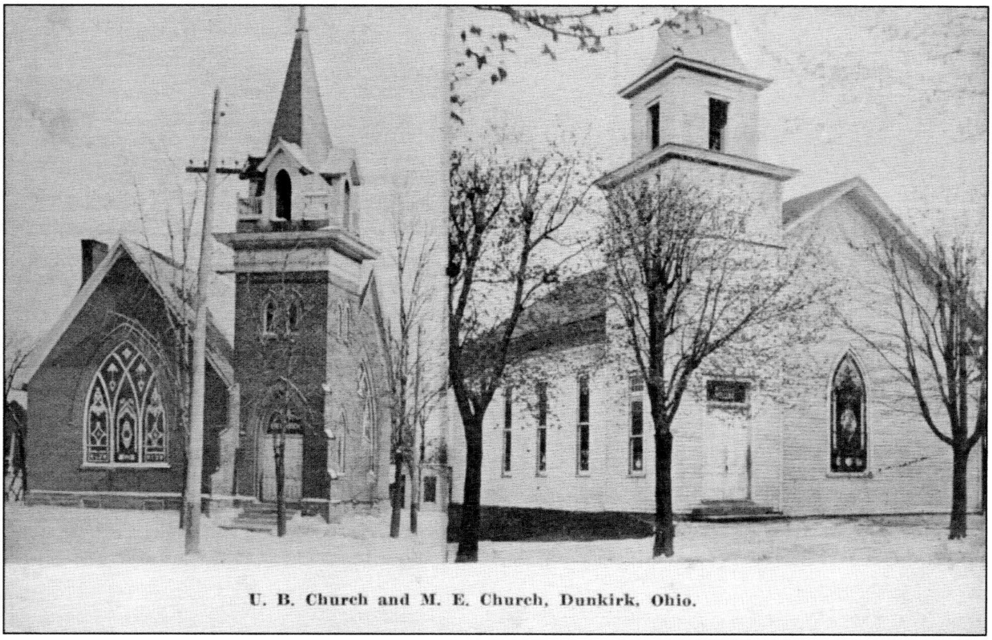

Nelson F. Faze, co-owner of the Faze & Moses dry goods store, published this 1914 winter view of the First United Brethren Church (left) and Wesley Methodist Episcopal Church in Dunkirk. In 1968, the Methodist Conference purchased the United Brethren Church and renamed it the Grace United Methodist Church.

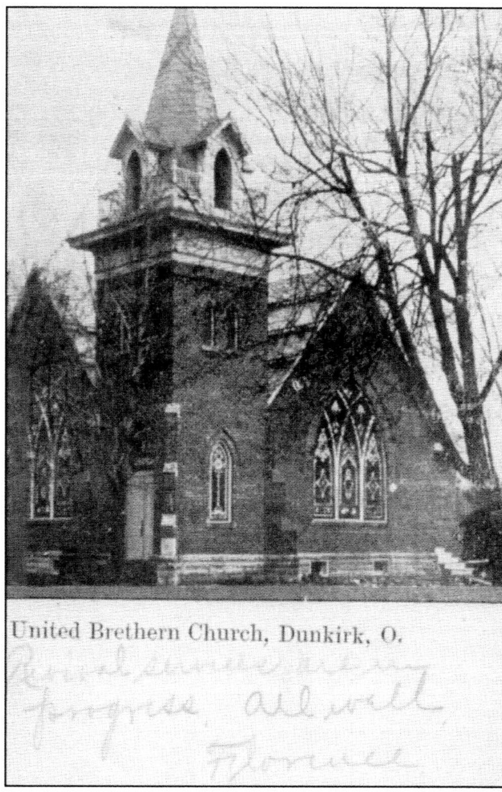

The Evangelical United Brethren Church in Dunkirk was organized in January 1860 and erected its first church at the intersection of Wayne and East (Walnut) Streets for $2,000. The French brothers, local businessmen, donated the lot for the church. It was dedicated in November 1860. The current brick church was erected in 1902.

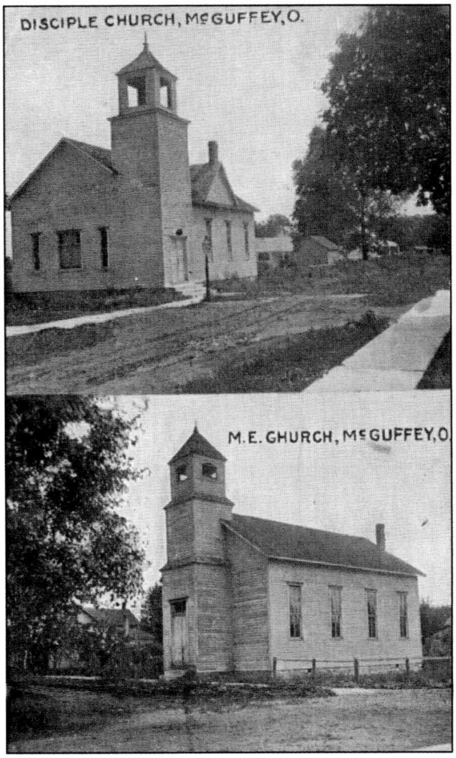

James W. Bowen published a series of postcards of sites around the Scioto Marsh, including this c. 1912 combination image of the Disciple Church and Methodist Episcopal Church in McGuffey. The Church of Christ (Disciples) constructed its wood-frame church on Columbus Street in the 1890s. The Methodist Episcopal Church was a wood-frame church erected about 1900.

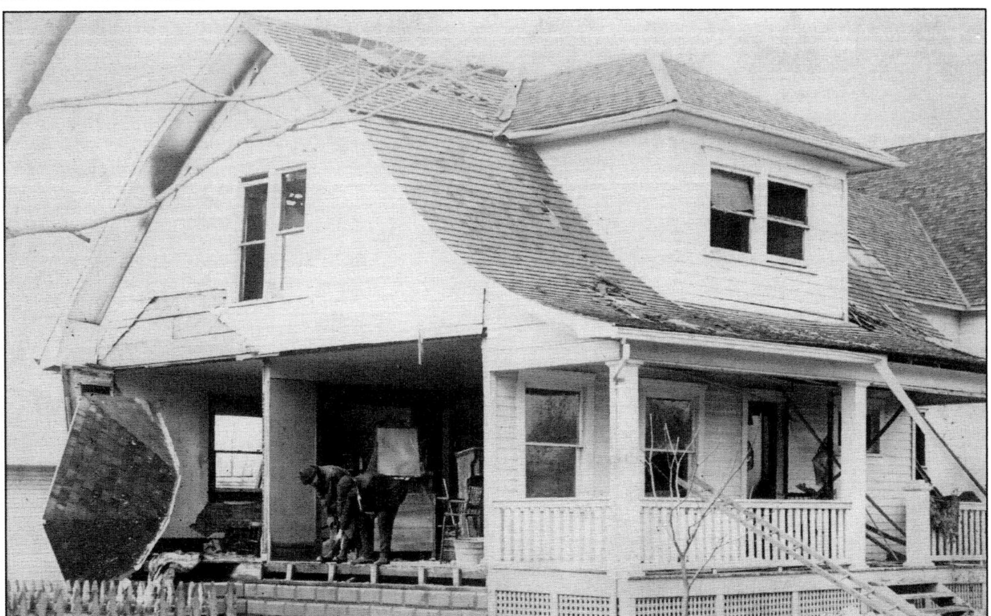

Prior to the Civil War, the Methodist Episcopal and United Brethren congregations erected a small log church at local gathering spot "Kingsley Corner" near Alger. This became the Methodist church following the war. A frame church was erected on Main Street in 1871. The current church was dedicated in January 1916. This photograph shows local workers examining one of Alger's parsonages following a severe storm in the 1910s.

Eight

Recreation

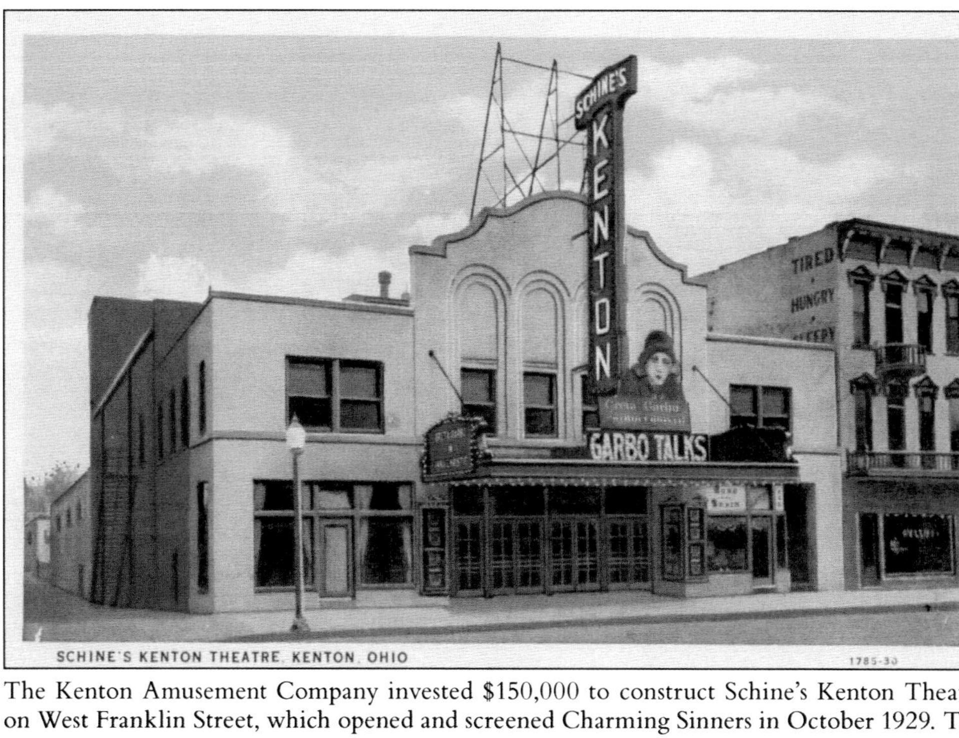

The Kenton Amusement Company invested $150,000 to construct Schine's Kenton Theatre on West Franklin Street, which opened and screened Charming Sinners in October 1929. The marquee promotes Greta Garbo's first talkie, *Anna Christie*, in 1930. Designed in the Spanish Colonial style, the theater featured air-conditioning plus murals in the lobby and auditorium. Converted into a three-screen movie house in 1993, it continues to show films today.

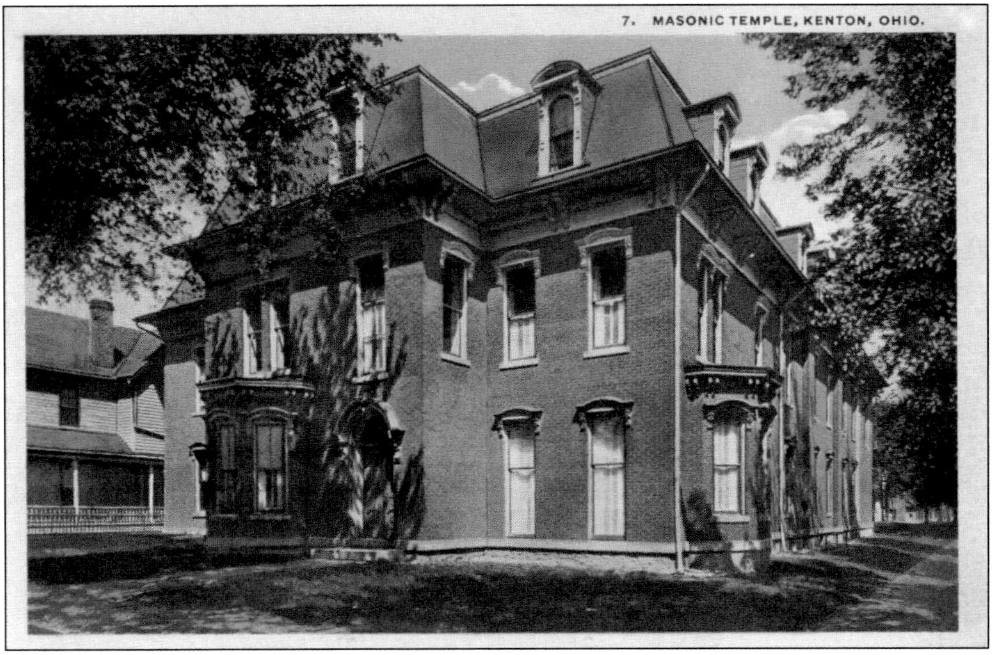

Kenton's Latham Lodge No. 154, Free and Accepted Masons, seen here about 1930, was chartered in September 1848. Early meetings were held at various locations downtown, including the Reese Hotel and the Cary & Kinnear Block, until the Masonic Block was completed on the west side of the courthouse square in 1877.

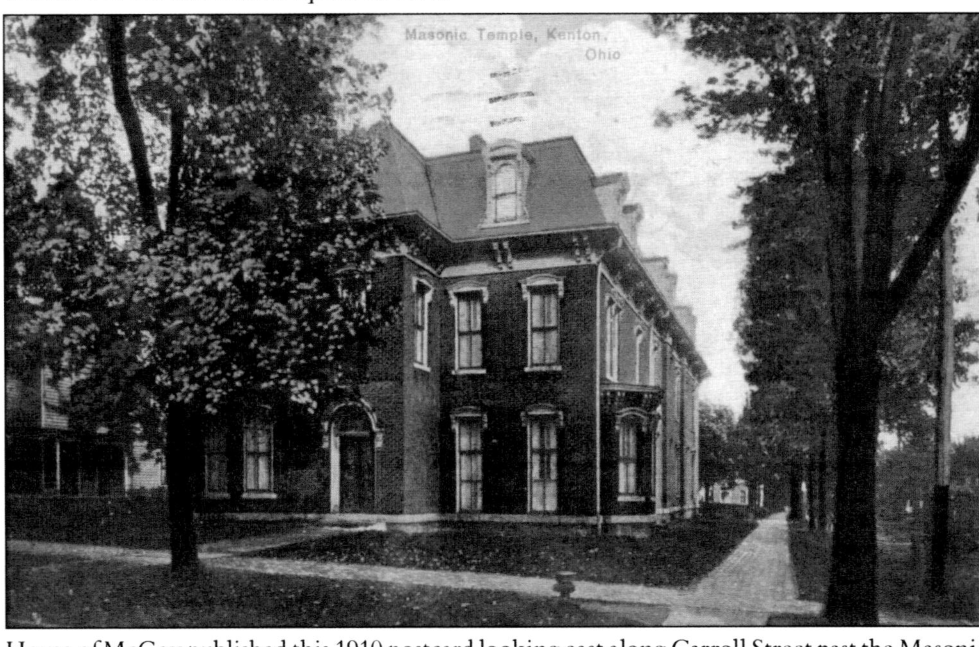

House of McCoy published this 1910 postcard looking east along Carroll Street past the Masonic Lodge toward the Hardin County Jail. In 1901, the Masonic Temple Association was organized and purchased the former Charles Merriman home at the corner of North Main and East Carroll Streets. The building was renovated and enlarged, and in February 1902 the Masonic Temple was dedicated.

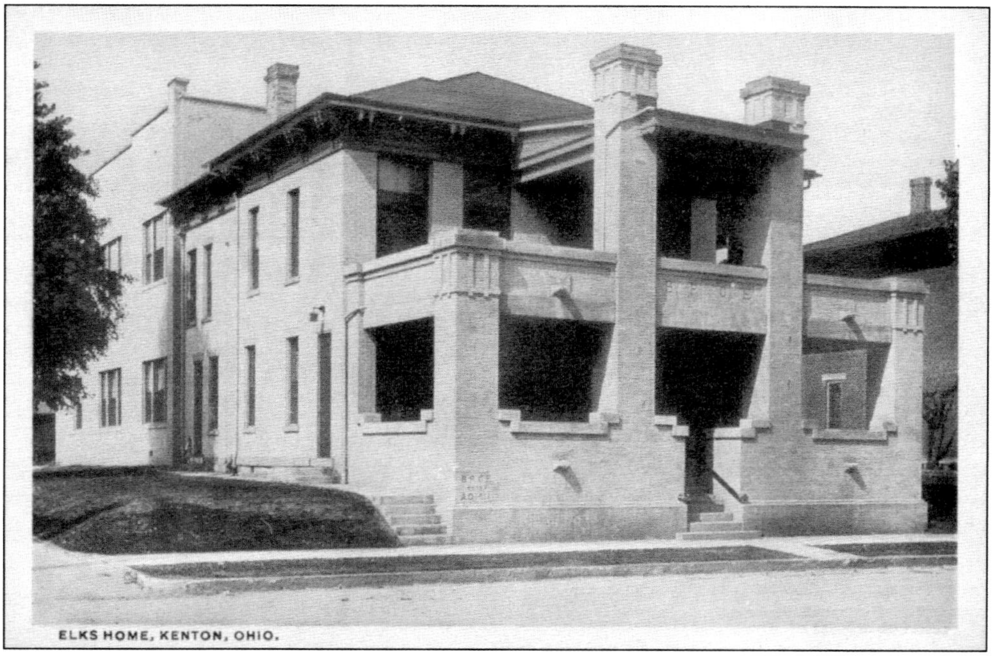

Benevolent Protectorate of Elks Lodge No. 157 was founded in February 1890. In 1897, the Elks Hall was on the second floor of a building at the corner of West Franklin and North Detroit Streets. By 1910, the Elks lodge had relocated to the second floor of the Palucci Block on West Columbus Street, one door east of the Kenton Telephone Company.

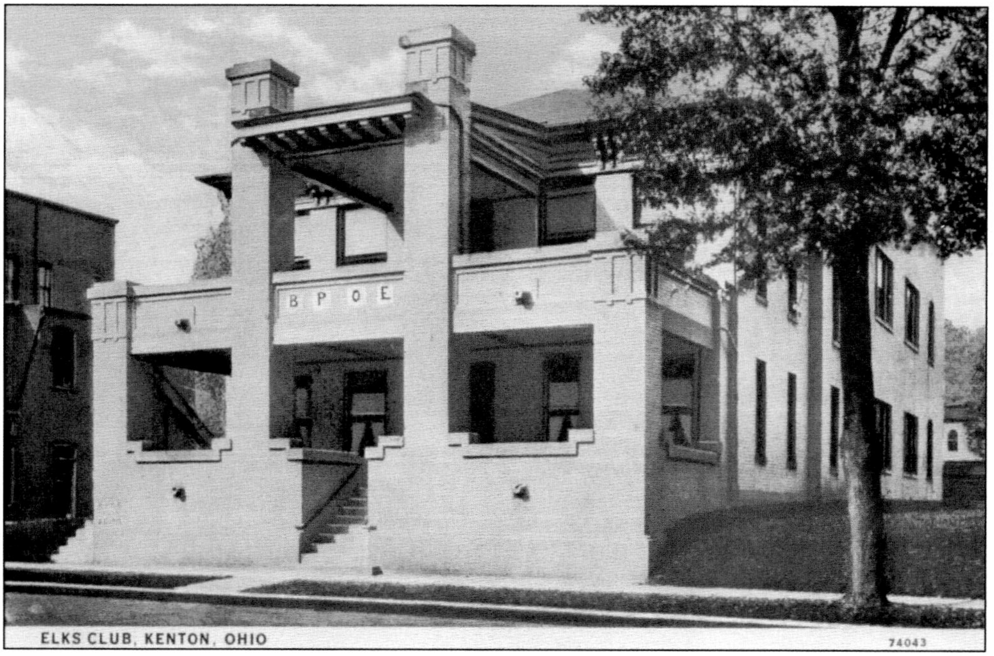

The Elks lodge is seen from the intersection of East Franklin and North Wayne Streets about 1940. After several locations downtown, including the Letson Block and the Munson Block, a permanent home was constructed in 1911 on East Franklin Street across from where the Home Savings and Loan Company is today.

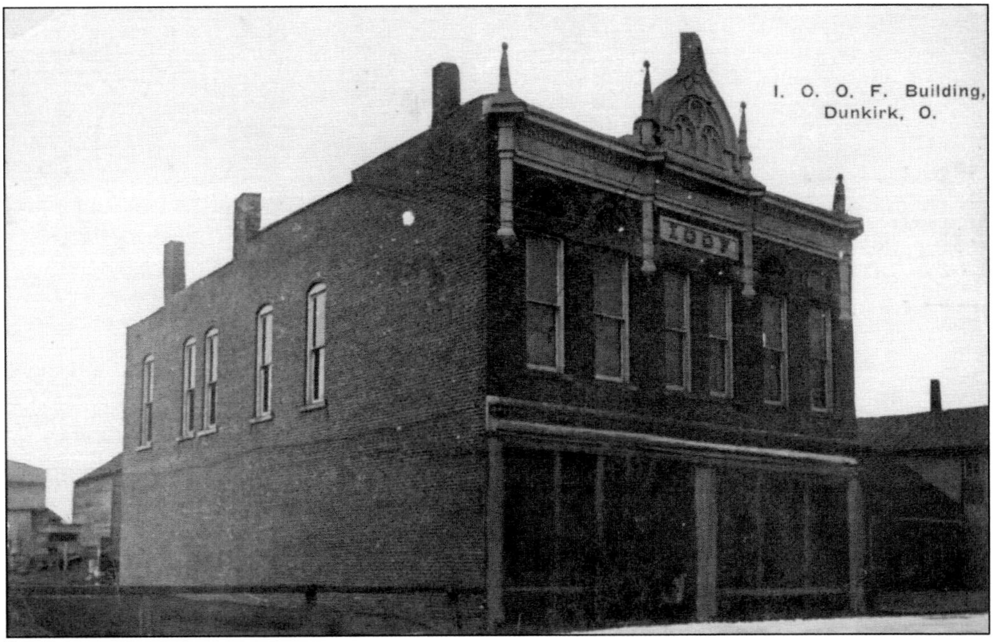

Dunkirk Lodge No. 624, International Order of Odd Fellows, was incorporated in June 1876. In 1897, the lodge met in a second-floor room of the Opera House Block. This view shows the IOOF building in Dunkirk as it appeared about 1915. The lodge consolidated with the Arlington Odd Fellows about 1941 and sold the building to the Dunkirk VFW Post 3516.

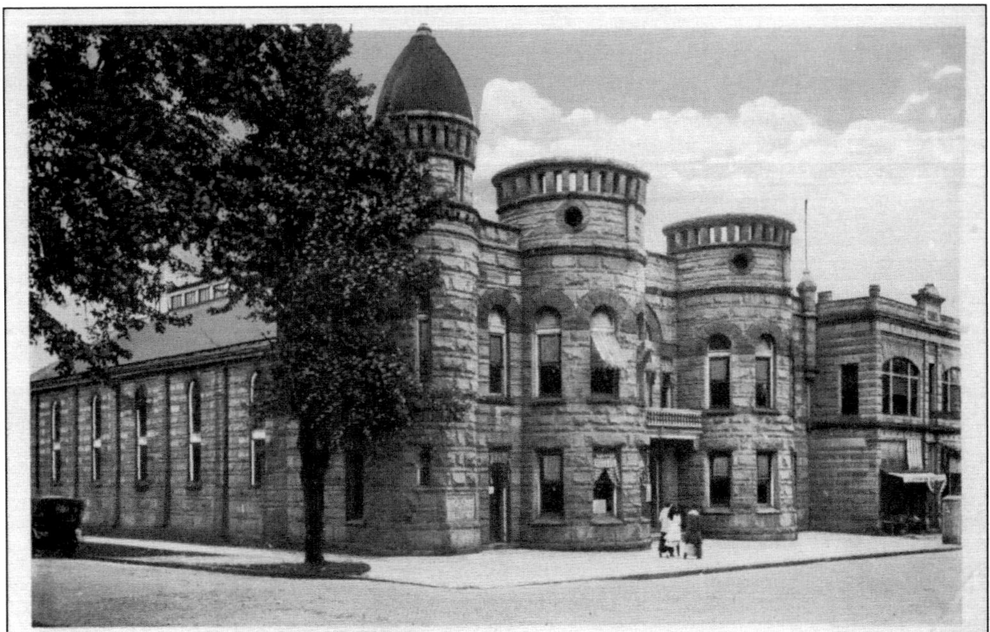

Lintz's Drug Store in Kenton published this 1920 image of the Hardin County Athletic Club, located in the Hardin County Armory, which hosted numerous basketball games. Jim Thorpe and the Oorang Indians faced Kenton's club here in 1923. Kenton's Company I of the Ohio Volunteer Infantry claimed the basketball national championship in 1900.

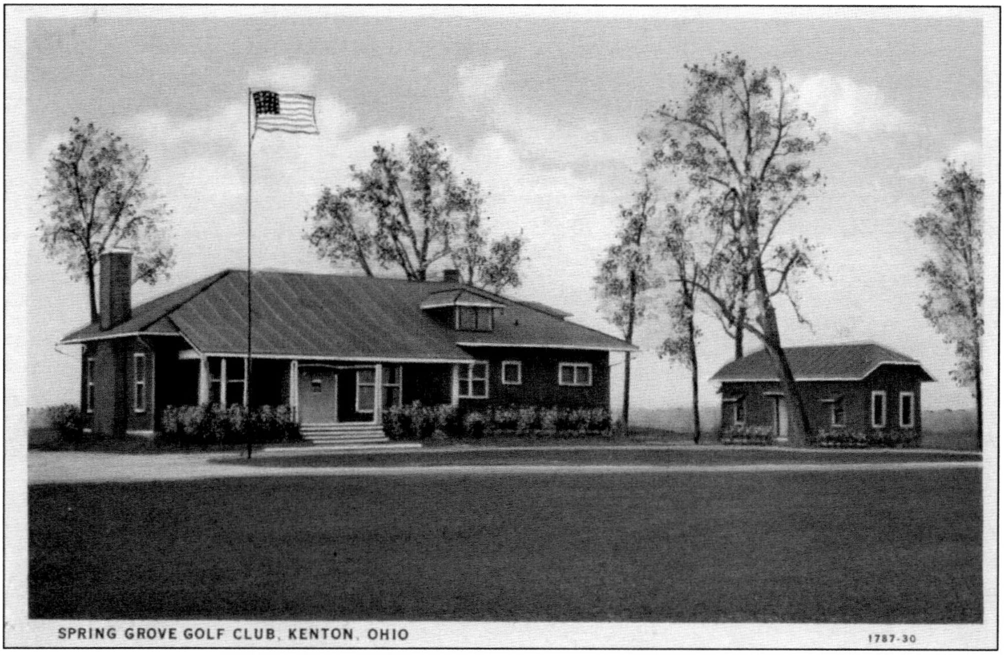

Spring Grove Golf Club, east of Kenton along the Harding Highway (State Route 309), opened its nine-hole course in July 1927. The clubhouse featured a golf shop, and Del Thompson served as its first golf professional. Tennis courts were installed later in the year. Eventually, a shelter house, swimming pool, and fishing lake were added.

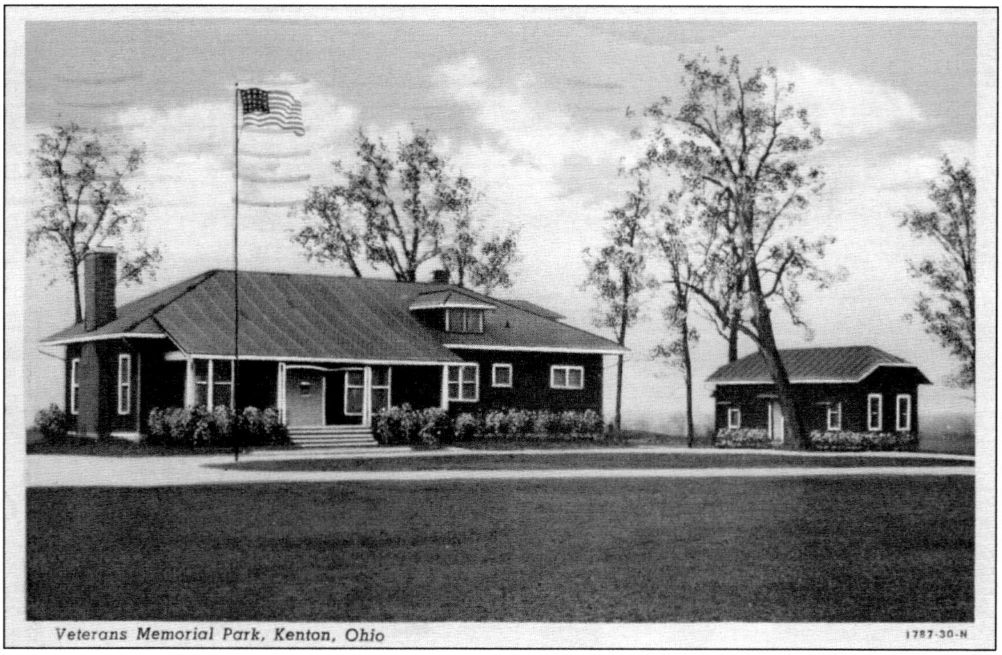

The local golf course was renamed Veterans' Memorial Park to honor the county's veterans after World War II. Its nine-hole course was expanded to an 18-hole course in the late 1990s, closing off an access road and encompassing Boy Scout Lake. The Kenton News Agency published this postcard during the 1940s.

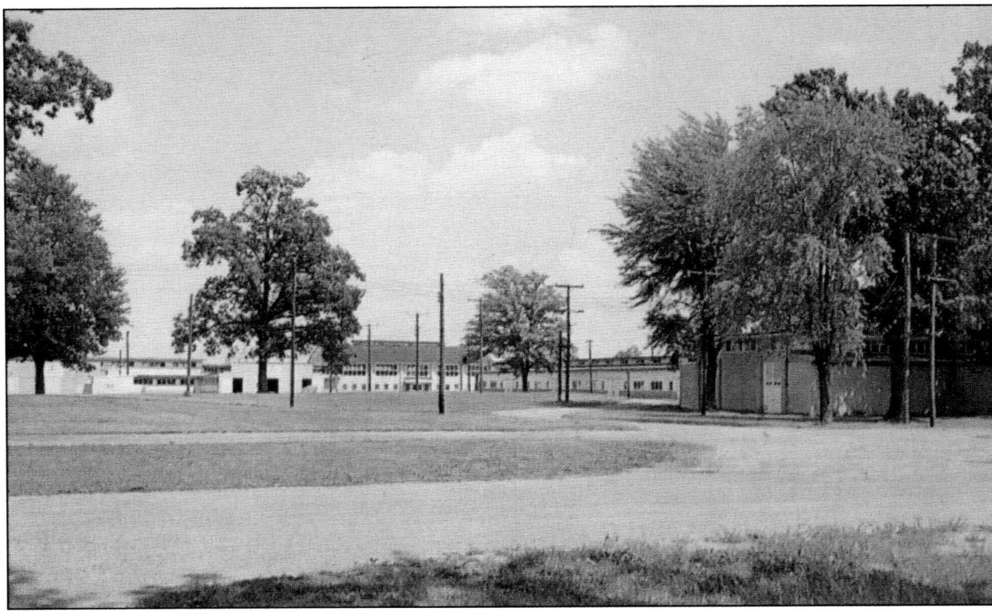

The Hardin County Agricultural Society was organized in 1851. Property south of Kenton was purchased for the Hardin County Fairgrounds in 1881. A fire destroyed the grandstand and most of the buildings, forcing the fair to close from 1926 to 1939. The fairgrounds reopened, and a rebuilding program between 1940 and 1947 resulted in over 20 structures, including the William Britton Grandstand.

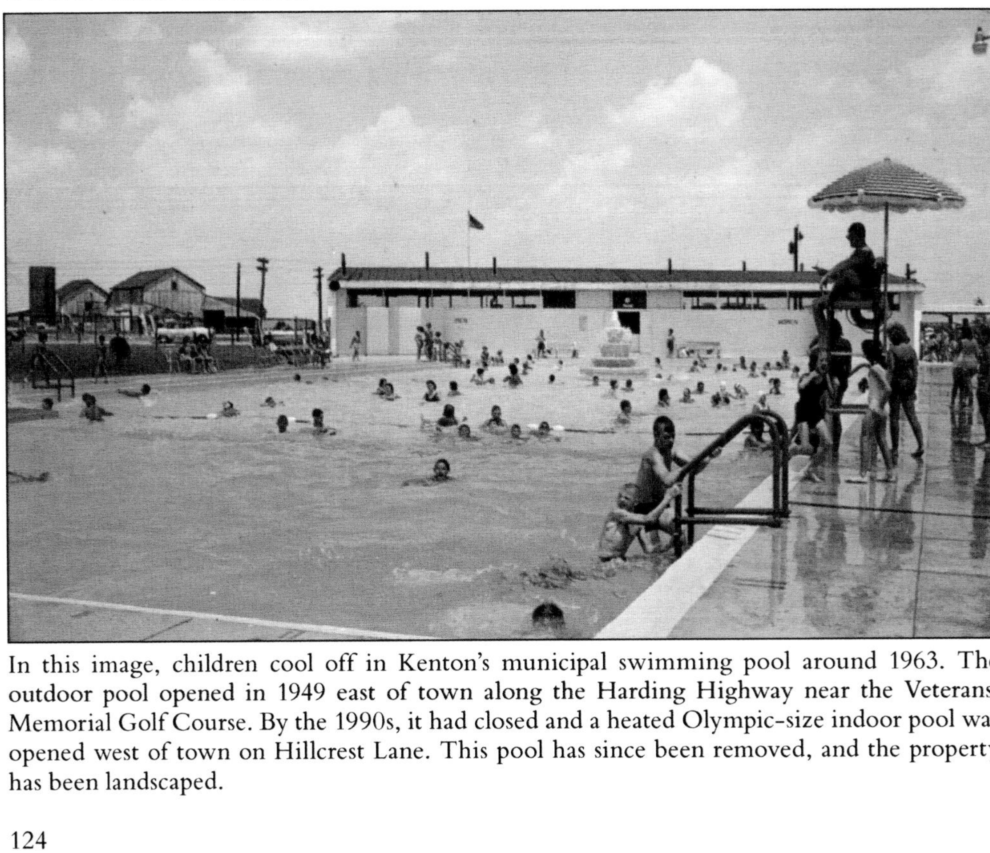

In this image, children cool off in Kenton's municipal swimming pool around 1963. The outdoor pool opened in 1949 east of town along the Harding Highway near the Veterans' Memorial Golf Course. By the 1990s, it had closed and a heated Olympic-size indoor pool was opened west of town on Hillcrest Lane. This pool has since been removed, and the property has been landscaped.

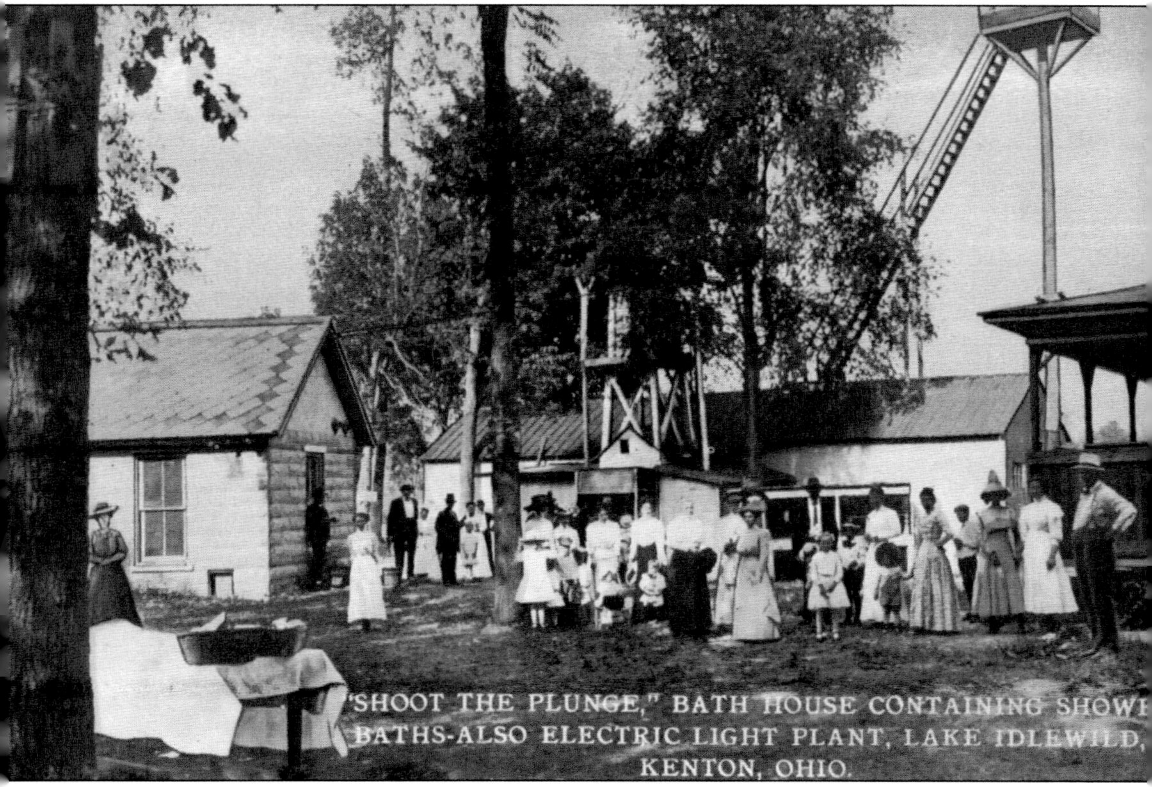

Walnut Hill was a 280-acre farm north of Kenton along the Dunkirk Pike (State Route 68) purchased in 1892 by Judge Lucius Salisbury. The property included a spring-fed lake known as Lake Idlewild, which provided ice for the town during winter. In 1898, Lucius and his son Arthur improved the lake with a pavilion, bandstand, bowling alley, bathhouses, magnetic showers, and 40 rowboats. The amusement park also featured a swimming area with diving boards plus separate sections for boating and fishing. Shortly after the park opened, the US Bureau of Fisheries enticed local fishermen by stocking the lake with 100 largemouth bass. Numerous reunions, picnics, baseball games, and dances were held here. Henry Pfeiffer and Harry Duckham purchased the park during the 1920s. In 1929, the park hosted an open-air boxing card, one of several cards promoted in Hardin County during the late 1920s. The pavilion burned down in July 1938 and was never rebuilt. The park closed shortly afterwards, and the property is now in private hands.

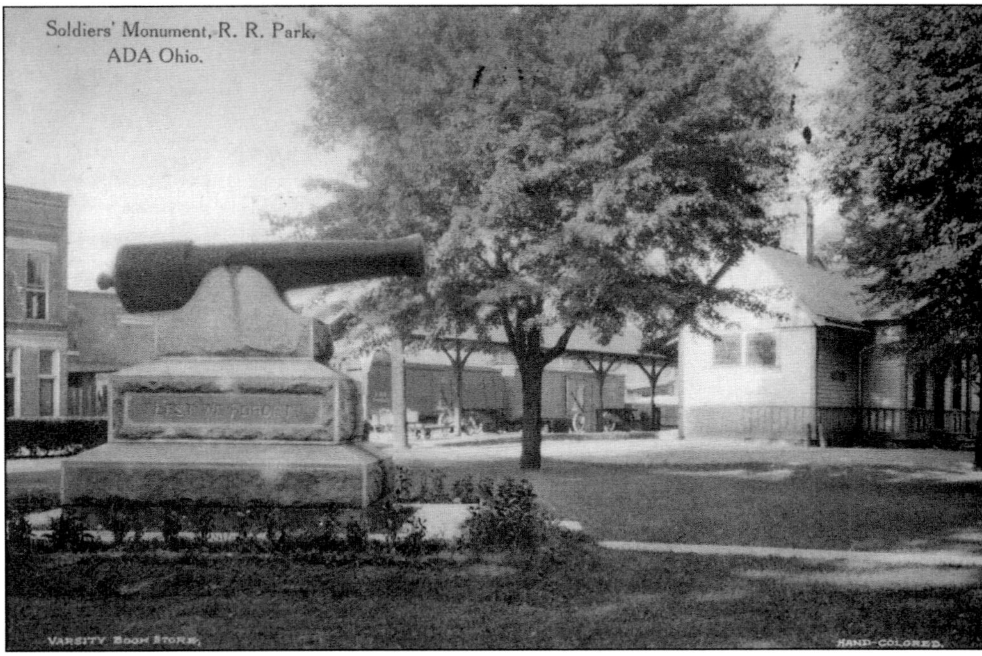

The Varsity Book Store published this 1915 image of the Soldiers' Monument at Railroad Park on Central Avenue in downtown Ada. The park features the restored 1887 Pennsylvania Railroad Depot and a flower garden surrounding the cannon. A Pennsylvania Railroad caboose, built in 1945, was renovated in the early 1990s and placed beside the depot in 1994.

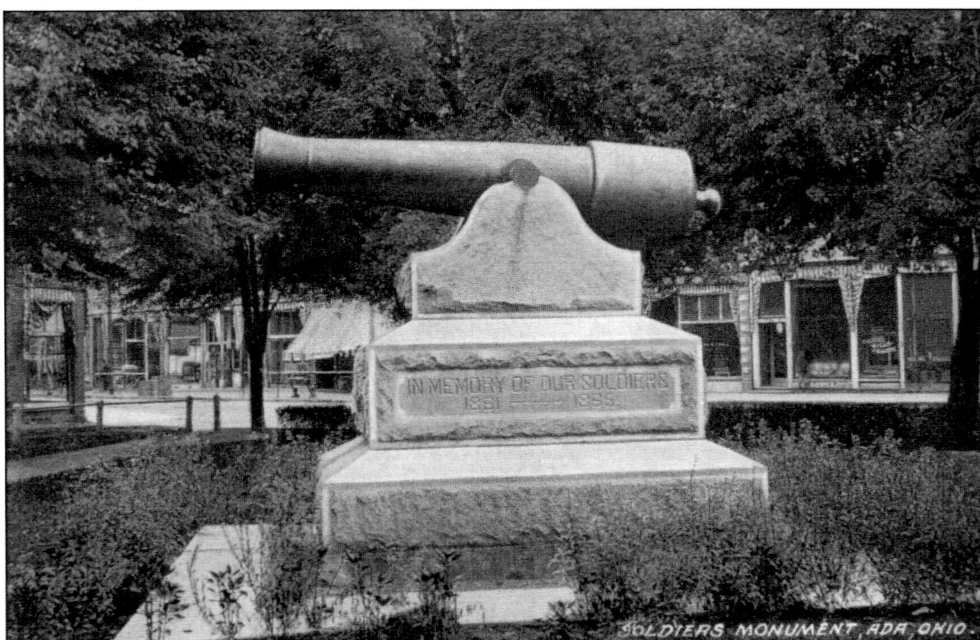

The Civil War siege gun, from Fort Mifflin, Pennsylvania, was installed on Memorial Day in 1903. The monument replaced two earlier brick and wooden memorials. It is said that the cannon still points toward Fort Sumter, South Carolina. The Doling Steam Bakery on South Main Street can be seen across the street from the monument.

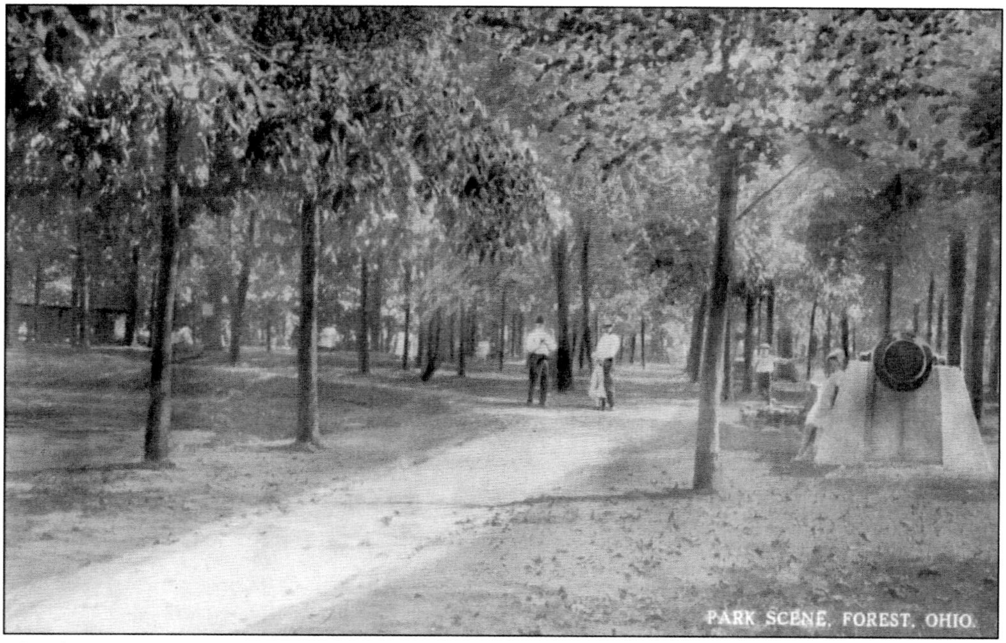

The five-acre Gormley Park, located along Mary Street, was donated in 1881 by the heirs of John Gormley. This 1914 postcard includes one of the two Civil War cannons (1906) and the historic log cabin (1908). The park's hand-dug lake provided water for the city and served as a swimming hole until 1960 when the community pool was built.

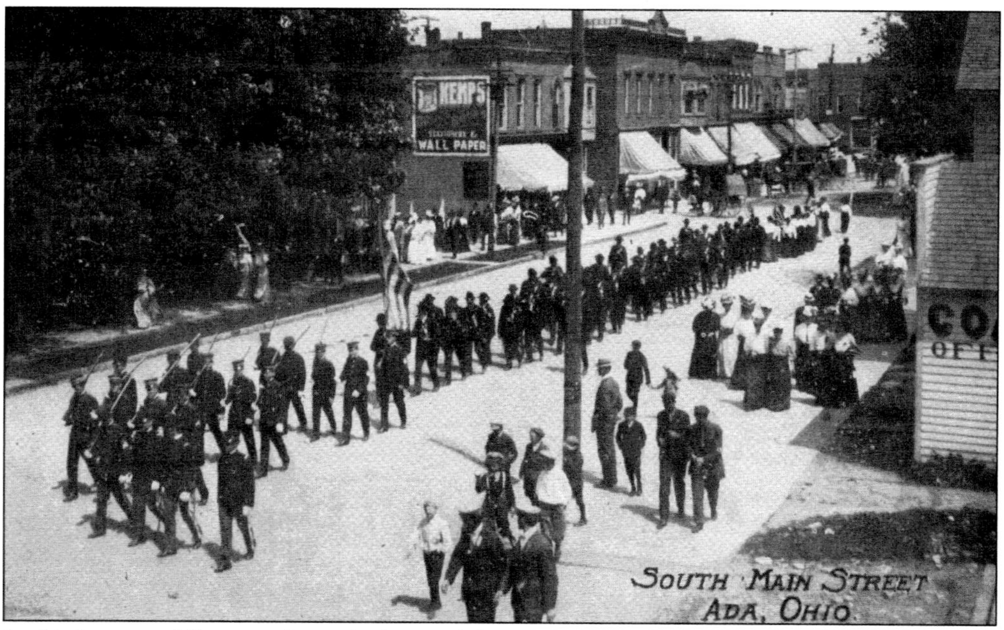

In this image, soldiers march south along Ada's Main Street past the Kemp Drug Store in a 1908 military parade. David Kemp purchased the Runkle Drug Store at 125 South Main Street and reopened the store with his wife, Laura, in 1877. Upon his death in 1894, Laura operated the store with her son-in-law Newton W. Tobias until her death.

www.arcadiapublishing.com

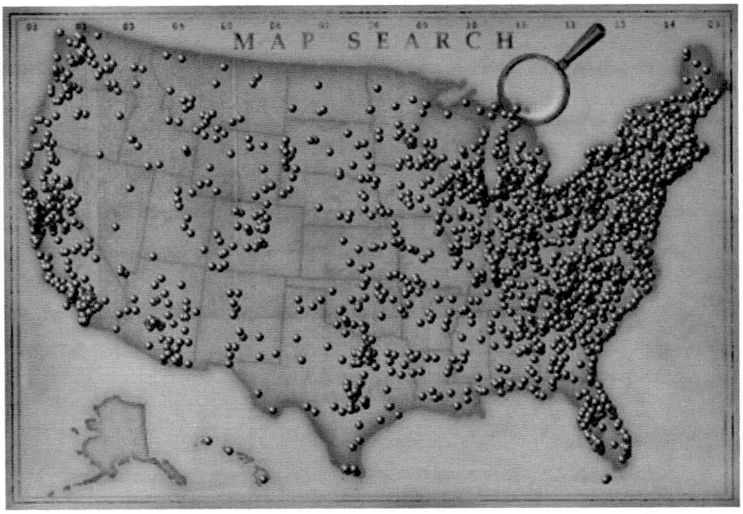

Discover books about the town where you grew up, the cities where your friends and families live, the town where your parents met, or even that retirement spot you've been dreaming about. Our Web site provides history lovers with exclusive deals, advanced notification about new titles, e-mail alerts of author events, and much more.

MADE IN THE USA

Arcadia Publishing, the leading local history publisher in the United States, is committed to making history accessible and meaningful through publishing books that celebrate and preserve the heritage of America's people and places. Consistent with our mission to preserve history on a local level, this book was printed in South Carolina on American-made paper and manufactured entirely in the United States.

This book carries the accredited Forest Stewardship Council (FSC) label and is printed on 100 percent FSC-certified paper. Products carrying the FSC label are independently certified to assure consumers that they come from forests that are managed to meet the social, economic, and ecological needs of present and future generations.

FSC
Mixed Sources
Product group from well-managed forests and other controlled sources

Cert no. SW-COC-001530
www.fsc.org
© 1996 Forest Stewardship Council

Find Your Place in History.